Yale Studies in English
Richard S. Sylvester, Editor
Volume 170

BLAKE

in the Nineteenth Century

His Reputation as a Poet
From Gilchrist to Yeats

by Deborah Dorfman

Yale University Press, New Haven and London, 1969

Library of Congress catalog card number: 69–13904

150231

Designed by Marvin Howard Simmons,
set in Times Roman type,
and printed in the United States of America by
The Colonial Press Inc., Clinton, Massachusetts

Distributed in Great Britain, Europe, Asia, and
Africa by Yale University Press Ltd., London; in
Canada by McGill University Press, Montreal; and
in Latin America by Centro Interamericano de Libros
Académicos, Mexico City.

Published with assistance from the
Kingsley Trust Association Publication Fund
established by the Scroll and Key Society of
Yale College.

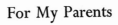
For My Parents

CONTENTS

ACKNOWLEDGMENTS

My principal obligations are to the efforts of scholars and editors of Blake, especially the work of John Sampson, Geoffrey Keynes, David V. Erdman, and Northrop Frye. I am indebted more than I can say to Harold Bloom of Yale University for suggesting the subject of this book to me as a thesis topic, and for advice, encouragement, and assistance throughout its progress. I wish also to thank Martin Price of Yale, who gave sympathetic and tactful assistance in the early stages of the manuscript.

I am grateful to Helen Hennessy Vendler, who read through the manuscript and suggested improvements. William S. Wilson III advised on two chapters, and my colleague R. L. Greene contributed helpful editorial suggestions. Hazard Adams furnished details on the Yeats-Ellis edition; G. E. Bentley Jr. supplied information about John Linnell. A special debt is owed Mrs. Landon K. Thorne of New York City, who gave permission to quote from unpublished Rossetti letters and manuscripts in her Blake collection. Much of this material is now available in a four volume edition of D. G. Rossetti's *Letters,* being brought out by the Clarendon Press.

The librarians at the Yale University libraries, where most of my research was done, have been courteous and accommodating. Yale, Temple, and Wesleyan Universities made available fellowship funds, research grants, and released time from teaching. My typists—Betty German, Irene Cecchini, and Marcia Astley—were dependable and efficient.

Among many friends, colleagues, former teachers, and

others who assisted with particular services I would like to thank Warren Chernaik, George Creeger, E. Talbot Donaldson, Cecil Lang, Yvonne Noble, Richard Ohmann, Toby Spiselman, and Edwin Wolf.

Finally, I am very grateful to Mary Shuford, Merle Spiegel, and Wayland Schmitt of Yale Press for valuable editorial guidance.

A regret is that I have not had the opportunity to use a new edition, with extensive corrections, of Gilchrist's *Life of Blake,* which Ruthven Todd is currently preparing.

As for errors and infelicities, I am of course responsible.

D.D.

LIST OF ABBREVIATIONS

The following short references have been used in the text and notes:

E-B	*The Poetry and Prose of William Blake,* ed. David V. Erdman with a commentary by Harold Bloom, New York, Doubleday, 1965. Unless specified to the contrary, all quotations from Blake are from this edition.
Blake, ed. Keynes	*The Complete Works of William Blake,* with Variant Readings, ed. Geoffrey Keynes, London, Oxford University Press, 1966.

WORKS BY BLAKE

Ahan	*The Book of Ahania*
Amer	*America, a Prophecy*
BLos	*The Book of Los*
DC	*A Descriptive Catalogue*
EG	*The Everlasting Gospel*
Eur	*Europe, a Prophecy*
FR	*The French Revolution*
FZ	*Vala, or The Four Zoas*
GA	*The Ghost of Abel*

GP	*The Gates of Paradise*
Grave	Illustrations to Blair's *Grave*
IM	*An Island in the Moon*
Jer	*Jerusalem*
Job	Illustrations to the *Book of Job*
MHH	*The Marriage of Heaven and Hell*
Milt	*Milton*
Note-Book	The *MS Note-Book* or *Rossetti MS*
NT	Illustrations to Young's *Night Thoughts*
"PA"	"[A Public Address]" from the *Note-Book*
Pick MS	*Pickering MS*
PS	*Poetical Sketches*
SE	*Songs of Experience*
SI	*Songs of Innocence*
SIE	*Songs of Innocence and of Experience*
SLos	*The Song of Los*
Thel	*The Book of Thel*
U	*The First Book of Urizen*
VDA	*Visions of the Daughters of Albion*
"VLJ"	"[A Vision of the Last Judgment]" from the *Note-Book*

GILCHRIST'S *LIFE OF BLAKE*

Two editions in the nineteenth century:

Alexander Gilchrist, *The Life of William Blake, "Pictor Ignotus," with Selections from His Poems and Other Writings*, 2 vols. London, 1863.

Alexander Gilchrist, *The Life of William Blake, with Selections from His Poems and Other Writings,* enl. ed., 2 vols. London, 1880.
Unless specified to the contrary, volume and page references are to the 1880 edition.

Life (or *Life of Blake*)   Refers to Volumes *1* and *2*.
Life (no italics)   Refers to Volume *1* only.
Selections   Refers to Volume *2* only.

(Note: After 1880, Gilchrist's Life was twice reprinted: by editors W. Graham Robertson [London, John Lane, 1906] and Ruthven Todd [New York, Everyman, 1942, and rev. ed. 1945]. The Selections was not issued with the Life, or reprinted in full, after 1880.)

OTHER EDITIONS OF BLAKE'S WRITINGS AND CRITICAL STUDIES, LISTED CHRONOLOGICALLY

Wilkinson   *Songs of Innocence and Experience,* by William Blake, ed. with a Preface by James John Garth Wilkinson (1839), London, New-Church Press, 1925.

Swinburne   Algernon Charles Swinburne, *William Blake: A Critical Essay,* London, 1868.

Aldine   *The Poetical Works of William Blake, Lyrical and Miscellaneous,* ed. with a Prefatory Memoir by William Michael Rossetti, London, Aldine, 1874.

EY   *The Works of William Blake, Poetic,*
                                Symbolic and Critical, eds. Edwin J.
                                Ellis and William Butler Yeats, 3
                                vols. London, 1893.
                                1, The System; *2,* The Meaning; *3,*
                                The Books

Sampson (1905)   *The Poetical Works of William*
                                Blake, ed. John Sampson, London,
                                Oxford University Press, 1905.

OTHER BOOKS (ABBREVIATIONS AND SHORT TITLES USED IN THE NOTES)

Blake Bibliography   Geoffrey Keynes, *A Bibliography of*
                                the Writings of William Blake, New
                                York, Grolier Club, 1921.

B-N   G. E. Bentley, Jr., and Martin K.
                                Nurmi, *A Blake Bibliography: An-*
                                notated Lists of Works, Studies, and
                                Blakeana, Minneapolis, Minn., Uni-
                                versity of Minnesota Press, 1964.
                                References are to item numbers.

Anne Gilchrist   H. H. Gilchrist, *Anne Gilchrist, Her*
                                Life and Writings, with a Prefatory
                                Notice by William Michael Rossetti,
                                London, 1887.

S. L.   *The Swinburne Letters,* ed. Cecil
                                Lang, 6 vols. New Haven, Yale Uni-
                                versity Press, 1959–62.

Thorne Coll.   Thirty unpublished letters from
                                D. G. Rossetti to Anne Gilchrist,
                                with Rossetti's autograph manu-
                                scripts of some passages in the 1863

	and 1880 editions of the Life; owned by Mrs. L. K. Thorne of New York City. Mrs. Thorne has kindly allowed me to quote from the letters.
Blake, Coleridge, Wordsworth, Lamb, Etc.	Henry Crabb Robinson, *Blake, Coleridge, Wordsworth, Lamb, Etc.,* ed. Edith J. Morley, New York, Longmans, Green & Co., 1922.
Letters, ed. Keynes	*The Letters of William Blake,* ed. Geoffrey Keynes, New York, Macmillan, 1956.
Letters of Blake, ed. Russell	*The Letters of William Blake, Together with a Life by Frederick Tatham,* ed. A. G. B. Russell, New York, C. Scribner's Sons, 1906.
Letters Concerning Whitman, Blake, and Shelley	William Michael Rossetti, *Letters to Anne Gilchrist Concerning Whitman, Blake, and Shelley,* eds. Clarence Gohdes and Paull Franklin Baum, Durham, N. C., Duke University Press, 1934.
Life, ed. Todd	Alexander Gilchrist, *The Life of William Blake,* ed. Ruthven Todd, rev. ed. with additional notes, New York, Everyman, 1945.
Life of Linnell	Alfred T. Story, *The Life of John Linnell,* 2 vols. London, 1892.
On Books and Their Writers	Henry Crabb Robinson, *On Books and Their Writers,* ed. Edith J. Morley, 3 vols. London, J. M. Dent & Sons, 1938.
Tatham, Memoir of Blake	See *Letters of Blake,* ed. Russell, above.

CHAPTER ONE

Introductory

During the 1850s in England a well-informed art critic of the younger generation would have known of William Blake only from Allan Cunningham's generally unsympathetic account in his *Lives of the Painters* and the engraved designs to Robert Blair's *The Grave*. Blake had died in 1827 and seemed to be making his way to oblivion; those who remembered the man or had bought his works were settling into old age. Then Alexander Gilchrist, a young writer on art who had just completed a life of the painter William Etty and was looking for a new subject, visited London and happened to see a number of Blake's designs. He saw too a set of Blake's engraved *Inventions to the Book of Job* and at once began work on *The Life of William Blake, "Pictor Ignotus."* It was published, with an accompanying volume of Selections from Blake's prose and poetry, in 1863, almost two years after the death of the biographer.

Gilchrist's memorable trip to London took place probably in 1854. In 1856 he moved himself, his wife Anne Burrows Gilchrist, and their children to 6 Great-Cheyne Row, London, where they lived as intimate next-door neighbors to Thomas Carlyle, Gilchrist's idol and the dominant intellectual personality of the early Victorian age. Except for two years, Gilchrist devoted the six years of life left to him to "a record of Blake's life and works." [1]

1. "Memoir of Alexander Gilchrist," by Anne Burrows Gilchrist, *Life, 2,* 373. For Gilchrist's life and his work on Blake, see this "Memoir" and also *Anne Gilchrist,* pp. 40–77. For the date of his visit to London, see *Life, 1,* 407–08. This and much preliminary work were

Gilchrist set out to refute Cunningham's conception of
Blake as a madman. Rather, Blake was an "enthusiast" whose
difficulty lay mainly in his originality and whose eccentricity
was a mode of self-defense; the Selections would confirm this
view of the man and the artist. Addressing itself to those for
whom Blake was an insane genius or else a quarrelsome ego-
maniac, Gilchrist's was to be a work preeminently of vindication.

A ferocious and conscientious researcher, a man whom
Carlyle called a genius in the "chase of Books," [2] Gilchrist
sought out both Blake's works and printed references to him.
He also spoke with the poet's surviving friends, the most important of whom were John Linnell and a group that had
called themselves the "Ancients." Linnell was a very successful landscape painter who had been Blake's close friend and
patron during the last nine years of his life; it was he who
commissioned the *Job* engravings. The "Ancients" were artists who had formed a youthful discipleship around Blake in
his last two years, calling his rooms in Fountain Court "The
House of the Interpreter." As he had studied Yorkshire for
Etty's biography, so Gilchrist immersed himself in Blake's
London; by 1855 he had spoken to nearly every living person who remembered Blake and had traced out the events of
his life that were recorded in the accounts of Cunningham
and the lesser-known biographers Benjamin Heath Malkin
and John Thomas Smith.[3] He looked at all the books and

------

accomplished while the Gilchrists were living at Guildford (1854–56).
The two years 1856–58 Gilchrist spent looking after the estate of his
deceased brother; he also helped Carlyle (see Chap. 4), wrote some
art criticism, and remained in communication with Samuel Palmer
(Blake's old disciple), although there was no sustained work done on
the *Life.*

2. *Anne Gilchrist,* p. 50.

3. Benjamin Heath Malkin, Esq., *A Father's Memoirs of His Child*
(London, 1806); John Thomas Smith, *Nollekens and His Times:
Comprehending A Life of that Celebrated Sculptor; and Memoirs of
Several Contemporary Artists, from the Time of Roubiliac, Hogarth*

artwork he could, including two major nineteenth-century Blake collections belonging to John Linnell and Richard Monckton Milnes (Lord Houghton after 1864), and he borrowed books, letters, and memorabilia. A notion of what he assembled may be inferred from this entertaining outburst by his neighbor Jane Welsh Carlyle, written three months after he died.

> Since poor Mr. Gilchrist's death there seems to have been a prevailing idea that I am the natural person thro' whom all applications for lent "books" and "papers" is to [be] made to Mrs. Gilchrist!! Now it is anything but an agreeable mission . . . and I have complied several times, with reluctance, but I protest *going on* with this sort of thing, which must be making me perfectly odious to the poor woman and with which I have no business!
>
> Tell Mr. [Henry Crabb] Robinson, who I was believing peacefully laid at rest years and years ago, to write a note himself to the Widow, stating precisely *what* the papers are, and I have no doubt they will be safely restored to him.[4]

All these researches and testimonies Gilchrist set out to compose on a canvas prepared by his reading of Carlyle; what emerged was a unified and consistent image of Blake, an exemplary life which the Victorian public admired, whether or not they cared for Blake's poetry and painting.

It was not until he had nearly completed work on the bi-

---

and Reynolds, to that of Fuseli, Flaxman and Blake (2 vols. London, 1828), 2, 461 ff. Allan Cunningham, *Lives of the Most Eminent British Painters, Sculptors, and Architects* (6 vols. London, 1830), 2, 143–87. All quotations from Cunningham's Life of Blake are from the second edition, which Cunningham enlarged but did not otherwise alter. For more on Blake's biographers and on Cunningham's second edition, see Chap. 3.

4. *Letters of Jane Welsh Carlyle to Joseph Neuberg (1848–1862)*, ed. Townsend Scudder (London, 1931), pp. 32–33 and n., p. 39; letter dated by Scudder February 15, 1862.

ography that Gilchrist learned of the manuscript *Note-Book* owned by Dante Gabriel Rossetti, a major biographical sourcebook for writers after him. Rossetti reported to his friend William Allingham, the poet:

> A man (one Gilchrist, who lives next door to Carlyle, and is as near him in other respects as he can manage) wrote to me the other day, saying he was writing a life of Blake, and wanted to see the manuscript by that genius. Was there not some talk of *your* doing something in the way of publishing its contents? I know William [that is, William Michael Rossetti] thought of doing so, but fancy it might wait long for his efforts; and I have no time, but really think its contents ought to be edited, especially if a new *Life* gives a "shove to the concern." . . . I have not yet engaged myself in any way to said Gilchrist on the subject, though I have told him he can see it here if he will give me a day's notice.[5]

Once they met, Rossetti "took a more than usual fancy" to Gilchrist. He admired his abilities as an art critic; and while engaged in his own painting and in preparing his translations of *The Early Italian Poets* and though beset by anxieties about his wife's health, he found time to advise about the plates for

5. *Letters of Dante Gabriel Rossetti to William Allingham 1854–1870,* ed. G. B. Hill (New York, [1897]), p. 237. Letter dated Nov. 1 (1860). See also William Rossetti's "Prefatory Notice," *Anne Gilchrist,* p. viii; *Dante Gabriel Rossetti: His Family Letters With A Memoir* by William Michael Rossetti (2 vols. London, 1895), *1,* 211; and William Michael Rossetti, *Some Reminiscences* (2 vols. New York, 1906), *1,* 304. In this account, William Rossetti mistakenly dates the Rossettis' first communication with Gilchrist 1859.

For more on Allingham's plan to "do something," see Chap. 3.

Gilchrist's informant concerning the *Note-Book* was William Bell Scott (painter, poet, engraver, and a member of the Pre-Raphaelite circle) or possibly the painter James Smetham (W. B. Scott, *Autobiographical Notes: . . . 1830–1882,* ed. W. Minto [2 vols. London, 1892]; *Life, 2,* Chap. 39; *Anne Gilchrist,* p. 57). For more on Smetham and Scott, see Chap 7.

Gilchrist's *Life* and frequently to visit Gilchrist's home.[6] Often he called with Algernon Charles Swinburne. Madox Brown, Edward Burne-Jones, and probably William Bell Scott also went there, and sometimes Rossetti brought other artists to see the Blake collection that Gilchrist had assembled. Rossetti seems to have made the *Life of Blake* a Pre-Raphaelite enterprise even while Gilchrist was alive; he suggested Mrs. Edward Burne-Jones as copyist for the Visionary Heads: "she really draws heads with feeling . . . —besides Jones would be there to give help without trouble to himself." In June 1861 Rossetti wrote Gilchrist that he had told the engraver Weigall "for the future to let me see his first drawing," this upon happening to see a "plate he is doing for your book, a *Job* border with the America headpiece in the middle." [7]

Rossetti read nothing of what Gilchrist had written, however, until the first proofs came (of Chapters One through Eight) in November 1861. On the 19th of that month, Rossetti wrote, "I have been reading with great pleasure (and corresponding impatience to go on) the two first sheets of Blake" [8] (galleys probably), in a letter Gilchrist never saw.

6. W. M. Rossetti, *Some Reminiscences, 1,* 304; *Dante Gabriel Rossetti: His Family Letters, 1,* 211; and W. M. Rossetti, "Prefatory Notice," *Anne Gilchrist,* pp. viii–ix. D. G. Rossetti, Madox Brown, and perhaps others of the Rossetti circle were in close communication with Gilchrist until he died in autumn 1861.

7. *Anne Gilchrist,* pp. 86 and 89 for quotations, and see pp. 88–89. D. G. Rossetti writes to Madox Brown of "having spent an evening at Gilchrist's . . . with Burne Jones & Swinburne" about a week before Gilchrist died. (*Ruskin; Rossetti; Pre-raphaelitism: Papers 1854–1862,* ed. William Rossetti [London, 1899], pp. 294–95.) A painter friend and a follower of D. G. Rossetti, G. P. Boyce, records in his diary for May 4, 1861: "With Rossetti and Swinburne to Gilchrist's, 6 Cheyne Row. Madox Brown looked in also. Spent a most interesting evening looking over some books of Blake's showing marked originality and marvellous imagination" (G. P. Boyce, "Boyce's Diaries: 1851–1875," *The Old Water-Colour Society's Nineteenth Annual Volume,* ed. Randall Davies [London, 1941], p. 40).

8. *Anne Gilchrist,* p. 95.

On November 30th he died of scarlatina. Surviving him were four children, three having to be nursed through illness, an unsettled estate of proofs, manuscript, and notes, and his remarkable widow.

Extraordinary as she was, Mrs. Gilchrist did not rise immediately to immortalize William Blake. Time elapsed, during which Rossetti sent letters urging her to go on with the book, and offering his help in the project. Even after his wife died under painful circumstances less than three months later, he repeated his offer, volunteering this time his brother William's help. Mrs. Gilchrist now gratefully accepted. In March 1862 she wrote to William Michael Rossetti asking assistance with the extracts from Blake for the biography. (This was the beginning of a correspondence that was to produce "An Englishwoman's Estimate of Walt Whitman" [1870]—originally a letter from Mrs. Gilchrist to William Rossetti on reading *Leaves of Grass* in the first English edition, which Rossetti had brought out.) In early summer the presses started up again, and D. G. Rossetti went to work on the Selections.[9]

The entrance of the Rossettis, with Swinburne, into collaboration brought to bear purposes and modes of apprehending Blake which, unlike Gilchrist's, were neither moralistic nor didactic. To Rossetti Blake looked a Pre-Raphaelite artist-poet, medieval, sensuous, and spiritual—the Blake-image adored by aesthetes of the 1870s and 1880s. Gilchrist's book, as eventually issued, has even some few suggestions of the apostle of individual freedom (co-spirit with Walt Whitman) and the art-for-art's-sake Blake. These were the work of William Rossetti, with Swinburne in the background—as, in general, was all indication of the broader scope of Blake's ideas (beyond his theories of painting). Nevertheless, the circumstances and exigencies of coauthorship proved frustrating. Out of an aroused interest in the prophetic books and

9. Ibid., pp. 104, 122. See, too, the warm "Prefatory Notice" written by William Rossetti (pp. vii ff.). "An Englishwoman's Estimate" appears on pp. 287 ff.

a dissatisfaction with the *Life,* Swinburne wrote the second major book of the mid-century Blake revival, *William Blake: A Critical Essay* (1868). William Rossetti's long-definitive edition of *The Poetical Works of William Blake* with a Prefatory Memoir (the Aldine Blake), published in 1874, summed up the achievement of the group that took up and carried forward Gilchrist's decisive initiative.[10]

To appreciate what Gilchrist accomplished, it is necessary to consider how taste, opinion, and Blake's own life-history conspired to make one of the most remarkable English poets appear to the cultivated world at large—if it could be said to know of him at all in 1855—a madman, with no poetic reputation to speak of, a gifted "but alas! insane" [11] designer and engraver.

10. The mid-century statement is closed by the second edition of Gilchrist's *Life,* published in 1880. This new "enlarged" edition is in fact a summary comment: there are significant changes—revisions, not simply additions—that clearly show the influences of the more enlightened and sympathetic view of Blake's prophetic poems found in the criticism of Swinburne and, to some extent, of William Rossetti; see especially Chaps. 10, 12, 14, and 21 in the two editions; and Chap. 6, nn., below; also my study "Blake in 1863 and 1880: The Gilchrist *Life,*" *BNYPL, 71* (April 1967), 216–38.

11. The remark is from a review of Cunningham's *Lives, Edinburgh Review, 59* (April 1834), 53. Nothing had happened to change this judgment by Gilchrist's time.

CHAPTER TWO

Knowledge and Opinion of Blake During His Lifetime

To Gilchrist Blake seemed always to have been entirely neglected, but this was not strictly the case. Though never widely
known or appreciated, Blake was not simply an obscure and
solitary engraver. He was active in the London art world,
especially in the 1790s, and—as twentieth-century scholars
have at last convinced us, despite the tradition that Gilchrist
perpetuated—he led much of his life "in this world." [1] Blake
himself said (in about 1810) that his "Inventive Powers & his
Scientific Knowledge of Drawing is on all hands acknowl-
edgd" ("PA," E-B, p. 560, and see *DC*, p. 529). The designs
to *The Grave* were almost famous.

1. See Harold Bruce, *William Blake in This World* (New York,
Harcourt Brace & Co., 1925); Mona Wilson, *Life of William Blake*
(rev. ed. [with additional notes] New York, 1949), Chap. 6; Ruthven
Todd's notes to the Everyman edition of Gilchrist's *Life* (rev. ed.
New York, 1945), cited hereafter as *"Life*, ed. Todd"; G. Keynes,
Blake Studies (London, 1949); and especially David Erdman, *William
Blake: Prophet Against Empire* (Princeton, 1954). My account of
Blake's part in the issues of the London art world is based almost
exclusively on Erdman, Chaps. 3 and 25. For Blake's career in the
1790s, especially the commissioning of *NT* and its association with
projects such as Boydell's Shakespeare gallery and Fuseli's Milton
gallery, see Chap. 14. See, too, Gilchrist's *Life, 1*, Chaps. 22–26.
B-N's short prefatory account of "Blake's Reputation and Inter-
preters" (pp. 3 ff.), is particularly useful for the period up to about
1810. The book was published after all my own work was finished and
too late for me to use it very extensively; their work generally con-
firms Erdman's biographical remarks, however, and tends to support
my own discussions.

As a poet, and as poet and illustrator in one, Blake certainly was little known, but this was in part his own doing. Only two of his works ever appeared in letterpress, though without doubt many more could have; and of the two, the *Poetical Sketches* was privately printed and then given to Blake to distribute on his own. The other, *The French Revolution: Book One* (1791), exists in a single copy, generally supposed to be a proof, that the radical publisher Joseph Johnson suppressed when the government began to make things difficult for revolutionary sympathizers. Neither book was reviewed, listed, or advertised. The remainder of his poetry, aside from works left altogether in manuscript, Blake himself engraved (both drawings and letterpress) and printed off on demand. Sometimes he had nothing ready for a prospective buyer.[2] As for the sale and advertising of such works, Blake refused (apparently) to become implicated in the hustling and "puffing" of the booksellers' trade. He resisted and resented R. H. Cromek, the one bookseller who "puffed" his designs (for Blair's *Grave*). That Blake was too uncompromising even for his friends to help is shown by the many letters extant pro-

2. Robert Southey recalled that when he wanted to buy a copy of *SIE*, Blake had none ready. See his letter to Caroline Bowles, dated May 8, 1830, containing a description of Blake's Exhibition of 1809 and a recollection of the man; *The Correspondence of Robert Southey with Caroline Bowles*, ed. E. Dowden (London, 1881), pp. 193–94.

For the publishing history of *PS*, see *Life, 1*, Chap. 4 and Sampson (1905), Bibliographical Preface to *PS*. Sampson's important edition is described more fully in Chap. 5, n. 11. From Blake's neglect to correct proofs, and his indifference to the sale (*PS* exists in 22 extant copies, most inscribed to friends, according to Keynes, *Blake Bibliography* [see too Blake, ed. Keynes, p. 883]), it has been thought that by 1783, when he had begun to work out a more individual style, Blake saw *PS* as mere juvenilia (Harold Bloom, *Blake's Apocalypse* [New York, Doubleday, 1962], Chap. 1).

On *FR*, see *Life, 1*, Chap. 11; *The Poetical Works of William Blake, with The French Revolution . . .* , ed. John Sampson (London, 1913), p. xxxi; *Life*, ed. Todd, p. 373; and Erdman. See too G. E. Bentley Jr., "William Blake as a Private Publisher," *BNYPL, 61* (1957), 539–60.

posing his name for engraving jobs he never took. Cunningham's interpretation was that Blake unreasonably "thought
that he had but to sing songs and draw designs, and become
great and famous"—and that the world in general therefore
slighted him.[3]

In London art circles Blake was known as an exponent of
republican art and a designer of abstract and allegorical subjects, and he was attacked on these grounds. His designs to
Edward Young's *Night Thoughts* (1797) were labeled absurdly "over-literal" and damned for excessive imagination.
Incompatible though they seem, both reactions object to a
"dangerous prevalence of imagination." Clearly imaged and
outlined, Death, Time, the soul, the "torrent of a sinful life,"
and like abstractions circle about the printed text; their actions—past Hours listening to the soul converse, the soul
mourning "along the gloom," and so forth—are rendered
literally. Setting aside for a moment all question of artistic
theory or merit, such unabashed exercise of vision (it remained for Yeats to see Blake as a "too literal realist of
imagination") was looked on by many at that time as un-
wholesome, overwrought, near-hallucinatory. So began the
persistent attributions of mental instability which put a seal on
Blake's worldly unsuccess.[4]

3. Cunningham, p. 153. For these difficulties, see Blake's *Note-
Book* epigrams on William Hayley, John Flaxman, Thomas Stothard,
Cromek, et al. Also letters by George Cumberland, Flaxman, Hayley.
and others, in *Letters*, ed. Keynes. See, too, letters in Russell, *Letters
of Blake;* Wilson, pp. 371–76, and passim; G. Keynes, "Blake's Minia-
tures," *TLS* (Jan. 29, 1960); *Life, 1,* Chap. 22 (for a letter from
R. H. Cromek to Blake); and Joseph Sandell, *Memoranda of Art
and Artists* (London, 1871), p. 31, in B-N, item 1909.

4. *The Farington Diary*, by Joseph Farington, R. A., ed. J. Grieg
(8 vols. London, n.d.), *1,* 141–42, entry for Feb. 19, 1796. See also
1, 151, entry for June 24, 1796; and *1,* 151–52, entry for Jan. 11,
1797. On the diary's accuracy, see *Life,* ed. Todd, pp. 377–78, and
Erdman.

As soon as his original work began to be known and recognized
(by some as "works of extraordinary genius and imagination" *Faring-*

B. H. Malkin in 1806 and Crabb Robinson in 1810, in an article on Blake written for a German periodical, refer to these objections against Blake.[5] Malkin speaks also of calumniators who "criticise the representation of corporeal beauty," as well as objecting to "the allegorical emblems of mental per-

___

ton Diary, 1, 151), Blake was classed with extravagantly imaginative artists such as Fuseli, Flaxman, and John Hoppner. Around the time of *NT,* one hears of Blake's "eccentric designs" influencing Stothard to "extravagance in his art" (ibid., *1,* 151–52, Jan. 11, 1797).

For the rise and turn of Blake's reputation on the failure, commercial and aesthetic, of *NT,* see *Life,* Erdman, B-N, pp. 4 ff., and Tatham's memoir (in Russell, *Letters of Blake*). For evidence of the Lambeth books being the ones most often mentioned in references to Blake, from Malkin (1806) through Cunningham's Life (*SIE, GP, Amer,* and *Eur*), see Henry Crabb Robinson, "William Blake: Künstler, Dichter und Religiöser Schwärmer," *Vaterländisches Museum* (Hamburg, Jan. 1, 1811), trans. K. A. Esdaile, in "An Early Appreciation of William Blake," *The Library,* 5 (July 1914), 229–56 (the article was reprinted in German by H. G. Wright, *MLR, 22* [April 1927], 137–54) and J. Watkins and F. Shoberl, *Biographical Dictionary of the Living Authors of Great Britain and Ireland* (1816). See also G. Keynes and E. Wolf, *William Blake's Illuminated Books: A Census* (New York, 1953) for the proportionately large number of extant copies of the Lambeth books.

In 1799 Blake writes to his friend George Cumberland, "I live by Miracle. . . . Since My Young's Night Thoughts have been publish'd, Even Johnson & Fuseli have discarded my Graver" (*Letters,* ed. Keynes, p. 38).

For a reference to Blake's "depraved fancy," see a review of Stanley's *Leonora* with three designs by Blake, *The British Critic* (Sept. 1796), in Erdman, p. 265. On Yeats, see below, Chap. 8, n. 41.

5. Page references for Malkin's *A Father's Memoirs* are cited in parentheses in the text. Malkin's short biographical and critical sketch of Blake (who drew the portrait of the dead child, Thomas Heath Malkin, for the edition) appears in an Introductory Letter to T. Johnes of Haford dated Jan. 4, 1806. For more on Malkin's biography of Blake see Chap. 3. References to Crabb Robinson's article, "William Blake: Künstler, Dichter und Religiöser Schwärmer, *Vaterländisches Museum,* are from the translation by K. A. Esdaile in *The Library;* the article was written during the year 1810, and printed in Jan. 1811. For more on Crabb Robinson see pp. 17 f. below.

fections" (p. xxiii). Crabb Robinson mentions the same criticisms: Blake's offenses against decency in some of the designs
to *The Grave* (published in 1808) and, "most offensive," the
representations of the reunion of the body and soul in which
"equal clearness of form and outline" is given to both; of the
soul wearing an expression of reluctance as it leaves the body;
of their passionate reunion at the resurrection, and so on.

In a review of the *Grave* designs in Leigh Hunt's *Examiner*
(1808), Robert Hunt coupled the "visionary" Blake with a
particular target of the *Examiner*'s wrath, "frantic" Henry
Fuseli, who wrote the introduction to the designs. Hunt condemned as absurd and outrageous both men's attempts to
connect visible and invisible worlds:

> Whatever is simply natural, such as "the death of a
> wicked strong man," is powerfully conceived and ex-
> pressed; nearly all the allegory is not only far fetched but
> absurd, inasmuch as the human body can never be mis-
> taken in a picture for its soul, as the visible can never
> shadow out the invisible world, "between which, there is
> a great gulph fixed" of impenetrable and therefore in-
> describable obscurity.[6]

6. "R. H.," "Blake's Edition of Blair's *Grave,*" *Examiner*, No. 32
(Aug. 7, 1808), pp. 509–10. Robert Hunt, Leigh Hunt's brother, regu-
larly wrote the "Fine Arts" column, in which the review appears.
(Leigh Hunt had nominated Blake an "Officer of Painting" in " 'the
Ancient and Redoubtable Institution of Quacks' " in "Miscellaneous
Sketches Upon Temporary Subjects &c.," *Examiner* [Aug. 28, 1808],
p. 558; cited in B-N, item 1394.)
    The *Examiner's* attack on both Blake and Fuseli had a history,
which Erdman reports at greater length: In 1806 R. Hunt attacked
Fuseli's painting *Count Ugolino* in *Bell's Weekly Messenger* (May
25); Blake defended Fuseli in a letter to the *Monthly Magazine, 21*
(July 1, 1806), pp. 520–21. Hunt's review of *The Grave* attacks both
Fuseli and Blake, and thanks the engraver Schiavonetti for redeeming
Blake's absurdities and indelicacies. Blake replied to attackers indi-
rectly in the *DC,* and was viciously attacked in turn by Hunt in his
review of Blake's Exhibition of 1809, *Examiner*, No. 90 (Sept. 17,

Hunt's comment,[7] like others directed against Blake's over-naturalistic abstractions, reflects a taste still prevalent, formed according to the principles Samuel Johnson had expressed in objecting to Milton's Sin and Death, and his angels—Milton's error in trying to embody unseen things.[8]

Hunt's second and "more serious" censure of "these most heterogeneous and serio-fantastic designs" is the objection, equally Johnsonian, of a man of Sensibility:

> At the awful day of Judgment, before the throne of God himself, a male and female figure are described in most indecent attitudes . . . an appearance of libidinousness intrudes itself upon the holiness of our thoughts.

Johnson had spoken of the religious feeling of his time as

1809). See Erdman for a full account of the context (Chap. 25); also *Letters,* ed. Keynes, pp. 156–57; *Life,* ed. Todd, p. 382.

S. Foster Damon has brought out an edition of Blake's designs to Blair's *Grave,* arranged in Blake's chosen order, and reprinting Fuseli's introductory note. See *Blake's Grave: A Prophetic Book* (Providence, Brown University Press, 1963).

7. Louis Crompton associates Hunt's criticisms with his brother Leigh Hunt's antipathy to emotional evangelicism—"sacro-sensualism" and "amatory Methodism," "Blake's Nineteenth Century Critics" (University of Chicago, diss., 1953), p. 47.

8. "John Milton," *Lives of the Poets* [1779–1781], ed. G. B. Hill (3 vols. New York, 1905), *1,* 184–85. Johnson writes, "To give [abstractions like Sin and Death] any real employment or ascribe to them any material agency is to make them allegorical no longer, but to shock the mind by ascribing effects to non-entity." Of the mixture of material and spiritual,

> Another inconvenience of Milton's design is that it requires the description of what cannot be described, the agency of spirits. He saw that immateriality supplied no images, and that he could not show angels acting but by instruments of action; he therefore invested them with form and matter. . . . [He] should have secured the consistency of his system by keeping imma-teriality out of sight. . . . But he has unhappily perplexed his poetry with his philosophy. . . . The confusion of spirit and matter . . . pervades the war in heaven.

being more "delicate" if not more fervent than that of earlier
times and disposed to find wit or lightness in sacred things
"offensive." The late eighteenth and the nineteenth century
was not a time for the heroic nudes either of Michelangelo or
of Blake in his "Ancient Britons." (One of the *Grave* illustrations was later bowdlerized for an American edition.)[9]

Blake's continuing support of a grand republican art even
after the French dictatorship and English repression was
evidenced in his Exhibition of 1809, with its *Descriptive
Catalogue*. "The Ancient Britons," and the "Spiritual Forms"
of "Nelson Guiding Leviathan" and "Pitt Guiding Behemoth"
emulate works seen in vision "on walls of Temples, Towers,
Cities, Palaces . . . in the highly cultivated states of Egypt,
Moab" (E-B, p. 522). Robert Hunt, again reviewing Blake,
concluded "that Blake was whitewashing the war policy associated with Pitt and Nelson." Hunt "pronounced that
Blake's reputation was a civic malady so 'pernicious' that it
had become 'a duty to endeavor to arrest its progress.' " In a
vicious personal attack, Hunt went on to denounce Blake as
"an unfortunate lunatic, whose personal inoffensiveness se-
cures him from confinement." The *Catalogue,* Blake's manifesto in behalf of line, imaginative vision, and national art,
was a "farrago of nonsense, unintelligibleness, and egregious
vanity, the wild effusions of a distempered brain." [10]

9. Johnson, "Abraham Cowley," ibid., *1,* 49 ff. See Blair's *Grave*
(New York, A. L. Dick, 1847), where the "Meeting of a Family in
Heaven" has been "gently bowdlerized" (*Life,* ed. Todd, p. 384).
On the heroic nudes, see Erdman.

10. Robert Hunt, "Mr. Blake's Exhibition," quoted and described
in Erdman, pp. 419–20. Erdman writes that Blake felt his paintings
carried forward the "ethical and historical tradition of Mortimer and
Barry" (p. 37, and see "PA," "VLJ," and *DC* for Blake on Ideal
and Republican art). In politics his antagonism to the Pitt government and hatred of its war policy should have appealed to Hunt and
the *Examiner,* but Hunt failed to grasp Blake's "recondite republicanism" (in "Pitt" and "Nelson"), and thought Blake was putting "a
halo" on the Pitt government (pp. 419–20).

In addition to its ideological statement, the *Catalogue* contained Blake's attempt (poorly, or perhaps defiantly, calculated) at self-vindication, particularly with regard to his "Chaucer's Pilgrims":

> Such are the characters that compose this Picture, which was painted in self-defence against the insolent and envious imputation of unfitness for finished and scientific art; . . . This has hitherto been his [Mr. Blake's] lot —to get patronage for others and then to be left and neglected, and his work, which gained that patronage, cried down as eccentricity and madness; as unfinished and neglected by the artist's violent temper, he is sure the works now exhibited, will give the lie to such aspersions.
>
> [E-B, p. 528]

Blake accused Thomas Stothard, R. A., and Cromek, publisher of *The Grave,* of having plagiarized his idea for a painting and an engraving of the procession of the pilgrims to Canterbury. Stothard's oil of this subject had been exhibited in 1807 and achieved some renown. This, together with Stothard and Cromek's much advertised difficulties in completing and publishing their engraving, had given a certain notoriety to the Chaucer subject and to Blake's accusations. Since Stothard and Cromek did not finally present their engraving until about 1814, the affair was kept alive; Gilchrist in 1863 writes that the Stothard engraving "had an extraordinary sale as everybody knows" (*Life, 1,* Chap. 26). Thus even after Blake's Exhibition paintings were forgotten, echoes of the quarrel perpetuated an image of Blake the complainer and accuser, if not the paranoiac.

The Exhibition and *Catalogue,* Blake's major effort to reverse the decade-long trend of abuse and misconceived criticism, failed disastrously. Blake was confirmed a madman, a self-inflated visionary whose claims to prophetic insight were compared with the special powers assumed by religious cranks and assured lunatics. He never afterward put himself before the world.[11]

Nonetheless, a few notable individuals, although they carried away with them an unshakable conviction of Blake's insanity, were able to discern in the Exhibition something of its author's genius. On Robert Southey it produced a "melancholy impression" he never forgot.

> Some of the designs were hideous, especially those which he considered as most supernatural in their conception and likenesses. In others . . . nothing but madness had prevented him from being the sublimest painter of this or any other country. . . . His madness . . . [was] evident . . . fearful.[12]

In 1811 Blake read to Southey parts of *Jerusalem,* "a perfectly mad poem. Oxford Street is in Jerusalem." [13]

11. Blake was classed with religious fanatics like Joanna Southcote and lunatics like Richard Brothers (Tatham's *Life,* in Russell, *Letters of Blake*). Henry Crabb Robinson observed that "Excessive pride equally denoted Blake & Barry [another seer of visions]" (journal entry for Jan. 30, 1815, *On Books and Their Writers.* All references to Crabb Robinson's diaries will be to the date of entry).

After 1810, Blake did try to get *Jer* read; possibly a "puff" by T. G. Wainewright ("Janus Weathercock") in "Mr. Weathercock's Private Correspondence," *London Magazine, 1* (Sept. 1820), 300, is a friendly push (see Chap. 3, n. 3).

More sympathetic references to Blake after 1810 speak of him as an unrecognized and little known artist (see William Carey, *Critical Description and Analytic Review of "Death on a Pale Horse"* painted by Benjamin West, R. A., with desultory references to the works of some ancient masters, and living British Artists . . . [London, 1817], p. 9 [a reference to *The Grave*] and pp. 128–36; and see pp. 18 f. below).

12. Letter to Caroline Bowles, cited above.

13. Crabb Robinson's Diary, *On Books and Their Writings,* July 24, 1811. The entry reads: "Late to C. Lamb's. . . . Southey had been with Blake & admired both his designs & his poetic talents at the same time that he held him for a decided madman. Blake, he says, spoke of his visions with the diffidence that is usual with such people & and did not seem to expect that he shd. be believed."

More fateful for Blake's eventual fame was the visit of Henry Crabb Robinson. Crabb Robinson was a student of German Romantic philosophy and psychology, an admirer of Wordsworth, and had interested himself in the revival of primitive and Elizabethan poetry. He knew the brief sketch in *A Father's Memoirs* in which Malkin had compared Blake with the Elizabethans and had spoken of his "enthusiastic and high-flown ideas on the subject of religion," his "warm imagination," and undisciplined genius. After visiting the Exhibition, Crabb Robinson induced Charles Lamb to go; he also introduced Lamb, Hazlitt, Wordsworth, and others to *Songs of Innocence and of Experience*.[14] In addition, he composed his essay for the German periodical, in which he called attention to Blake as an English genius of the sublime Shakespearean type, one of "those faces . . . in which nature has set something of greatness which she has yet left unfinished." He referred to the "union of genius and madness" and genius' affinities with the childlike and the mystical—notions not very widely allowed at this time (1810) as evidence of sublimity. The article was not reprinted before the twentieth century, nor was it known in England; nevertheless, to some among his own generation, Crabb Robinson communicated a way of

14. Crabb Robinson's "Reminiscences" (collected from memory and from the diaries he began keeping in 1811), for the year 1810, record that he had visited Blake's Exhibition and bought four copies of the *DC* (*On Books and Their Writers, 1,* 15). One of the copies was for his friend Charles Lamb. His diary for Mar. 10, 1811 records his reading Blake's *SIE* to Hazlitt. For Hazlitt's reaction, see Chap. 5, n. 34. On May 24, 1812, he read them to Wordsworth: "He was pleased with some of them, and considered Blake as having the elements of poetry a thousand times more than either Byron or Scott." For others to whom Crabb Robinson introduced Blake's poems see entry for Jan. 12, 1813.

The most important person to whom Crabb Robinson spoke of Blake was, of course, Alexander Gilchrist. Their meeting came about through Samuel Palmer, in 1855 (*On Books and Their Writers,* June 20, 1855). For Palmer see Chap. 3, pp. 57 ff.

valuing Blake—in particular, of coming to terms with Blake's
"madness." [15]

Lamb especially had been attracted by Blake's "marvellous
strange pictures . . . mystical and full of vision" and his
unorthodox opinions about art. He also recalled Blake's criticism, in *A Descriptive Catalogue,* of the General Prologue to
the *Canterbury Tales* as one of the most spirited commentaries
he had ever read on the subject. "I must look on him as one
of the most extraordinary persons of the age," Lamb wrote in
1824;[16] although Blake was living only a short distance away,
in Fountain Court, Lamb did not know that he was still alive.

In his very last years, while it did not significantly widen
his audience, Blake does seem to have drawn some distinguished attention. Samuel Taylor Coleridge, for one, met him
in 1825 or 1826, probably at the salon of Mrs. Aders. Coleridge visited Blake at Fountain Court, and according to Crabb
Robinson talked "finely about him." [17] And, perhaps not

15. Esdaile, "An Early Appreciation of William Blake." In his
Reminiscence for "1810," Crabb Robinson writes: "I was amusing
myself this spring by writing an account of the insane poet, painter,
and engraver, Blake." For Crabb Robinson's other references to
Blake's insanity, see journal entries for April 6, 1828 and Aug. 4,
1836; and Chap. 3, p. 35. Crabb Robinson's article is cited in a
sketch of Blake that appeared in *Neues Algemeines Künstler-Lexicon
. . .* Bearbeitet von Dr. G. K. Nagler (Munchen, E. A. Fleischman,
1835), *1,* 519–22. In 1830, parts of Cunningham's Life of Blake were
translated for *Zeitgenossen,* and are reprinted by Nagler.

16. *The Letters of Charles and Mary Lamb,* ed. E. V. Lucas (3
vols. New Haven, 1935), *2,* 424–27 and n.; letter addressed to
Bernard Barton, dated May 15, 1824 (on Barton, see Chap. 3, pp.
29 f. and 55).

Crabb Robinson may have given one copy of *DC* to Hazlitt, who
echoes Blake on Chaucer's Pilgrims in one of his lectures on Spenser
and Chaucer (1818). Hazlitt writes, "Chaucer, it has been said,
numbered the classes of men, as Linnaeus numbered the plants"
(*Lectures on the English Poets, Works of Hazlitt,* ed. P. P. Howe
[21 vols. London, J. M. Dent & Sons, 1930–34], *5,* 24).

17. See a letter to Dorothy Wordsworth, dated Feb. 1826. Henry
Crabb Robinson, *Coleridge, Wordsworth, Lamb, Etc.,* p. 16.

surprisingly, Blake's name is sometimes linked by critics with that of Coleridge. For the most part the comparison is superficial, but it seems likely enough if one remembers how little was known about Blake's thought. Both men were reputed to be mystical, obscure, and unstable. They appear in such groupings as Coleridge, Blake, and Edward Irving (the head of the Catholic Apostolic Church); Coleridge, Blake, and Landor; Coleridge, Flaxman, and Blake.[18] A witness to a meeting of the two reported that "Blake and Coleridge, when in company, seemed like congenial beings of another sphere, breathing for a while on our earth: which may be perceived from the similarity of thought pervading their works." [19]

Although in 1865 a reviewer of Gilchrist's *Life* speculated that "had his whole training and career been different, [Blake] might have been the Coleridge of his time," the two were seldom associated after 1830. Coleridge was outside the

18. *On Books and Their Writers,* Jan. 8, 1826, Jan. 27, 1811, Feb. 2, 1827.

19. "The Inventions of William Blake," *London University Magazine, 2* (Mar. 1830), 323 n. The writer of the footnote, apparently, is not the writer of the article. For more on "The Inventions . . ." see Chap. 3, pp. 42 ff.

20. Review of Gilchrist's *Life, Quarterly Review, 107* (Jan. 1865), 11. The review, unsigned, may be by Francis T. Palgrave (*S.L.,* No. 53, *1,* 94).

C. H. Herford, *The Age of Wordsworth* (London, G. Bell and Sons, 1897 and 1916), contrasted a rare and, to him unmanly strain of poetry found in "Blake and Chatterton—Coleridge and Keats" to a more robust realism. The realism of Cowper and Crabbe and the "supernatural" strain of "visionaries" like Blake converge in the *Lyrical Ballads* (pp. xi and 152). In 1894, William Macneile Dixon saw Blake as combining Wordsworth's "innocence" and Coleridge's "mystic vision" (*English Poetry from Blake to Browning* [London, 1894], p. 35; cited by Crompton, "Blake's Nineteenth Century Critics," p. 30 n.). See too Walter Pater, *Appreciations* (London, 1889), pp. 98–99.

Crompton notes that Coleridge's association with the thought of Kant, Hegel, and other German philosophers, linking him to a conservative religious and political tradition, discouraged comparison

liberal tradition of the Blake revival.[20] His comments on
Blake's poetry are, however, prophetic of the central problems
Blake presented to the entire nineteenth-century sensibility,
even at its most sympathetic.

Coleridge read Blake's *Songs of Innocence and of Experience* in 1818 in a copy lent him by his friend Charles Augustus
Tulk, a Swedenborgian. He wrote to Reverend Henry F. Cary
that Blake "is a man of Genius—and I apprehend a Swedenborgian—certainly a mystic emphatically." In a letter to Tulk
he rated each poem in the *Songs* according to whether "It gave
me pleasure," "great pleasure," pleasure "in the highest degree," or "not at all" (his favorites being "The Little Black
Boy" and "Night").[21]

Coleridge wrote Tulk that he objected to "Infant Joy" (in
Songs of Innocence) because "a Babe two days old does not,
cannot, *smile*—and Innocence and the very works of nature
must go together." Where the eighteenth-century mind's objection to the *Night Thoughts* illustrations was founded on a
Johnsonian dim view of sacred poetry—that "the sanctity of
the matter rejects the ornaments of figurative diction" [22]—the
difficulties of a newer mentality with Blake may be seen in
Coleridge's comment that "Infancy is too holy a thing to be
ornamented." Coleridge's obstacle, his quarrel with Blake's

---

between him and Blake ("Blake's Nineteenth Century Critics," Chap.
1).

21. *Collected Letters of S. T. Coleridge,* ed. Earl Leslie Griggs
(4 vols. London, 1956–59), *4,* 834; letter to Rev. H. Cary dated
Feb. 6, 1818. Coleridge continues, "You perhaps smile at *my* calling
another poet a *Mystic;* but verily I am in the very mire of commonplace common-place compared with Mr. Blake, apo- or rather—ana-
calyptic Poet, and Painter!" For more on Cary and Blake, see Chap.
3, p. 52. The letter to Tulk is dated [Feb. 12, 1818], ibid., *4,* 836–38.
For more on Tulk, see Chap. 3, n. 25.

22. "Isaac Watts," *Lives of the Poets, 3,* 310. See also "Abraham
Cowley," ibid., *1,* 49 ff., where Johnson writes that "sacred history" is
"a subject indisposed to the reception of poetical embellishments"
(p. 51).

"despotism of symbols" is Blake's quarrel (in reverse) with nature and the natural man. All Blake critics among the post-Romantic Victorians echo Coleridge's problem in one way or another, insofar as they share the nineteenth century's legacy from Rousseau, faith in nature and piety toward the natural heart.

Coleridge also wrote that he found himself "perplexed" by "The Little Vagabond": he was alive to a "mood of mind" which rejects the remote and repressive God of the Churches, but he could not move along with it into an over-sentimental religious humanism. This perplexity leads him to a second objection to the *Songs*—this time, paradoxically, from the side of orthodoxy—concerning the absolute existence of evil and the need to accuse or restrain the natural man. His remarks point to the last stanza; and Coleridge almost certainly takes it that Blake, if not actually speaking in his own person, agrees with his speaker. "The Little Vagabond" ends

And God like a father rejoicing to see,
His children as pleasant and happy as he:
Would have no more quarrel with the Devil or the Barrel
But kiss him & give him both drink and apparel.

[E-B, p. 26]

The common error among "Scholars of Em. Sw. [Emanuel Swedenborg]," Coleridge writes, "is that of utterly demerging the Tremendous incompatibilities with an evil will that arise out of the essential Holiness of the abysmal Aseity [that is, of the unknowable Other], in the love of the eternal Person— and thus giving temptation to weaker minds to sink this Love itself into *good nature*"—an error which causes Coleridge to retreat from the poem as one he "cannot approve altogether." But, he continues, "still I disapprove the mood of mind in this wild poem so much less than I do the servile blind-worm, wrap-rascal Scurfcoat & *fear* of *modern Saints*. . . . Anything rather than *this* degradation of Humanity [To this Coleridge remarks in a footnote, "With which how can we utter

'Our Father'?"] and there-in of the incarnate Divinity!" Evidently, one dialectical mind is clashing with another; however, Coleridge seems not to perceive the ironies in the two poems. The critic Joseph Wicksteed observed that Coleridge failed "to realize the profound element of Blakean humour mingled with Blake's scathing tongue. It is Swedenborg who is almost humourless, not Blake, and S. T. C. reads W. B. in the misleading light of Swedenborg." [23] Taking him for a Swedenborgian may have prevented Coleridge from noting that in Blake the solution to a dualistic god is not a love of the natural man and that in "The Little Vagabond" the two alternatives, Church and Ale-house, merge—the ossifying with the stupefying. Moreover, in reading "Infant Joy," Coleridge, like other readers at the time, was not open to irony in poems on childhood. The tension, evident already in Coleridge, between a belief in nature and an ethical recognition that restraints are needed is one that Swinburne later works out very largely through his study and criticism of Blake.

After Crabb Robinson himself finally made Blake's acquaintance in 1825, also at Mrs. Aders', he visited him and brought friends (and sometimes prospective buyers) such as the young German painter Gotzenberger, whom he reported as saying that "Blake [is] the first and Flaxman . . . the second man he has seen in England." He tried, though unsuccessfully, to arrange a meeting between Blake and Wordsworth.[24] These last years are the time when the Shoreham

23. G. Keynes, "Blake with Lamb and His Circle," *Blake Studies,* p. 98 n.

24. In the letter to Dorothy Wordsworth cited above, Crabb Robinson suggested a meeting between Blake and Wordsworth. But although Blake was interested, Wordsworth apparently was not. He answered Crabb Robinson's letter himself, did not allude to Blake, and the subject was dropped (*Blake, Coleridge, Wordsworth, Lamb, Etc.,* pp. 14 ff.). For Gotzenberger, see *On Books and Their Writers,* Feb. 2, 1827.

disciples made Blake's rooms in Fountain Court their shrine and when his *Inventions to Job* were recognized by the Royal Academy.

In spite of this last-minute attention, Blake never overcame his obscurity, and he died in 1827 without having altered his reputation of insanity.[25] After his death, Allan Cunningham could write that "few men of taste could be ignorant" of Blake's "merits," and in 1863 an irate reviewer of Gilchrist's *Life* protested that he would like to know to whom Blake was "Ignotus." [26] However, the truth seems to have been that by

Crabb Robinson, before and after Blake's death, spoke of him, recited his poems, and interested people in his designs (ibid., Jan. 8, 1826; Feb. 18, 1826; Jan. 8, 1828; May 20 and 22, 1838; Nov. 15, 1847; Apr. 16, 1848; Apr. 27, 1848; Jan. 18, 1851). His famous verbatim records of Blake's opinions on Wordsworth, Milton, and Dante; free love, education, and so forth, date from 1825–27. In 1852, he collected his notes into a "Reminiscence of Blake" (reprinted in *Blake, Coleridge, Wordsworth, Lamb, Etc.*, pp. 18 ff.). These were used by Gilchrist who took some liberties in transcribing.

There is a record of Blake's having attended a dinner party, given by Lady Caroline Lamb, at which Byron was present. Blake's *GA*, 1822, the only book engraved after *Jer*, is addressed "To LORD BYRON in the Wilderness" (see *Diary Illustrative of the Times of George the Fourth* . . . [By Lady Charlotte Bury] . . . , ed. John Galt [4 vols. London, 1839], *3*, 345–48; entry dated Jan. 21, [1820]). There is no record of what Byron knew or thought of Blake.

25. "Mad Blake" persists into the present day. In an article on the career of Theodore Roethke, Stanley Kunitz recalled:

Eventually he [Roethke] more than half-believed that the springs of his disorder were inseparable from the sources of his art, and he could brag of belonging to the brotherhood of mad poets that includes William Blake, John Clare, and Christopher Smart, with each of whom he was able to identify himself as "lost."

[*The New York Review of Books* (Oct. 7, 1963)]

26. Cunningham, *2*, 177 and *Athenaeum*, No. 1880 (Nov. 7, 1863), 600. For more on this review, see Chap. 4, p. 86.

The *Athenaeum*'s reviewer was probably a man acquainted with those who had known Blake personally, and whose wife, as a child, had met Blake. On reading the review, Crabb Robinson guessed the author to be Augustus DeMorgan (*On Books and Their Writers,*

the time Cunningham wrote (1830) it was mainly a small circle of personal acquaintances who still *honored* Blake. A reviewer of Cunningham's *Lives* criticized the author for his absorption with such crude personalities as Blake, Fuseli, Cosway, and Barry: Blake, he said, "the able, but, alas! insane author of some very striking and original designs" barely deserves to be named among painters. The same reviewer excludes Blake's name from a list of ten fine painters of poetical subjects.[27] One anonymous writer in 1830 did, however, indicate quite succinctly the state of Blake's reputation, as well as the simplest way of accounting for it.

> We are perfectly aware of the present state of public opinion on this kind of man, but we know at the same time, that every genius has a certain end to perform, and always runs before his contemporaries, and for that reason is not generally understood,—This is our candid opinion with respect to Blake.[28]

Nov. 24, 1863). For the DeMorgan family's contacts with Crabb Robinson, see *William De Morgan and His Wife,* by A. M. W. Stirling (New York, 1922). For Mrs. DeMorgan's meeting with Blake (She is the beautiful little girl to whom Blake wished happiness—see *Life, 1,* 353), see *Three-score Years and Ten: Reminiscences of Sophia Elizabeth De Morgan,* ed. M. A. De Morgan (London, [1895]), pp. 66–68.

27. *Edinburgh Review* (see Chap. 1, n. 11).
28. "The Inventions of William Blake," p. 320.

CHAPTER THREE

Knowledge and Opinion of Blake
Up to Gilchrist

The First Biographers

The Memoir of Blake by "honest, prosaic," "gossiping" John Thomas Smith which appears in *Nollekens and His Times* (1828) consists mostly of anecdotes. It includes twenty-four lines of Blake's poetry; a discussion of his method of coloring; and a description obtained from Richard Thomson, librarian at the London Institution,[1] of *America, Europe,* and *Songs of Experience.* Smith concentrates on Blake's marriage to Catharine Boutcher, his death, and the question of assessing blame in the Cromek-Stothard affair. Smith's points of emphasis were repeated by Cunningham (who vindicated Stothard and Cromek) and then by Gilchrist (who devoted a chapter to "Blake v. Stothard and Another") and by every nineteenth-

1. References are to the second edition of Smith, *Nollekens, 2,* 461–94. The description of J. T. Smith is Gilchrist's (*Life, 1,* 367).

Smith, Keeper of the Prints and Drawings in the British Museum, consulted John Linnell, Frederick Tatham (one of the Shoreham disciples), Mrs. Blake, and John Varley. His Memoir contains two important letters written by Blake: to John Flaxman (Sept. 21, 1800) and to Ozias Humphreys (Feb. 1808) (see Blake, ed. Keynes, pp. 801–02 and 442–44).

For more on Smith and his sources, see *Life, 1,* passim; Alfred T. Story, *James Holmes and John Varley* (London, 1894); John Thomas Smith, *A Book for a Rainy Day* (London, 1845), Recollection for "1784," pp. 81–82 (reprinted in Arthur Symons, *William Blake* [New York, 1907], p. 387). I am indebted also to a private letter from Professor G. C. Bentley, Jr.

century writer on Blake's life thereafter. Gilchrist also looked into and developed Smith's important firsthand recollection of Blake and the so-called Mathew circle in the 1780s. But for Gilchrist the special appeal of Smith's Memoir, as of Malkin's earlier one,[2] was that Smith sides with Blake's apologists: "I believe," the sketch begins,

> it has been invariably the custom of every age, whenever a man has been found to depart from the usual mode of thinking, to consider him of deranged intellect, and not unfrequently stark staring mad. . . . Bearing this stigma of eccentricity, William Blake. . . .
>
> [p. 461]

One passage recommended itself particularly to Gilchrist— Smith's insistence on Blake's inward piety and his Bible reading. This passage suggests that *Jerusalem* was then known[3]

2. Malkin (*A Father's Memoirs*) refers to accusations of insanity against Blake:

> Mr. Blake has long been known to the order of men among whom he ranks; and is highly esteemed by those, who can distinguish excellence under the disguise of singularity. Enthusiastic and high flown notions on the subject of religion have hitherto, as they usually do, prevented his general reception, as a son of taste and of the muses. The sceptic and the rational believer, uniting their forces against the visionary, pursue and scare a warm and brilliant imagination, with the hue and cry of madness.
>
> [p. xxiii]

3. Blake's *Jer* was not as unknown as, for example, another late book, *Milt*. For evidence of his trying to get a hearing for *Jer,* see Chap. 2, n. 11. Crabb Robinson knew of *Jer* from Southey (see Chap. 2). T. G. Wainewright's "puff" in the *London Magazine, 1* (1820) called *Jer* "an ancient, newly discovered, illuminated manuscript, which has to name JERUSALEM THE EMANATION OF THE GIANT ALBION!!!! It contains a good deal anent one '*Los,*' who, it appears, is now, and hath been from the creation, the sole and fourfold dominator of the celebrated city of *Golgonooza!*" The most convincing evidence is that *Jer* is alluded to by writers on Blake after his death (see pp. 31 f., 45 below).

and that because of it, possibly, Blake was reputed to be an atheist.

> As for his later poetry . . . though it was certainly in some parts enigmatically curious as to its application, yet it was not always wholly uninteresting and I have unspeakable pleasure in being able to state that though I admit he did not for the last forty years attend any place of Divine worship yet he was not a Freethinker as some invidious detractors have thought proper to assert, nor was he ever in any degree irreligious. Through life, his Bible was everything with him; and as a convincing proof how highly he reverenced the Almighty, I shall introduce the following lines. [The concluding stanza of the Address to the Deists follows.]
>
> [2, 465]

From Malkin's life (1806) Gilchrist learned the story of Blake's youth among the monuments of Westminster Abbey. "[All] the ornaments appeared as miracles of art, to his Gothicized imagination" (p. xxxi), writes Malkin in a passage that inspired Gilchrist and, especially, the Pre-Raphaelites and their followers to affirm Blake's medievalism. Malkin was also the inspiration for Gilchrist's approach to Blake's poetry. Writing of Blake's lyrics, Malkin classes him with the Elizabethans, whom he sees in terms of early Romantic taste:

> this untutored proficient . . . has made several irregular and unfinished attempts at poetry. He has dared to venture on the ancient simplicity; and feeling it in his own character and manners, has succeeded better than those who have only seen it through a glass. His genius in this line assimilates more with the bold and careless freedom, peculiar to our writers at the latter end of the sixteenth, and former part of the seventeenth century, than with the polished phraseology, and just, but subdued thought of the eighteenth.
>
> [p. xxv]

In 1806 this may have been avant-garde endorsement; Malkin's reviewers passed it over. One compared Blake rather with the eighteenth-century hymn writer Isaac Watts, a "mere versifier"—but better than Blake.[4] By the time that Cunningham wrote his Life, Romantic poetry and taste were sufficiently established for him to commend Blake's lyric poems as "deep [in] melody and poetic thought," although, at the same time, he held them to be "defective" in "structure of verse" and "inharmonious" in arrangement. In a section that he added later in 1830 Cunningham also stressed Blake's affinities with primitive poetry: "something more may be said, for there is a simplicity and a pathos in many of his snatches of verse worthy of the olden muse" (pp. 146 and 185).[5]

Cunningham's Life was the most influential and the only one much read before Gilchrist's. Cunningham treated his subject as a curiosity, at times a misguided genius, and frequently as a conceited lunatic; he deals with the question of Blake's vision in terms of the "visionary fits to which Blake was so liable" (p. 168). He preferred to accept John Varley's story of the Visionary Heads (Blake's portraits of William Wallace, Edward I, the Ghost of a Flea, etc., who came to pose

4. [Christopher Lake Moody], "Monthly Catalogue. Biography," Monthly Review, N.S., 51 (Oct. 1806), 217. An analogy between Blake's SI and Watts's hymns has been reintroduced into twentieth-century Blake criticism, where it comes up as an ironic illumination about some of the SI.

See a notice of Malkin's sketch in "Half-Yearly Retrospect of Domestic Literature," Monthly Magazine, 22 (Jan. 1806), 633. Blake's poems, says the writer, do "not rise above mediocrity." Blake " 'seems chiefly inspired by . . . Divine Nonsensia,' " according to a review in the British Critic, 28 (Sept. 1806), 339 (see B-N, item 640). For the poems that Malkin printed, see Appendix.

5. All quotations are from the second 1830 edition; see Chap. 1, n. 3. Unlike Smith's Nollekens which went out of print after the second (1829) edition, Cunningham's Lives went into a number of editions. These reprinted the shorter first edition "Life of Blake" (see B-N, item 1059).

for him in vision): that they were likenesses of ghosts Blake claimed he saw, even though John Linnell actively contradicted such literalism. Varley's story became a central instance of Blake's insanity;[6] Gilchrist gives an entire chapter (Chap. 28, "John Varley and the Visionary Heads") to what is after all a series of minor drawings.

On the subject of Blake's private life, however, Cunningham was solicitous. Writing to Linnell for information in 1829 he says, "I knew Blake's character, for I knew the man. I shall make a *judicious* use of my materials, and be merciful where sympathy is needed." [7] Blake's courtship and marriage, his devotion to art and unceasing labor, his cheerfulness in the face of poverty and neglect, and his edifying death (all from Smith's Memoir) are pressed for the maximum of sentiment and melodrama. Cunningham embroidered Smith's account of Blake's saintly death with a long deathbed speech which was subsequently quoted in at least two articles written in the 1840s. His picture of Blake starving in a garret is probably an elaboration of an obituary notice that alluded to Blake's "penury." All of this continued to move sentimental hearts and inspired tributes from minor poets, including two lady bards, Mrs. Felicia Hemans ("The Painter's Last Work") and an American, Mrs. Elizabeth E. Eames ("Love's Last Work"). The Quaker poet and Woodbridge Wit, Bernard Barton, writer of "household" and occasional verse, sent the following effusion to John Linnell after reading Cunningham's Life:

6. See Cunningham's Life of Blake, 169–73. For Linnell on Varley, see *Life of Linnell,* pp. 159–62. Varley's written account of how the Ghost of a Flea and of some of the engraved Heads came to be done appeared in a pamphlet he wrote, *A Treatise on Zodiacal Physiognomy* (1828), a very rare work, which Rossetti lent to Gilchrist (*Anne Gilchrist,* p. viii). For allusions to Blake in connection with the Visionary Heads, in the period 1830 to 1863, see B-N, items 763, 791, 792, 1094, 1382, 1575, and 1765.

7. *Life of Linnell, 1,* 246.

TO MR. LINNELL, OF BAYSWATER

"Yet he was reduced, one of the ornaments of the age,
to a miserable garret and a crust of bread, and would
have perished from want, had not some friends, neither
wealthy nor powerful, averted this disgrace from coming
upon our country."—*Cunningham's "Life of Blake."*

Patron and friend of him who had but few
   Of either, justly worthy of the name,
   To smooth his rough and thorny path to fame;
Methinks with honest pride thou must review
That best of patronage, which took the hue
   And form of friendship, by its generous aim,
   To save our age and country from the shame
Which from neglected genius must accrue!
Nor wealth nor power the wretched garret sought,
   Where he, the gifted artist, toil'd for bread.
'Twas thine the balm of sympathy to shed,
To soothe his wounded feelings while he wrought
Bright forms of fancy, images of thought,
   Or held high converse with the glorious dead.

BERNARD BARTON.[8]

8. Ibid., *1*, 194. The obituary sketching Blake's "penury" appeared
in the *Literary Gazette* (Aug. 18, 1827), 540–41. Symons reprints it
along with two others (pp. 345–349): *Gentlemen's Magazine, 98*
(Oct. 1827), 377–78 and *Annual Register* [for 1827] *69* (1828),
253–54. See in addition, B-N, items 645, 691, and 744.

Mrs. Hemans' poem first appeared in *Blackwood's Edinburgh Magazine, 31* (Feb. 1832), 220–21, where she writes that the work was
" 'suggested by the closing scene in the life of the painter Blake,
which is beautifully related by Allan Cunningham.' " For her subsequent revisions, see B-N, item 1344. She may have inspired Mrs.
Eames's poem in the *Southern Literary Messenger, 9* (Sept. 1843),
559–60. Blake's married life also provoked interest: see Caroline
Bowles' letter to Southey inquiring about the fate of Mrs. Blake, *The
Correspondence of Robert Southey with Caroline Bowles,* dated
April 1830; and Mrs. D. L. Child, "Mrs. Blake, Wife of William

Cunningham's treatment of Blake's vision relies on ready-made criticisms about fancy overcoming judgment, about excessiveness (and excesses) of imagination. There are quotations from the *Descriptive Catalogue* to demonstrate Blake's gigantic conceit as well as his scornful prejudices against Rubens and Rembrandt, against drawing from life, and against oil-painting and chiaroscuro. *The Book of Urizen* (which Cunningham seems to have read) is described in a tone of mystified hilarity, and the opening of *Jerusalem* is printed as evidence of insanity.

One student has noted Cunningham's connection with the Scottish school of "Common Sense" critics who placed artistic value on "naturalness." This would accord with his strong preference for the *Songs of Innocence* and the designs to *Job* over the prophetic books.[9] Cunningham sees Blake's mis-

Blake," *Good Wives* (Boston, 1833), pp. 128–33, B-N, item 1024.

For essays on Blake in periodicals, printed in the 1840s and 50s and deriving from Cunningham, see *"Death's Door* by W. Blake," *Howitt's Journal,* 2 (Nov. 24, 1847), 321–22; William Allingham, "Some Chat About William Blake," *Hogg's Weekly Instructor, N. S.* 2 (1849), 17–20 (see below); "Death of Blake the Painter," *Arthur's Home Magazine,* 3 (Mar. 1854), 220, B-N, item 690; also B-N, item 700. For references in dictionaries and encyclopedias (English, American, French, and German), usually based on Cunningham, see ibid., items a672, 697, 790, a880, 1705, 1706, 1731, 1849, 1852, 1987, 1988. B-N prints a year-by-year "Table of Type-Printed References to Blake before 1863," pp. xvii–xviii.

9. See Crompton, "Blake's Nineteenth Century Critics," pp. 58 ff. for an analysis of Cunningham's criticism.

Apart from possible philosophical sources of his critical position, Cunningham might simply be applying the commonplace that echoes Johnson on Milton: that his ability to portray angels meant he could not portray human beings ("John Milton," *Lives of the Poets, 1*). Eighteenth-century attitudes had by no means disappeared from literary criticism of the 1830s; and also, as has been noted, Cunningham employs not only Common Sense "naturalness" but the essentially Romantic criterion of "deep melody."

The only other book length study dealing more or less directly with my subject is Jacob Walter's *William Blakes Nachleben in der*

guided aesthetic doctrines working against his success as an
artist, particularly in such a work as "Chaucer's Pilgrims."
"The picture is a failure. Blake was too great a visionary for
dealing with such literal wantons as the Wife of Bath and her
jolly companions. The natural flesh and blood of Chaucer pre-
vailed against him" (p. 164).

Cunningham is most severe when he speaks of Blake's
prophetic books: if we judged Blake's "worth" only on the
basis of *Jerusalem, Urizen, America,* and *Europe,* "we would
say that . . . he was unmeaning, mystical, and extravagant"
(p. 181). The *Job* designs are Blake's only late work of
which Cunningham approves; "in such things Blake shone;
the Scripture overawed his imagination, and he was too devout
to attempt aught beyond a literal embodying of the majestic
scene." He never overlays "the text with the weight of his
own exuberant fancy" (p. 175).

Blake, in Cunningham's treatment, tends to split into two:
there is the young man of originality and lucid genius; the
older Blake is obscure and deranged. This dichotomy re-
appears in the biographical approaches of Wilkinson, Gilchrist, and, through Gilchrist, almost every writer after him.
And although the Life seems at times less a serious critical
work than a piece of journalism which evades Blake's complexity, still Cunningham wrote coherently within a rationalistic tradition and also provoked answers from opposing schools
of thought (see below, pp. 41 ff.).

In the second edition of the *Lives* (Vol. 2), Cunningham
added a quotation from Charles Lamb's letter on the Exhibition of 1809, which singled out for praise Blake's Chaucer
criticism in the *Descriptive Catalogue* and manifested sym-

Englishen Literatur des Neunzehnsten und Zwanzigsten Jahrhunderts
(Schaffhausen, 1925 and 1927), which mainly deals with verbal
echoes of Blake in Swinburne, James Thomson, D. G. Rossetti, and
W. B. Yeats.

pathy, admiration, and appreciation for Blake.[10] The weight of Lamb's name and testimony might have balanced Cunningham's treatment of the Exhibition and the *Catalogue*.

Frederick Tatham (one of the Shoreham Disciples) wrote his "Memoir of Blake" with Cunningham in mind; he explained and seconded Blake's principles in the *Descriptive Catalogue* and defended Blake against the ridicule directed at his visions. The Memoir was never published, however, and was lost until after Gilchrist's death. Swinburne used it for one or two anecdotes about Blake's hatred of injustice, and Edwin J. Ellis drew on it for his speculations about Blake's marriage in the Ellis-Yeats edition of Blake's writings.[11] But

10. Lamb's letter (see Chap. 2, n. 16) was written to Bernard Barton.

In 1824 Barton wrote to Lamb to find out whether he had written Blake's "The Chimney Sweeper" (*SI*). (Lamb had contributed the poem to an anthology for chimney sweepers.) In his answer to Barton (1824), Lamb referred to Blake's poems as well as to the *DC*.

Cunningham's Life of Blake renewed Barton's interest. Barton (and Lamb too) knew Cunningham, and his name as well as Lamb's appears in Cunningham's additional passage. Possibly then, Barton (perhaps with Lamb's approval) influenced Cnnningham not only to print parts of the letter but also to add another section on Blake's poetry. The passages added, are at pp. 169–70 (quotation from Lamb) and p. 183 beginning "Of Blake's merits as a poet" to the end.

"The Chimney Sweeper" appeared in *The Chimney-Sweepers' Friend, and Climbing Boy's Album* [comp. James Montgomery] (London, 1824), pp. 343–44. (Montgomery, a hymn writer and later one of the Woodbridge Wits, wrote a prose imitation of Blake's poem, for the anthology.) See, too, *The Letters of Charles and Mary Lamb*, 2, pp. 426–27, n.; J. Holland and J. Everett, *Memoirs of the Life and Writings of James Montgomery, 1* (London, 1854), 38; and G. Keynes, "Blake with Lamb and His Circle," *Blake Studies*, p. 88.

11. Tatham's "Memoir of William Blake" (in Russell, *Letters of Blake*, pp. 1 ff.) was written in 1831 or 1832. Bound up with a copy of *Jer*, it came to light in 1864 (Ibid.; p. 21 n.) and incorporates

coming to light only after Gilchrist's Life, Tatham's Blake,
as opposed to Cunningham's, never greatly affected the pre-
vailing picture of the poet. This is regrettable, for in addition
to the usual pieties about his marriage and death, Tatham's
Memoir is the only one which shows Blake in his worldly as
well as his unworldly and other-worldly aspects: humorous,
ironic, vastly learned, as well as mystical, gentle, and perverse.

Early Critical Opinion—The Mystic, the Madman, and the Seer

Edward Fitzgerald, in the course of analyzing *Hamlet,* compares Shakespeare with Blake, applying the criteria of sublimity (both in nature and in man) commonly subscribed to
by such admirers of Blake as there were in the 1830s:

> I take pleasure in reading things I don't wholly under-
> stand; just as the old women like sermons: I think it is of
> a piece with an admiration of all Nature around us. I

---

an attempt at interpreting this poem. Tatham's biography clearly
distinguished Blake's visions from ghosts and from the hallucinations
of madmen:

> The Cock Lane ghost story, the old women's tales and the
> young bravo who defies the ghost in the tap-room, that he
> shudders at in his walk home, are foolishly mixed up with
> Blake's visions. They are totally different; they are mental
> abstractions. . . . These visions of Blake seem to have been
> more like peopled imaginations and personified thoughts. . . .
> Richard Brothers has been classed as one possessing this power,
> but he was really a decided madman; he asserted that he was
> nephew to God the Father, and in a mad-house he died, as
> well indeed he might. Brothers is only classed with Swedenborg
> in order to ridicule Swedenborg and bring him into contempt.
> Blake and Brothers, therefore, must not be placed together.
>
> [p. 21]

For anecdotes from Tatham's "Memoir" in Swinburne, see pp. 77–79
and 84 of Swinburne's *William Blake.*

think there is a greater charm in the half meanings and glimpses of meaning that come in through Blake's wilder visions: though his difficulties arose from a very different source from Shakespeare's.

He adds that his "particular interest in this man's writing and drawing" comes "from the strangeness of the constitution of his mind." To one writer in 1833 Blake is an "embodied sublimity." George Darley praised Blake's "sublime and singular genius." In 1835, Bulwer-Lytton termed the designs for *Night Thoughts* "one of the most astonishing and curious productions which ever balanced between the conceptions of genius and the ravings of insanity." Crabb Robinson for twenty years after he knew Blake also enjoyed speaking of his "interesting insanities," and much of Blake's attraction for Lamb was due to the appeal of the eccentric.[12]

12. *Letters of Edward Fitzgerald,* ed. J. M. Cohen (Centaur Classics, Carbondale, Southern Illinois University Press, 1960), p. 6, letter dated Nov. 19, 1833; and p. 5, letter dated Oct. 25, 1833. "Bits of Biography: Blake, the Vision Seer, and Martin, the York Minster Incendiary," *Monthly Magazine,* 15 (Mar. 1833), 244–45. The rest of this piece is an account of ghosts and Blake's literal belief in their reality. The conception—like Fitzgerald's idea of Blake who made "drawings . . . of Alexander the Great, Caesar, etc., who he declared, stood before him while he drew"—comes from reading Cunningham's Life (*Letters of Fitzgerald,* Oct. 25, 1833). C. C. Abbott, *The Life and Letters of George Darley* (London, Oxford University Press, 1928), p. 165. (In 1831 Darley writes to his good friend Allan Cunningham, "Your Blake is the only thing better than your Flaxman." He goes on to flatter Cunningham in a light vein, not taking the book very seriously [p. 98].) Edward Bulwer-Lytton, *The Student: A Series of Papers* (2 vols. London, 1835), 2, 152–55. See also his *A Strange Story* (2 vols. London, 1862), 2, 167–68. Crabb Robinson, *On Books and Their Writers,* Apr. 6, 1828; and *Letters of Charles and Mary Lamb* (see Chap. 2, n. 16). A reviewer (possibly William P. Carey) of Varley's *Treatise on Zodiacal Physiognomy* (see above, n. 6) writes that " 'the madness of poor Blake (sublime as in some remains of him we possess, it was) is too serious a subject to be jested with' " ("Literary Novelties," *Literary Gazette* [Oct. 11, 1828], 654. See B-N, item 728). Abraham Raimbach re-

Blake could be fitted recognizably into the category of the "personality of genius" that had been naturalized in England from German thought (largely through the efforts of Crabb Robinson and Coleridge), and was subsequently elaborated by Carlyle. Not restricted to any particular medium of expression or to the artist at all for that matter, the conception was neither aesthetic nor as yet moral. So far as Blake was concerned, it simply included him (as had Crabb Robinson's article of years before) among the "whole race of ecstatics, mystics, seers of visions and dreams." [13] Such classification of Blake belongs mainly to the period between 1800 and 1840 but persisted into the 1860s.

A slightly later sensibility would see in Blake's separation from the world mainly a happy self-sufficiency; but John Clare, who once wrote that Blake was "brave by instinct and honest by choice," [14] John Ruskin, and Landor saw it more as courageous, even martyred, resistance in the face of the "grim Satanic mills." Art and social concern had not yet become mutually irrelevant; it "was still possible in the general cultural situation of the Early Victorian period, at least in theory, to conceive of poetry as an effective social and moral force, and so far in England it had occurred to no one to claim

ferred to Blake's "insane Genius" (*Memoirs and Recollections of the Late Abraham Raimbach, Esq.,* . . . , ed. M. T. S. Raimbach [London, 1843]; in B-N, item 1796).

13. Robinson, "William Blake: Künstler, Dichter und Religiöser Schwärmer," Esdaile, p. 249.

In 1826 Hazlitt classed Blake among "mystical artists (like Varley, Sharp, Cosway, and Flaxman) who in order to relieve the "literalness of their profession," "pass their time between sleeping and waking, and whose ideas are like a stormy night, with the clouds driven rapidly across, and the blue sky and stars gleeming [sic] between" ("On the Old Age of Artists," Essay Nine of *The Plain Speaker, Works of Hazlitt,* ed. P. P. Howe, 7, 95). The essay appeared anonymously in 1826.

14. *The Prose of John Clare,* ed. J. W. and A. Tibble (London, Routledge & Paul, 1951), p. 228. Only the single sentence is printed under "Fragments" written between 1825 and 1837. (Not in B-N).

autonomy for the aesthetic experience." [15] To Walter Savage
Landor, the very impressiveness of Blake's aspirations might
have warranted declaring him "the greatest of poets" (spoken
in 1838 to a company that included Crabb Robinson, Monckton Milnes, and Carlyle). Landor's own ambitions had been
shaped by the promise of the French Revolution; he had left
England a disappointed and disillusioned republican early in
the century and probably never read Blake until, on a visit in
1837, he picked up "some of the writings . . . at an old
bookseller's in Bristol" and became "strangely fascinated."
For Landor *America, Europe,* and the *Marriage* may have
realized the epic poems of liberty he himself never effectively
brought to life. Of his own ambitions he wrote:

> Lately our poets loiter'd in green lanes,
> Content to catch the ballads of the plains;
> I fancied I had strength enough to climb
> A loftier station at no distant time
> And might securely from intrusion doze
> Upon the flowers thro' which Ilissus flows.
> In those pale olive grounds all voices cease,
> And from afar dust fills the paths of Greece.
> My slumber broken and my doublet torn,
> I find the laurel also bears a thorn.

About Blake he noted once in a private notebook, "Never
did a braver or a better man carry the sword of justice." [16]

15. Alba H. Warren, Jr., *English Poetic Theory, 1825–65,* Princeton Studies in English, No. 29 (Princeton, 1950), p. 20. See also
Jerome Buckley, *The Victorian Temper* (Cambridge, Mass., 1951).

16. For Landor's comments and his poem, see: *On Books and
Their Writers,* May 20, 1838; a note written by Landor in a MS note-
book from the Browning and Fairfax Murray Libraries (sold at
Sotheby's) quoted in Keynes's *Blake Bibliography,* p. 335 n.; and
The Poetical Works of Walter Savage Landor, ed. S. Wheeler (3 vols.
London, Oxford University Press, 1937), *2,* 476. See also John Forster,
Walter Savage Landor: A Biography (2 vols. London, 1869), *2,* 322–
23.

Landor's biographer writes that Landor became "anxious to have

For Ruskin, especially after the publication of Gilchrist's *Life* in 1863, Blake was preeminently the poet of "Auguries of Innocence," filled with social passion and compassion and with mad prophetic wrath. He compared Blake with Benjamin Haydon, contrasting their respective insanities; he ascribes Haydon's to "weakness of insolent egotism" but speaks of Blake's "conscientious agony of beautiful purpose and warped power." [17] Ruskin is speaking here of an ethical insanity, a sort of honorable madness, and as he grew older he saw Blake more and more in the terms of his own frustrations and agonies. In one of his letters (to a painter friend, and alluding to her taste for the ghastly) he notes, "We [that is, the English] have had one grand man of the same school—William Blake—whose 'Book of Job' fail not to possess yourself of—

---

collected as many more [of Blake's writings] as he could, and enlisted me in the service," but Forster never had the time or energy for it (Forster, *2,* 322–23).

Landor's comments are probably the most unqualified praise of Blake voiced by a Romantic poet; the reason they come down to us at all is that Landor lived so long (he died in 1864); and Gilchrist's *Life of Blake* made any famous man's recollections or comments about Blake of value, whereas earlier appreciations of an accepted lunatic may not have been recorded in print.

17. *A Cestus of Aglaia* [1865–66], *Works of John Ruskin,* ed. E. T. Cook and Alexander Wedderburn (39 vols. London, 1907), *19,* "Liberty," 133. All quotations from Ruskin are from this edition.

Ruskin saw Blake's work soon after he met and became a friend of Blake's Shoreham disciple George Richmond (see below) in Rome in 1840. (Richmond subsequently painted a number of portraits of Ruskin over the years.) Ruskin almost bought a portfolio of Blake's drawings but ultimately kept only *Let Loose the Dogs of War* (see *Works, 36,* 32–33 and also xxvii; and the annotated lists of Blake's designs, *Life,* 1863, *2*). Ruskin is said to have owned also a fine, colored copy of *Jer,* which he cut apart and distributed to friends (see A. M. W. Stirling, *The Richmond Papers* [London, 1926]; R. H. Wilenski, *John Ruskin* [N. Y., F. A. Stokes Company, 1933], pp. 163–64 and n.; and Keynes and Wolf, *William Blake's Illuminated Books, A Census,* p. 111). On his owning *NT,* see B-N, item 1875.

if it come in your way; but there is a deep morality in his horror—as in Dante's." And in a note to his statement in 1856, "All sincere and modest art is, among us, profane," Ruskin says that "Blake was sincere, but full of wild creeds, and somewhat diseased in brain." (Knowing nothing at this time of Rossetti's indebtedness to Blake's *Note-Book*,[18] he excepts from his generalization about the profanity of sincere art a "new Phase," Pre-Raphaelite art.) Ruskin later turned his interest to Blake's poems and praised them in Pre-Raphaelite language. His response to the mind that created them is, by 1872, manifestly and painfully self-projective:

> The impression that his drawings once made is fast, and justly, fading away. . . . But his poems . . . are written with absolute sincerity, with infinite tenderness, and . . . [are] the words of a great and wise mind, disturbed, but not deceived, by its sickness; nay, partly exalted by it.[19]

18. See, in order of citation, *Letters, 36,* 109–10 (written in about 1850); *Modern Painters, 3,* Part iv, *5,* 323 n. See *ibid.,* pp. 137–38 for comments on the designs to *Job* which D. G. Rossetti quoted in Chap. 39 of Gilchrist's Life.

19. *The Eagle's Nest* [1872], *22,* 138. Ruskin's title comes from the Motto to *Thel.* See, too, pp. 151 and 470.

Ruskin writes movingly also of "religious madness" in Blake, thinking perhaps of his own Rose LaTouche. The passage is not on personal suffering however; Ruskin reviews a number of figures who might have been great spokesmen, prophets—but because they were estranged from the world about them, remained inarticulate.

> [Blake found] refuge for an entirely honest heart from a world which declares honesty to be impossible, only in a madness nearly as sorrowful as its own;—the religious madness which makes a beautiful soul ludicrous and ineffectual; and so passes away, bequeathing for our inheritance for its true and strong life, a pretty song about a tiger, another about a birdcage ["A Robin Redbreast in a cage/ Puts all Heaven in a rage" from "Auguries of Innocence"], two or three golden couplets, which no one will

While recovering from a breakdown, brought on by Carlyle's death and the feeling that the moral-prophetic burden of the age now rested on him alone, Ruskin wrote that his last terrible siege had shown him "what kind of temper Blake worked in." [20]

In the 1840s and 1850s, however, there were not many to whom madness might be understood as frustrated evangelicism or a portion of sublime genius. Southey, exhibiting what was certainly the prevalent temper, anatomized Blake in *The Doctor* (1847), along with other curiosities of life and literature; and by 1859 a book *On Hallucinations* has Blake in Bedlam, as "Example 28" of "Hallucinations Involving Insanity," combined hallucinations of "sight and hearing." [21] It

---

ever take the trouble to understand,—the spiritual portrait of the ghost of a flea,—and the critical opinion that "the unorganized blots of Rubens and Titian are not art."

[*A Cestus of Aglaia* (1865–66), *Works, 19, 56*]

Ruskin continued to mine the "Auguries" in particular for aphoristic touchstones on pain, destruction, and prophetic frustration (see *Fors Clavigera* [1877], *Works, 29,* 36 and 577; *Bibliotheca Pastorum* [1877], *Works, 31,* 187.)

20. Letters to George Richmond, *Letters, Works, 37,* 361. See also a letter to Charles Eliot Norton on the same subject of Ruskin's identification of Blake's mental disorder with his own, ibid., p. 569.

21. Robert Southey, *The Doctor* (London, 1847), *6,* 116–27 and *7,* 160–63. A section on ugliness (in *6*) deals with *DC,* the "Ancient Britons"—one of Blake's "worst pictures"—and the "Mad Song" (*PS*) (which Southey reprints); Blake is "that painter of great but insane genius . . . of whom Allan Cunningham has written so interesting a memoir." The passage in *7* repeats the story of the spirit of a flea visiting Blake, from Varley's *Treatise on Zodiacal Physiognomy* (see n. 6).

In the first piece (*6*), Southey attributed Blake's knowledge of the three who escaped the disaster at Camlan, the ugliest, strongest, and most beautiful men (cf. *DC*) to William Owen, the "Welsh-headed" storehouse of "Cymric tradition and lore" (p. 117). His letter to Caroline Bowles written in 1830 (see Chap. 2, n. 2) recounts the influence of Owen upon Blake's imagination.

For "Example 28," See A. Briere de Boismont, M. D., *On Halluci-*

is with this attitude toward Blake that Gilchrist had to contend.

Among the important early writings about Blake—important because there is so little—are two articles that appeared about the time of Cunningham's Life and which, in different ways, are more appreciative of Blake's visionary imagination: "The Last of the Supernaturalists" in *Fraser's Magazine* and "The Inventions of William Blake" in the *London University Magazine*.[22] "The Last of the Supernaturalists" is more dependent on Cunningham for biography and criticism. Its approach to the relationship between genius and madness is more ethical than psychological; the writer concludes, not that Blake's "madness . . . was really the elements of a great genius ill-sorted" [23] (as Crabb Robinson and others held) but that outward circumstance (in the abstract) may pervert the *quality* of genius, especially where there is either a weak character or a lack of guidance. Genius, as it is for Carlyle, is primarily a divinely conferred, nonspecialized potentiality. Had Blake, "the mystic, the spiritualist, the supernaturalist," been given advice, education, and guidance, he might have been "like Goethe . . . a perfect man . . . yielding in merit to few of his prophetic brethren, [and] would have been honoured by them and by mankind as a truly inspired *Vates*" (pp. 218–19). In this there is a foreshadowing of the unfulfilled Carlylean "prophet-hero" to be found in Gilchrist's presentation of Blake.[24] According to the writer, Blake was a

---

nations: A History and Explanations . . . (1854), trans. R. S. Hulme, F. L. S. (London, 1859), Chap. 3, pp. 83–85. See Wilson, *Life of Blake*, pp. 347 ff. for the genesis of de Boismont's story.

22. "The Inventions of William Blake," 318–23 (see Chap. 2, n. 19); and "William Blake, The Last of the Supernaturalists," *Fraser's Magazine, 1*, No. 2 (Mar. 1830), 217–35.

23. See *Letters of Edward Fitzgerald*, p. 5 (Oct. 25, 1833).

24. Thomas Carlyle, *On Heroes, Hero-Worship and the Heroic in History* [1841], *Works of Thomas Carlyle*, Centenary ed., 5 (London, n.d.). Carlyle has been suggested as the writer of this essay, and it is listed by his bibliographer Dyer, on the basis of A. S. Barrett's argu-

man of genius who found himself "alone in the world" (p. 219), could not support that isolation, and longed to find a refuge in a world of childhood. This meant abdicating the responsibilities of an adult, rejecting the "laws of mutuality" (p. 227), abstaining from one's appointed task: "he wished ever for a calmer and more quiet retreat, where man's sinfulness should never meet his eye . . . the blessed retreat of childhood and innocence" (p. 220). Cunningham had simply attributed to neglect Blake's turning away from the active world; but in this article Blake's withdrawal, ultimately into insanity, is construed as the escapism of unsupported genius and offended innocence.

The writer for the *London University Magazine*[25] is more

ment that the writer's diction and acquaintance with German philosophy point to Carlyle (*TLS* [Apr. 26, 1928]). The *Fraser's* article is Carlylean in its sympathetic tone to a fellow Scotsman (Cunningham) and in its long digression on Vitalis who turned his back on human help and failed in the Appointed Task. Yet that Gilchrist should have lived next door to Carlyle, communicating with him daily about his Blake book and seeing Carlyle's own *Works* through the press (see Chap. 4), without knowing or saying that Carlyle had written on Blake, seems unthinkable. The essay has also been ascribed to a disciple of Coleridge John Abraham Heraud, or to William Maginn, who wrote for *Fraser's* at this time (Miriam Thrall, *Rebellious Fraser's* [New York, Columbia University Press, 1934], pp. 267–68). Crompton agrees that neither author is admissible ("Blake's Nineteenth Century Critics," p. 65 n.).

25. The article is unsigned. Keynes thinks one of the Shoreham disciples, possibly Palmer, wrote it (*Blake Bibliography,* p. 375). However, since Gilchrist never mentions it, any one of the Shoreham group is unlikely. Crompton guesses the author to be B. H. Malkin (on circumstantial evidence). My own suggestion, also on circumstantial evidence, is that a Swedenborgian strain of Blake interest was responsible for it, the author possibly being Charles Augustus Tulk, who introduced Coleridge to *SIE* in 1818 (see Chap. 2). My guess is based upon: 1) the article's repeated references to Blake and Flaxman (a Swedenborgian and Tulk's friend) together (and not Fuseli who is more commonly linked with Blake); 2) the evidence of the author's having known about *Jer* without having read deeply in it (e.g., he speaks of "Albion, with *which* the world is very little ac-

in the spirit of Landor and Ruskin than of the *Fraser's* critic
and is the most confident concerning Blake's sanity; he en-

quainted" [pp. 320–21, italics mine]); he perhaps knew one who, like
Flaxman (and few others), read the poem and pronounced it
"grand"; 3) the article's similarities to the Swedenborgian Garth
Wilkinson's preface to *SIE* (see below) and the fact that Tulk lent
Wilkinson his copy of *SIE* and interested him in Blake; 4) the fact
that an "Augustus Tulk" of Duke St., Westminster, is among those
listed for Honors and Prizes at London University in 1829 (*London
University Magazine, 1* [1829], 250).

According to Wilkinson, Tulk (1786–1849) was "a Friend of
Blake's" (G. Keynes, "Blake, Tulk, and Garth Wilkinson," *The
Library*, Ser. iv, *26*, No. 3 [Dec. 1945], 190–91); there is extant a
copy of *PS* inscribed to Tulk by Blake and as a rule all the *PS* are
inscribed and were given to friends—George Cumberland, Anna Flaxman, Thomas Butts, John Flaxman, Samuel Palmer (*Blake Bibliography*, p. 78). A "fringe" Swedenborgian, Tulk with John Flaxman
founded the London society to publish the writings of Swedenborg in
1810. He was a political and social liberal, a writer for journals, and
after 1820 a member of Parliament. Tulk was interested in a rational
mysticism founded on Swedenborgian writings; and was particularly
drawn to Berkeley, to whose work he introduced the young J. J. Garth
Wilkinson in the 1830s. For Wilkinson's early intellectual tutelage
under Tulk, see Clement John Wilkinson, *J. J. Garth Wilkinson; A
Memoir of His Life* (London, 1911).

Blake's connection with Swedenborgian thought dates from about
the time of *MHH;* among his Swedenborgian friends were Flaxman,
Thomas Butts (his chief patron), Frances O. Finch (one of the
Shoreham disciples) (see Erdman, *William Blake: Prophet Against
Empire*, p. 456). Crabb Robinson's German article records some contemporary (1810) hearsay that Blake was invited to join by Joseph
Proud (1745–1826), minister of the New Church (Esdaile, 240). *DC*
is sympathetic to Swedenborg; and in 1818 Coleridge was under the
impression that Blake was a Swedenborgian.

In *MHH*, "Swedenborg is the Angel sitting at the tomb: his writings
are the linen clothes folded up" (E-B, p. 34). But in *DC*, Number
VIII, "The spiritual Preceptor, an experiment Picture," the subject of
the picture being taken from Swedenborg's Visions, Blake advises
painters and poets to seek "foundations for great things" in the works
of Swedenborg: "the reason [the works of this visionary] have not
been more attended to, is, because corporeal demons have gained a
predominance" [E-B, p. 537].

lists Blake as the arts' spokesman for the writer's own ideal of a new England. He envisons a national political renaissance to be based on a peculiarly English ideal philosophy (which is yet conformable to current German idealistic principles) and supported by sympathetic artists who would "love and instruct" England (p. 320). As uncompromisingly antimaterialistic artists, Blake and John Flaxman, along with Coleridge as philosopher, should be "forerunners" of a "more elevated and purer system which has even now [1830] begun to take root" in their country: "they have laid a foundation for future minds—Coleridge, for the development of a more internal philosophy—Blake and Flaxman, for a purer and more ennobling sentiment in works of art" (p. 318).

The *London* writer attributes both the neglect of Blake's work and the imputations of insanity not to disorder in Blake but rather to the rationalistic and scientific preoccupations of English thought. There is no consideration of Blake's having retreated, no interest in his psychological makeup; obscurity is not taken to imply insanity. He suggests, "Perhaps 'reason stumbles all night over bones of the dead' [sic] [26] as Blake has elegantly expressed it" (p. 320). Only in England, where "little attention is paid to the works of the mind, and . . . much to natural knowledge," could Blake, with Flaxman, have been thus "buried in obscurity" (pp. 320, 318). Had he been a German artist,[27] Blake would have "by this time . . . had commentators of the highest order upon every one of his effusions" (p. 320). English critical skepticism toward Blake's kind of work is countered with a combined defense, definition, and commendation of his extreme antimaterialism: Blake

26. "They stumble all night over bones of the dead," "The Voice of the Ancient Bard," *SIE,* E-B, p. 32.

27. Crompton notes that this is the first instance in English criticism of Blake's work and thought being specifically related to the thought of his time—that is, to ideas of German Romanticism ("Blake's Nineteenth Century Critics," pp. 61 ff.). Crompton also notes that the *London* writer is the first to attempt an analysis of a prophetic poem (*Jer*) and to defend Blake's obscurities.

"contemplated the natural world as the mere outbirth of thought." Like Novalis, he "lived and existed in that world for which we are created" (p. 320). The *London* writer makes the unequivocal pronouncement—not to be heard again in Blake criticism until the end of the century—that Blake's writings[28] are, all of them, wholly sane: his "wandering flights" have "every one of them . . . been well-digested in the brain of a genius"; he goes on to advise readers, in a Blake-like metaphor, that reason alone will inhibit the understanding of such a genius: "[W]e should endeavour rather to unlock the prison-door in which we are placed, and gain an insight into his powerful mind than rail and scoff at him as a dreamer and madman" (p. 320). The writer's attempt to convey Blake's meaning and purpose in *Jerusalem,* the work singled out by Cunningham and others as indisputably insane, is a further vindication of Blake's art. What would appear to be madness is, in effect, pure prophecy: "Horrid forms and visions pervade this Albion, for they were the only representative, in his opinion, of the present state of mankind" (p. 320). More generally, the *London* critic vindicates Blake's (and Flaxman's) ideal art, their efforts at direct representation of spiritual experience; and, probably thinking of the *Grave* designs, he rejects the common charge attached to Blake's work since the 1790s that "sensual representation" in itself defiles spiritual existences:

> Flaxman and Blake thought it a still higher honour to be celebrated for their innocence and beauty of sentiment, than for a mere sensual representation of forms. Their internal aesthetic produced a similar external, not by any means inferior to the mere form-painter, and in this

28. The use to which the *London* writer puts Blake in proposing him as a forerunner of a national art suggests that he is familiar with parts of *DC,* and understands something of Blake's view of his art. Of Blake's other works, he has read *Thel, SIE,* and possibly parts of *Jer.* No other works are dealt with sufficiently so that one can know how extensively read in Blake the writer actually is.

respect superior, that there was a Promethean fire which
glowed in their productions, purifying the soul from the
gross imperfections of the natural mind.

[p. 320]

The "Promethean fire" of Blake's originality is seen as an
artistic corollary to a "freedom of thought" unknown to other
European nations. The high "sentiment" in the works of Blake
and Flaxman has been "practically, and not theoretically developed" (p. 320) only in the works of English artists; these
alone have succeeded in embodying in their art "a higher
principle . . . which conducts from the merely sensual delight of form to a contemplation of the beauties of the soul."

> The powers, then, of both mind and body having been
> freely exercised, the result is a genius, who stands forth
> as a representative of his race; and thus we may say,
> Blake in his single person united all the grand combina-
> tion of art and mind, poetry, music, and painting; we
> may carry the simile still further, and say, that as Eng-
> land is the least fettered by the minds of other nations,
> so Blake poured forth his effusions in his own grand
> style, copying no one . . . but breathing spirit and life
> into his own works; and though shaping forms from
> the world of his creative and sportive imagination, yet
> he still remembered he was a moral as well as intellectual
> citizen of England. . . . These ought to be the ruling
> principles of all artists and poets.

[p. 320]

Ultimately, the *London* writer is using Blake for his own
cause. He represents an extreme position in an intellectual
crusade against the rationalistic and Utilitarian spirit of his
time. And throughout the century Blake is to be recruited,
according to varying strategies, for rebellions against ma-
terialist ideas and philistine attitudes. As a critic the *London*
writer is superficial; however he prints a good deal of poetry,

five lyrics from *Songs of Innocence and of Experience* and thirty-seven lines of *The Book of Thel* (see Appendix, p. 272). His remarks are limited to pointing out that they are effective poems.

In demonstrating that a high regard for Blake's genius is compatible with a very slight acquaintance with his poems and paintings, "The Inventions of William Blake" is, along with the essay in *Fraser's,* wholly characteristic of the Victorian temper between 1825 and 1865. The first printed edition of *Songs of Innocence and of Experience* (1839) was inspired by very much the same feeling about Blake that one finds in "The Inventions of William Blake." The young Swedenborgian James John Garth Wilkinson printed them because they attested to the reality of immaterial things, demonstrating the superiority of the intuitions (which he terms "Spiritual phenomena") over sensational evidence (p. xiv).[29] As William Bell Scott, who met Wilkinson about this

29. All page references in parentheses in the text are to Wilkinson's "Preface." The text of his edition follows C. A. Tulk's copy of *SIE,* the one Coleridge borrowed (*Blake Bibliography,* pp. 121 and 265–67, and Chap. 3 n. 25 above). On Wilkinson's editing, see Chap. 5. Wilkinson includes Blake's "Dedication" from Blair's *Grave;* he dropped "The Little Vagabond," but restored it in a second printing. Interestingly, this poem was defended by the Swedenborgian Henry James, father of the novelist, with whom Wilkinson corresponded from about 1840 until the end of his life. See a letter from James signed "Y. S.", "William Blake's Poems," *Spirit of the Age, 1* (Aug. 25, 1849), 113–14; the poem is termed a comment on hollow orthodoxy. "True worship," James says, is "an offspring of delight" and "cannot be spontaneous, so long as the native passions or susceptibilities of the worshipper are unsatisfied"; it "flows from us spontaneously . . . having its spring in the perfect bliss of our daily sensible experience" "The Little Vagabond" is the poem Coleridge both approved and disapproved. (See Chap. 2, pp. 21–22).

Wilkinson's edition, privately printed, enjoyed a narrow circulation; Crabb Robinson learned of it when he met Wilkinson, in 1848 (see *On Books and Their Writers,* Apr. 16 and 27 and May 9).

Information on Wilkinson is from Clement Wilkinson, *Memoir of J. J. Garth Wilkinson* (see p. 190 on his "Tulkism").

Possibly Wilkinson's criticism is indebted to "The Inventions of

time, recalled, the young physician "discerned in them Swedenborgianism and spiritual magnetism." [30] The editor himself says he printed the poems to give impetus to a "new
Spiritualism" (p. xxii). Wilkinson's edition and prefatory
essay constitute the first effort to revive Blake and to do so
specifically on the basis of his poetry.

Wilkinson begins by attacking Cunningham's approach, and
through Cunningham the larger target—his philosophic coun-
trymen, Dugald Stewart, Thomas Brown, David Hume, and
all other materialistic philosophers (pp. xiv–xv). Incapable
"by Nature, or by Will, of dealing with . . . Spiritual phenomena" and committed to a set of "Mercantine ethics,"
Cunningham can understand vision only as *"Delusion";* he
treats of the primeval Golden Age "when Angels, who had
once been men, were in close communion with men,—only
to display his ingenuity in transmuting them into dirt" (p.
xiv). In the *Songs of Innocence,* Wilkinson perceives an innocence gone from his own time: "glimpses into all that is
holiest in the Childhood of the World and the Individual—
. . . sweetest touches of that Pastoral life, by which the
Golden Age may be still visibly represented to the iron one"
(p. xxii). Here there is no objection to representation as
such of the spiritual. Wilkinson is not willing, however, to
accept "naturalizing the spiritual" without further definition
and specific reservations. In one place, in fact, he objects to
Blake's merging the "higher in the lower, and sully[ing] the
spiritual by sinking it in the natural" (p. x). He was a Swedenborgian, a Christian, and a Victorian humanist; except for

---

William Blake": both argue the unfitness of Cunningham's rationalistic approach in dealing with Blake's sensibility; both dwell on antimaterialism.

30. W. B. Scott's memory of Wilkinson confuses his work on Blake
with a later preoccupation with spiritual magnetism dating from the
1850s, when Wilkinson published a volume of automatic poetry,
Improvisations from the Spirit (London, 1856) (Scott, *Autobiographical Notes, 1,* 298). For more on Scott, see below and Chap. 7.

Songs of Innocence and the designs to *Job, The Grave,* and *Night Thoughts,* everything of Blake's he saw appalled him by its indulgence in what he took to be personal nightmare:[31]

> Of the worst aspect of Blake's genius it is painful to speak. . . . In the domain of Terror he here entered [*Amer, VDA,* and "a host of unpublished drawings"], the characteristic of his genius is fearful Reality. He embodies no Byronisms—none of the sentimentalities of civilized vice, but delights to draw evil things and evil beings in their naked and final state. . . . Their human forms are gigantic petrifactions, . . . [with] stony limbs, and countenances expressive of despair and stupid cruelty.
>
> [pp. xix–xx]

For Wilkinson the insanity of these visions springs from the error and irresponsibility of the Romantic imagination. Having rejected the true sources of inspiration defined, according to the "true and unpopular doctrine" of Swedenborg, as the voices of souls who "have gone before us into the land of life" (p. xvi), Blake gave himself to an uncontrolled "interior naturalism, which he was . . . [as early as the time of writing *Thel*] beginning to mistake for spiritualism, listening as he did, to the voices of the ground" (p. vii). (At this point Wilkinson does accept Cunningham's interpretation of Blake's

31. Approval of *NT* is Wilkinson's only departure from the conventional estimate of Blake's work; he voiced profound horror on seeing a collection of Blake's drawings (*Memoir of Wilkinson,* pp. 26 and 30; letter dated July 17, 1839). On the whole, Wilkinson is a peculiarly mid-nineteenth century Englishman's Swedenborgian, finding his contemporary Swedenborgians in a deeper, more fruitful atmosphere than that of their founder, because the "modern plane of existence is human and social in . . . a new sense" where Swedenborg merely saw "through" the "Social World" (p. 199). Moreover, he was an admirer of Carlyle, and sent him both his biography of Swedenborg and his edition of *SIE*. (Carlyle replied with a letter of appreciative criticism [p. 35]; unfortunately, I have not been able to trace this.)

later years as a retreat into visionary solipsism.) Without
reason or faith in science, totally accepting the sovereignty of
personal vision, Blake's imagination rejected "Truth . . . in
the Divine-Human embodiment of Christianity" for "the loose
garments of Typical or even Mythologic Representation" (p.
xviii) and

> imbued itself with the superficial obscurity and ghastli-
> ness, far more than with the inward grandeur of primeval
> times. *For the true Inward is one and identical* [italics
> mine], and if Blake had been disposed to see it, he
> would have found that it was still . . . extant in the
> present Age. On the contrary, copying the outward
> form of the Past, he has delivered to us a multitude of
> new Hieroglyphics, which contain no presumable re-
> conditeness of meaning. . . . [The] Artist, not less than
> the man, was a loser, though it unquestionably gave him
> a certain power, as all unscrupulous *passion* must, of
> wildness and fierce vagary. This power is possessed . . .
> [by any man who yields] to the hell that is in him.
>
> [pp. xviii–xix]

Later in Wilkinson's own career, as in the nineteenth century
generally, all mythologies will be viewed as potential sources
of Divine Revelation (see Chap. 8); but in 1839, Wilkinson
finds eclectic systems and myths anti-Christian and anti-hu-
manist. His final approval of the *Songs of Innocence* is on the
score of their universality; here Blake "transcended Self, and
escaped from the isolation which Self involves" so that the
poems "belong to the ERA as well as to the Author" (pp.
xxi–xxii).

In his analysis of the pitfalls of the free imagination, Wilkinson makes the first comparison between Shelley and Blake.
In both poets self-reference and "ego-Theism" (p. xx) lead
to exclusiveness, esotericism, and finally to their own imaginative enslavement in false myth (for Blake) and paganism

(for Shelley). Wilkinson finds in both minds a movement toward "Pantheism, or natural-spiritualism" (p. xx). His phrase
is startling; it exactly prefigures the position which Swinburne
and James Thomson attributed to Blake and adopted for
themselves later in the century. Wilkinson also extends the
comparison of Blake and Shelley to their personalities. He
assimilates Shelley's angelism into the image of Blake portrayed by Cunningham and concludes that both poets, lacking
"vital heat . . . [and] substantial or practical Truth . . .
fail . . . to appeal to the universal instincts of Humanity"
(p. xx).[32]

The First Blakeans

Two representative Victorians, John Linnell and Samuel
Palmer, were Gilchrist's most important personal sources.
Each had been part of a circle in which Blake was included
toward the end of his life. At Linnell's house in Hampstead
Blake met the professional astrologer and occultist John
Varley, who believed in the literal reality of Blake's imaginations, even in the face of Blake's own explanations. A talented
and respected watercolorist, a spendthrift living in the shadow
of debtors' prisons, and an ebullient and likable crackpot, he
is quoted by Linnell as saying, "If it were not for my troubles,
I should burst for joy." Blake also met Varley's brother

32. On Shelley's reputation, particularly with respect to angelism,
see Sylva Norman, *The Flight of the Skylark* (Norman, Oklahoma
University Press, 1954).

For Wilkinson, Blake and Shelley illustrate "visionary tendencies"
which developed from "Materialism" (Shelley) on the one hand, and
"Christianity" on the other (Blake). Mistaking form for Truth, they
drew subjects from the types and shadows of Christianity: Shelley
from the Greeks, Blake from "Egyptian and Asiatic perversions of an
ancient and true religion." Both, centered in personal "Self-will" and
"self-intelligence" which Wilkinson equates with "the Anima Mundi
of the Philosopher" violated the universe and confounded Life and
Death "to suit their own fancies" (pp. xx–xxi).

Cornelius; the engraver James Ward; the Rev. Henry F. Cary, translator of Dante's *Divine Comedy;* and Dr. Robert John Thornton, whose *New Translation of the Lord's Prayer* Blake annotated and parodied in 1827. It was for Thornton's school text of Virgil's *Pastorals* that Blake executed the woodcuts which influenced Edward Calvert and Palmer. Linnell, sometimes with Blake, was a visitor to Mrs. Aders' salon, where Blake met Coleridge and Crabb Robinson. Of Blake's Linnell circle of acquaintances, John Varley and Dr. Thornton were dead when Gilchrist began work; Mrs. Aders and most of her acquaintances were dead, and her husband's Blake collection dispersed and untraceable. Except for James Ward who wrote to Gilchrist, only Cary, Cornelius Varley, and Linnell were available in 1855 to tell Gilchrist that Blake had been sane.[33]

Linnell was, along with the Shoreham disciple Frederick Tatham, Blake's unofficial executor. Each in his own way abetted Blake's long exile in private collections.[34] Tatham in-

33. Apart from Gilchrist's *Life,* the principal references for the Linnell circle and the Shoreham disciples are: Story, *Life of Linnell;* A. M. W. Stirling, *The Richmond Papers,* for George Richmond; A. H. Palmer, *Life and Letters of Samuel Palmer* (London, 1892); Geoffrey Grigson, *Samuel Palmer: The Visionary Years* (London, 1947); *A Memoir of Edward Calvert, Artist,* by Samuel Calvert [his third son] (London, 1893).

For Dr. Robt. Thornton, see *Life of Linnell, 1,* 147, 150–51; for John Varley, ibid., pp. 159–62, and Alfred T. Story, *James Holmes and John Varley* (London, 1894). For visits to Mrs. Aders' salon, see *Life of Linnell, 1,* 223, and *On Books and Their Writers,* Crabb Robinson's entries for 1825–26, passim. For Cary, see R. W. King, *The Translator of Dante: The Life of Henry Francis Cary* (London, M. Secker, 1925), pp. 170–71.

34. The early great Blake collections were those of Linnell, Thomas Butts (d. 1846) sold at auction in 1852, Mr. Aders (sold), and the Earl of Egremont. Bibliophiles Charles W. Dilke, Thomas F. Dibdin, and Isaac Disraeli owned Blakes. Disraeli, who possessed a number of the engraved books, urged his friend Dibdin to abandon his project of writing on Blake's designs—they were too monstrous for praise. The smallish collection of F. T. Palgrave—who was introduced to Blake's designs at Oxford when in 1845 Benjamin Jowett showed him a copy

herited from Mrs. Blake (in 1831) all of her husband's work that remained in her possession; soon after, as a diligent member of the Irvingite sect, he destroyed drawings, manuscripts, and engraved plates in the conviction that Blake's inspiration had been from the devil.[35] Linnell was reputed by many to be an opportunist; Crabb Robinson notes, after a meeting with Samuel Palmer in Wales:

---

of the *Inventions to Job*—and the large, very distinguished one of Palgrave's friend Monckton Milnes, date from the 1830s, 1840s, and 1850s. (Both men bought at the Butts sale.) Among collectors listed by William Rossetti (Rossetti compiled the annotated catalogue of Blake's designs and paintings for Gilchrist's *Life*), were many of the same names (Dilke, Palgrave, Milnes, the Earl of Egremont); also A. G. B. Russell. Collectors later in the century included Bernard Quaritch, W. A. White, and Frederick Locker-Lampson. (See *Charles Wentworth Dilke (1789–1864)*: *Papers of A Critic, Selected . . .* by . . . Sir C. W. Dilke, Bart. [2 vols. London, 1875], *1*, 51; Thomas Frognall Dibdin, *Reminiscences of a Literary Life* [2 vols. London, 1836], pp. 787–88 and n. and *A Library Companion* [London, 1825], pp. 740–42, n.; G. F. Palgrave, *Francis Turner Palgrave: His Journals and Memories of His Life* [London, 1889], pp. 26–27. On some early buyers, see G. Keynes, "New Blake Documents," *TLS* [Jan. 9, 1943], p. 24 and "History of the Job Designs," *Blake Studies*, p. 129).

By 1849, William Allingham complains that *SIE* is "scarcely ever . . . publicly offered for sale," the other books never. Only *Job, The Grave*, and *NT* are to be seen ("Some Chat about William Blake," p. 18).

35. The Irvingites—a fanatical sect, the Catholic Apostolic Church, formed and headed by the preacher Edward Irving—reached their highpoint in the early 1830s. Carlyle who had been Irving's closest friend for years (before the Irvingite days) assured Mrs. Gilchrist that Irving could not personally have advised such destruction (*Anne Gilchrist*, p. 131). Edward Calvert tried to persuade Tatham against the act (*Memoir of Calvert*, pp. 58–59); Grigson speculates that Palmer and George Richmond may have looked on with composure, thinking Blake's memory would be harmed if the writings were to be known (*Samuel Palmer: The Visionary Years*, pp. 37–38 and n.).

Tatham sold the works that survived the purge, mainly through booksellers (Russell, *Letters of Blake*, introduction). For more on sales, see *Life*, ed. Todd, p. 396.

I inquired whether Linnell is not a man of worldly wisdom. He [Samuel Palmer] understood the insinuation,
and said: "Only *defensively*," and he represented Linnell's conduct as having been very generous towards
Blake . . . contrary to my impression concerning Linnell.[36]

The fact is, however, that Linnell tried actively to sell only
those works of Blake's that he himself had commissioned—
the designs to the *Divine Comedy* and the engravings to *Job*
—and soon left off trying when he found that interest was
sparse. And since, with all good intentions, he kept adding
to his own Blake collection which he kept at his home, Red
Hill, and never lent out,[37] Linnell was ineffectual, to say the
least, in promoting recognition for his friend.

In 1855 Gilchrist found Linnell "an upright, truthful, if
somewhat hard man." [38] It was the same Linnell who twenty-

36. *On Books and Their Writers*, August 4, 1836. Crabb Robinson
had been skeptical of Linnell's disinterestedness from the first time he
met him with Blake (see his "Reminiscences of Blake," *Blake, Coleridge, Wordsworth, Lamb, Etc.*, p. 26; and a journal entry for Jan.
8, 1828, in *On Books and Their Writers*). According to Gilchrist,
Linnell's conduct toward Blake "had been throughout admirable"
(*Anne Gilchrist*, p. 130); Gilchrist's book helped vindicate Linnell to
others (see either W. R. Rea, "Review of Gilchrist's Life," *Fine Arts
Quarterly Review, 3* [Oct. 1864], 56–79 or "William Blake, *Art Journal, N. S. 3* [1864], 25–26).

37. Linnell bought Mrs. Aders' *SIE*, the Visionary Heads from
Varley, and other works, which were retained until the Linnell Sale
in 1918 (see provenances in *Blake Bibliography*). For more on
financial arrangements between Blake and Linnell, see *Life of Linnell,
1*, 169–70, 175 ff., and 243–45.
Linnell's unwillingness to lend out his Blakes is attested in a letter
written by Palmer (at this time Linnell's son-in-law), A. H. Palmer,
pp. 240–41. He (Linnell) did however show them to anyone who
asked (unpublished Linnell Papers; information in a private letter
from G. C. Bentley, Jr.).

38. *Anne Gilchrist*, p. 130. W. M. Rossetti thought him also a
stubborn man, on the basis of his one visit to Red Hill (*Letters Concerning Whitman, Blake, Shelley*, p. 6).

five years earlier had answered Bernard Barton's request to
dedicate his sonnet to the "Patron and friend of him who had
but few" (see p. 23) with the disclaimer: the poem "is not
applicable to me." The *Job* commission to Blake was no
"balm of sympathy . . ./ To sooth his wounded feelings
while he wrought/ Bright forms of fancy"; to prove it, Linnell
sent Barton "a plain copy of the Job for your inspection. The
price to you will be the same as the trade prices. £ 2, 12s.
6d." No sentimentalist, Linnell also corrected the bit of melodrama in Cunningham that had moved Barton to his effusion:
"Mr. Blake never was reduced to live in a garret, as asserted
in the Memoir; and I am sorry Mr. Cunningham did not avail
himself of the information I offered him." [39] Gilchrist finally
corrected Cunningham in print; in general Gilchrist dealt
"most carefully" with Linnell's comments and his letters, as
the biography indicates.[40] Stubborn, practical, authoritarian,
a successful landscape painter, and a tyrannical Victorian
father and father-in-law (to Samuel Palmer after 1838),
Linnell wrote Bible commentaries and for a short time thought
of becoming a Quaker but concluded that the sect was too
regimented for him. He baked his own bread, made his own
wine unless he got someone to ship it to him wholesale from
the Continent, and worried that his son might turn Roman
Catholic when he went to Italy to study painting. From Linnell, Alfred Story remarks, his son "learned the beauty of
cash payments." [41]

At the same time, Linnell appreciated Blake thoroughly;
and in the same brusque letter that rejected Barton's sonnet
he eloquently recalled Blake as

> more like the ancient patterns of virtue than I ever ex-
> pected to see in this world; he feared nothing so much

39. Russell, *Letters of Blake,* pp. 226–29; dated April 1830.
40. *Anne Gilchrist,* pp. 132–33; *Life, 1,* Chaps. 27, 28, and 30–38,
passim.
41. *Life of Linnell, 2,* 75.

as being rich, lest he should lose his spiritual riches. He
was at the same time the most sublime in his expressions,
with the simplicity and gentleness of a child, though
never wanting in energy when called for.

The largest body of personal testimony in Gilchrist's Life
came from Blake's Shoreham disciples, the so-called "Ancients," who had worshipped at the "House of the Interpreter"
when they were young, and remembered Blake in undimin-
ished glory. Unlike Shelley's friends, they did not hasten to
immortalize their hero, but it was proposed in 1827 at one
of their monthly meetings that each write down his memories
of Blake. Palmer kept a journal which Gilchrist later drew
upon, but Tatham alone wrote a substantial Memoir. Tatham
was also the only one of the disciples who may have tried to
capitalize on Blake, selling the drawings and manuscripts
which he had not destroyed; he is the villain in any Blake
saga and to the present time only Geoffrey Grigson has spoken
in behalf of the "angel of destruction." In 1838 Garth Wilkinson wrote to a friend that he had been "introduced by my
friend Mr. Elwell to a Mr. Tathans [sic] an artist, who pos-
sesses all the drawings left by Blake." [42] Gilchrist borrowed

42. Memoir of Wilkinson, pp. 29–30; letter dated Nov. 6, 1838. On
the proposal to write a memoir, see Memoir of Calvert, p. 19.
    The name "Ancients" derives from Edward Calvert and stock-
broker member John Giles' extravagant worship of Greek art and
thought (Life of Linnell, 1, 150). Grigson prefers the designation
"Shoreham Disciples," considering the group to be "The Palmer
Circle" (Chap. 4).
    In Pilgrim's Progress, Christian came to the House of the Inter-
preter, saying, "Sir . . . I am a Man that am come from the City of
Destruction, and am going to the Mount Zion, and I was told by the
Man that stands at the Gate, at the head of this way; that if I called
here, you would shew me excellent things. Such as would be a help to
me in my Journey" (ibid., Chap. 3, "Palmer and William Blake,"
p. 19).

the *Pickering MS* from him, and William Rossetti bought his Blake drawings. An itinerant portrait painter and evangelist when Gilchrist met him, Tatham made himself useful advising about the owners of Blake's works. For the *Life* he copied portraits of Blake and Mrs. Blake from the *Note-Book* in 1861.

George Richmond who was only sixteen at the time recalled his first meeting with Blake: it was " 'as if he were walking with the prophet Isaiah' " (*Life, 1,* 342). He later became a fashionable portrait painter for prominent and wealthy Evangelicals such as William Wilberforce, the Thornton family, and John Ruskin (whom he introduced to Blake's drawings in 1840). His later references to Blake in private papers (letters to Calvert mainly) do not absolutely bear out Grigson's opinion that his Shoreham intensities were an affectation. Edward Calvert, the disciple who may have tried to prevent Tatham's devastation, did a beautiful set of pastoral woodcuts modeled on Blake's. His later life was spent mainly in seclusion at Brixton, where he finished a few perfect pictures but declined to exhibit them; he recalled for Gilchrist Blake's spontaneous courtesy to a workman (*Life, 1,* 351). Francis O. Finch, a watercolorist pupil of John Varley,[43] wrote (or told) Gilchrist that Blake had "struck him as *a new kind of man,* wholly original, . . . in all things" (*Life, 1,* 343).

The disciple most lastingly influenced by Blake was Samuel Palmer, whose keen interest in Blake's biography and ardent temperament impressed Gilchrist who "must have been somewhat astonished to find an enthusiasm equal to his own, and no whit the fainter for long lapse of years." Palmer and his wife, Hannah Linnell Palmer, spent several evenings with the Gilchrists in congenial discussion over the Blake works which Gilchrist had accumulated. On one visit they were "so

43. Finch died in 1862; a tribute to him written by Samuel Palmer appears in *Life,* 1863, *1,* 298–300, n. In 1880, it was moved to Volume 2. On Richmond and Ruskin, see above, n. 17.

riveted and unaware of the time" that it was "three in the
morning!" when they thought of leaving.[44] Palmer had come a
long way from the time when, at nineteen, he first saw Blake,
who appeared to him "one of the Antique patriarchs, or a dying Michael Angelo." His diary account of this first meeting
(in 1824) continues:

> there was he making in the leaves of a great book (folio)
> the sublimest designs from his (not superior) Dante. He
> said he began them with fear and trembling. I said "O! I
> have enough of fear and trembling." "Then," said he,
> "you'll do." He designed them (100, I think) during a
> fortnight's illness in bed! And there, . . . did I show
> him some of my first essays in design; and the sweet
> encouragement he gave me (for Christ blessed little
> children) did not tend basely to presumption and idle-
> ness, but made me work harder and better that after-
> noon and night. And, after visiting him, the scene re-
> curs to me afterwards in a kind of vision: and in this
> most false, corrupt, and genteelly stupid town my spirit
> sees his dwelling (the chariot of the sun), as it were an
> island in the midst of the sea—such a place is it for
> primitive grandeur whether in the persons of Mr. and
> Mrs. Blake, or in the things hanging on the walls.[45]

Italy conventionalized Palmer's landscapes from the visionary
Beulah-world of the Shoreham period. Domestic life had
worn him. But even after money worries, neglect, and a lapse
of inspiration had combined to shrink and fray him, and his
glorious and erratic evangelical strain had declined into ha-
bitual formulas, sometimes into mere tediousness, the early
brightness never entirely forsook him. His very moving simplicity is felt in the eloquent and influential memorial letter
which he wrote in 1855 and which Gilchrist printed in the
Life (*1*, 344–47).

44. A. H. Palmer, pp. 109 and 256; letter dated June 1864.
45. A. H. Palmer, pp. 9–10. Journal for Oct. 9, 1824.

Blake, once known, could never be forgotten. . . . He
was energy itself, and shed around him a kindling influence; an atmosphere of life, full of the ideal. To walk
with him in the country was to perceive the soul of
beauty through the forms of matter.

To the Gilchrists Palmer was "especially delightful," a
"genial, scholarly artist." There is no sign that Alexander
Gilchrist regarded Palmer's veneration of Blake as either
excessive or naive. From the beginning Palmer helped Gilchrist with description and anecdote, and with various tasks.
After her husband's death he advised Mrs. Gilchrist and
contributed at least one important passage to the book, a
description of the designs to *The Marriage of Heaven and
Hell.*[46]

Palmer's influence on the *Life,* like his father-in-law's, was
conservative; both men were puritan in character. Although
the Shoreham disciples had dined on bread and apples in
the "valley of vision" when they were young, they were
neither Bohemians nor rebels. All of them grew up to be
exemplary Victorians.

The group of young men who were to become the most
influential shapers of Blake's reputation in the nineteenth
century began to learn about him in the 1840s. The Pre-
Raphaelites' articulate and glamorous chieftain (if not chief)
D. G. Rossetti liked Allan Cunningham's poems and folk
stories, read his Life of Blake, and became interested in
Blake's works. In 1847 Rossetti made what may be the most
famous purchase of his life (besides his wombat), the *Note-
Book,* sometimes called the *Rossetti MS.* He bought it for
ten shillings, loaned him by his brother, from William Palmer
(brother of Samuel Palmer), an attendant in the Antique

46. *Anne Gilchrist,* p. 57. For Palmer's contributions to the Life,
see Chap. 4.

Gallery of the British Museum, described by his nephew
A. H. Palmer as "a curiosity of weakness, ineptitude and
foolishness" whose "singular character," "baleful" actions,
and "connection with Frederick Tatham" resulted in Rossetti's lucky purchase.[47] William Rossetti recalls that his
brother then "proceeded to copy out across a confused tangle
of false starts, alternative forms, and cancellings, all the poetry
in the book, and I did the same for the prose." [48]

In 1848 D. G. and William Rossetti, John Everett Millais,
Thomas Woolner, William Holman Hunt, and Frederick
George Stephens formed the Pre-Raphaelite Brotherhood.
Blake's *Note-Book,* William Rossetti reports, "certainly stim-

47. See Wilson, *Life of Blake,* pp. 37–38; and a letter to Miss
Wilson from A. H. Palmer, dated Nov. 16, 1925, quoted in Grigson,
p. 145. Also Grigson, pp. 3, 38, and 134.

On the fly-leaf of the *Note-Book,* Rossetti wrote:

I purchased this original M. S. of Palmer, an attendant in the
antique Gallery at the British Museum, on the 30th April, 1847.
Palmer knew Blake personally, and it was from the artist's wife
that he had the present M. S. which he sold me for 10s. Among
the sketches there are one or two profiles of Blake himself.

D.G.C.R.

The Note-Book of William Blake, facsim., ed. Geoffrey Keynes (London, 1935), p. ix.

48. *Some Reminiscences, 1,* 302–03. (The transcriptions were probably made in 1847.) William Rossetti is unsure whether his brother
"may . . . have known a few of Blake's poems and designs before
reading [Cunningham's] graphic and diverting account of him" (*D. G.
Rossetti: His Family Letters, 1,* 109). To Hall Caine Rossetti said that
his first knowledge of Blake dated from about 1845 (when he was
sixteen or seventeen) (Hall Caine, *Recollections of Dante Gabriel
Rossetti* [Boston, 1898], p. 191).

The *Note-Book* transcriptions were headed "Verse and Prose by
William Blake (Natus 1757: obit 1827). All that is of any value in
the foregoing pages has been copied out. D.G.C.R." (*The Note-Book
of William Blake,* ed. Keynes, p. x). Rossetti's transcriptions are still
bound with the *Note-Book;* the transcriptions of the prose may have
been written on five "cut out" leaves (see Wilson, p. 334 and Appendix
IV, pp. 334 ff. a description of "The Rossetti MS").

ulated" his brother's rebellion against aesthetic sacred cows
of the time. Blake's "irrational epigrams and jeers against
. . . Correggio, Titian, Rubens, Rembrandt, Reynolds, and
Gainsborough . . . men Blake regarded as fulsomely florid,
or lax, or swamping ideas in mere manipulation" were "bal-
sam to Rossetti's soul, and grist to his mill." [49] Soon after
copying the *Note-Book,* Rossetti visited the continent, where
he saw the works in question for himself and decried them
(though from a not very Blakean, naturalistic standpoint)
echoing Blake's horror of "Blots & Blurs." [50]

> *Non noi pittori!* God of Nature's truth,
>   If these, not we! Be it not said, when one
>   Of us goes hence: "As these did, he hath done;
> His feet sought out their footprints from his youth."
> Because, dear God! The flesh Thou madest smooth
>   These carked and fretted, that it seemed to run
>   With ulcers; and the daylight of thy sun
> They parcelled into blots and glares, uncouth
> With stagnant grouts of paint . . .[51]

Rossetti's picture of Blake at this time was a sympathetic
idealization from Cunningham's Life; this short poem was
written in 1849 (though not published until 1898):

BLAKE
To the memory of William Blake, a Painter and Poet,
whose greatness may be named even here since it was
equalled by his goodness, this tablet is now erected—

49. *D. G. Rossetti: His Family Letters, 1,* 109 and D. G. Rossetti,
Works, ed. W. M. Rossetti (rev. and enl. London, 1911), p. viii.
50. Men think they can Copy Nature as Correctly as I copy Imagination this they will find Impossible. & all the Copies or Pretended Copiers of Nature from Rembrat to Reynolds Prove that
Nature becomes . . . to its Victim nothing but Blots & Blurs.
["PA," E-B, p. 563]
51. "Last Visit to the Louvre," sub-headed, "The Cry of the P.R.B.
after a careful Examination of the Canvases of Rubens, Correggio,
et hoc genus omne" (*Works,* p. 181).

years after his death . . . in poverty and neglect, by one
who honours his life and works.

Epitaph
ALL beauty to pourtray
Therein his duty lay
And still through toilsome strife
Duty to him was life—
Most thankful still that duty
Lay in the paths of beauty.[52]

Cunningham had spoken of Blake's unflagging industry in his
craft, but not in the cause of "beauty." The lines herald the
aesthetie-moralist mode of appreciation to be found in Rossetti's later writing on Blake.

Soon after copying the *Note-Book* (in 1847) Rossetti
showed the poems to his friend the Irish poet William Allingham, who approached at least one publisher about the possibility of printing them. Allingham at this time (1849) wrote
an article titled "Some Chat About William Blake" for *Hogg's
Weekly Instructor*. True to its title, it is a superficial piece,
with texts of the poems derived from Cunningham's *Life*.[53]

52. Ibid., pp. xxvii and 176.
53. Allingham's diary for Aug. 16, 1849 records that Slater, a
publisher, seemed "inclined to publish" a "new edition of Blake's
poems" (William Allingham, *A Diary*, ed. H. Allingham and D. Rad-
ford [London, Macmillan, 1907], p. 53). On the same day he visited
the British Museum with Coventry Patmore; they found "almost
nothing" of Blake's poems. See too Rossetti's letter to Allingham,
quoted on p. 4.
An interesting pre-Gilchrist reference occurs in G. W. Thornbury,
British Artists from Hogarth to Turner (2 vols. London, 1861), *2*,
26–44 ("The Prophet in Carnaby Market"), where Blake is classed
among a small, very un-English group of visionary artists: Louther-
berg, Cosway, Varley, Flaxman, and "good William Blake"—the
"Hell-Breughel, the Kaulbach, the Doré of English art" (pp. 26–27).
Thornbury's view is much like Ruskin's opinion of Blake at this period
(see pp. 38 f. above): As a matter of fact, Ruskin had commissioned a
biography of Turner from Thornbury and directed him in the writing
of it; possibly Ruskin also influenced Thornbury's criticism of Blake.

Allingham asserts the importance of Blake's poetry and deplores the scarcity and inaccessibility of Blake's works. However, he seems not to have persisted in his effort to publish a separate edition of Blake's poems. He and Rossetti followed their respective paths, Allingham into the writing of his own poetry and Rossetti into his painting and his translations of the early Italian poets.

In 1857 Rossetti met W. B. Scott and Swinburne through Edward Burne-Jones and showed them the *Note-Book*. Swinburne adopted "When Klopstock England defied" as his touchstone of the obscene lyric ("I have written a new ballad so indecent that it beats all the rest and is nearly up to Blake's Klopstock."); he also bought Blake's *Job* and Dante engravings.[54] But beyond their private circle Rossetti and his followers did little in this period to extend interest in Blake. When he collected his diary notes on Blake early in 1852 Crabb Robinson concluded his Reminiscences:

> since Blake's death Linnell has not found the market I took for granted he would seek for Blake's works. Wilkinson printed a small edition of his poems including the "Songs of Innocence & Experience" a few years ago. And Monckton Milnes talks of printing an edition. I have a few coloured engravings, but B[lake] is still an object of interest exclusively to men of imaginative taste & psychological curiosity. I doubt much whether these Memoirs will be of any use to this small class.[55]

If this is so, then it may be particularly noteworthy that Thornbury's remarks on Blake's poems contain the first comparison in print between Blake and Wordsworth: Blake is a "poet of no mean order; for he anticipated Wordsworth, rivalled our old dramatists in sustained majesty and worth, and at times vied with Shelley in nervous fire" (p. 27).

54. *S. L.*, No. 19, *1*, 27–28; letter (to W. B. Scott) dated Dec. 16, 1859. For "When Klopstock," see E-B, p. 491. For Rossetti and the so called second P.R.B., including William Morris, Swinburne, and Burne-Jones, see *D. G. Rossetti: His Family Letters, 1*, 194–95.

55. "Reminiscence of Blake," *Blake, Coleridge, Wordsworth, Lamb,*

Three years later Gilchrist began work on the *Life of William Blake, "Pictor Ignotus,"* Rossetti turned over the *Note-Book* to Gilchrist, and Allingham finally made good his old intention, printing four of Blake's poems in an anthology of lyric poetry, *Nightingale Alley*. The selections in Allingham's anthology reflect Pre-Raphaelite taste; his brief introduction attacking contemporary utilitarian theories of poetry manifests the language and values of the latent aesthetic movement: "As for the *use* of Poetry. . . . can [you] put . . . Love into a crucible. . . . [Poetry is] founded on the nature of man in mystic relation to the Universe." Allingham singles out "the celestial-infantine fancies of William Blake" in terms that anticipate the appreciations of Rossetti. The texts, "Introduction" and "The Blossom" from *Songs of Innocence,* and "The Angel" and "The Tyger" from *Songs of Experience,* evidence the nineteenth-century's practice of rewriting Blake's poetry,[56] which seems to have been an educational diversion for poets (Swinburne, Rossetti, and W. B. Yeats) and poetasters (Cunningham, William Rossetti, and Edwin Ellis).

Etc., p. 27; dated Mar. 1, 1852. Milnes' intention went back to the 1830s, when he wrote to Aubrey de Vere that he thought of publishing "some selections" (T. Wemyss Reid, *Life, Letters, and Friendships of Richard Monckton Milnes, First Lord Houghton* [2 vols. London, 1890], *1*, 220–21; dated "[?1838]").

56. *Nightingale Alley,* ed. "Giraldus" [ed. W. Allingham] (London, 1860), pp. vii and ix. (Allingham's wording suggests he has read *Thel*.) The poems appear on pp. 54–55, 116–17, 235, and 95–96 respectively. Allingham's version of "The Tyger" seems to be an amalgam of Blake's engraved version and of the abbreviated text of the poem found in Cunningham's *Life*; he prints "What dread hand *form'd thy* dread feet?" for Blake's "What dread hand? & what dread feet?" in line 12. Line 6 in Allingham is unique: "Burnt the *ardour* of thine eyes" for Blake's "Burnt the fire" (This may be a wrong memory of Cunningham's *"fervour."*) Allingham also cuts lines 15, 16, 17, and 18, so that the last stanza of the poem is composed of Blake's lines 13, 14, 19, 20 (E-B, p. 25). The other texts are fairly accurate.

CHAPTER FOUR

The Mid-Century Revival—Biography

On reading the Life in proof nearly a year after Gilchrist's death, Samuel Palmer was moved to suggest that Mrs. Gilchrist ask Thomas Carlyle to write a short preface: "I never saw a *perfect* embodiment of Mr. C.'s *ideal* of a *man in earnest,* but in the person of Blake." [1] Palmer's impression is hardly fortuitous. There is ample evidence, internal and external, of influence from Carlyle's *On Heroes, Hero-Worship and the Heroic* in Gilchrist's biographical procedure, his method of molding materials into the unified expression of a heroic life.

Gilchrist was, in fact, a disciple of the Chelsea Sage; while at work on his Blake he saw Carlyle's collected works through the press and did considerable research for the biography of Frederick the Great. He was in contact almost daily with Carlyle and Carlyleans,[2] sternly raised Evangelical and non-

1. A. H. Palmer, p. 248; letter dated Sept. 1862; see also *Anne Gilchrist,* pp. 141–42.

2. The evidence for Carlyle's direct influence on Blake's reputation remains unexplored. He was however connected with *Fraser's* in 1830 when "The Last of the Supernaturalists" appeared, whether or not he wrote the piece (see Chap. 3, n. 24). He was in touch with circles where Blake was known in the 1830s; he knew Wilkinson's edition of *SIE* (ibid., n. 31); and he owned a set of the *Job* engravings (*Anne Gilchrist,* p. 59).

Gilchrist introduced himself to Carlyle's notice when he sent him a copy of *The Life of William Etty, R. A.* in 1854; he was one of many admirers who did legwork and editing for Carlyle: "I have got a kind volunteer (young Barrister man, called Gilchrist, much an admirer, etc.) who will take the trouble of all that off my hands." "All that" refers to Carlyle's *Works,* published by Chapman, begin-

Conformist intellectuals; he had himself been bred in an
earnest non-Conformist household and, of course, he was in
communication with the Shoreham disciples—all of them but
Calvert sincere and uncompromising testers of their souls.

Revealing the "earnestness" of Blake's life, Gilchrist assumed the role of Carlyle's ideal biographer: "a whole epit-
ome of the Infinite, with its meanings, lies enfolded in the
Life of every Man. Only . . . the Seer to discern this same
Godlike [essence] . . . is wanting." [3] The biographer is, in
effect, the man who creates heroes. On first thought Blake
might seem unlikely material for apotheosis: he was unknown
and he was not a moral "Force." But the power to make
himself heard is not of paramount importance to the hero-
maker and hero-worshipper. Moreover, Carlyle writes in "The
Hero as Poet" that it cannot matter whether the Hero poet
"writes at all; and if so, whether in prose or in verse." This
will "depend on accidents." [4] The essential quality of the
great man or the genius is potentiality, elemental and non-
specific; "the hero can be Poet, Prophet, King, Priest, or what
you will, according to the kind of world he finds himself born
into" (p. 78). For Carlyle greatness lay primarily in the sincerity of a man's endeavors. Given Blake's accomplishments,

---

ning in October 1856, and monthly thereafter (*New Letters of Thomas
Carlyle,* ed. Alexander Carlyle [2 vols. London, 1904], *2,* 179; letter
dated June 20, 1856). See, too, p. 209.

While researching Carlyle's biography of Frederick II, Gilchrist consulted with him about the Life of Blake. Apparently Carlyle followed
it with interest and in Dec. 1859 gave Gilchrist an introduction to his
publisher (*Anne Gilchrist,* p. 74). (Ultimately, the Life of Blake was
published by Alexander Macmillan.)

3. "Biography" [1832], *Critical and Miscellaneous Essays, 3, Works
of Carlyle,* Centenary ed., *28,* 52.

4. "The Hero as Poet: Dante; Shakespeare" [1840], *On Heroes,
Hero-Worship and the Heroic in History. Works of Carlyle, 5,* 105.
In this and the following paragraph all single words in quotation
marks are from "The Hero as Poet" (pp. 78–114). Page references for
longer citations are given in parentheses within the text.

personality, and reputation as they were known to Gilchrist in 1855, he was an opportune subject.

Carlyle saw the fundamental moral earnestness which bound together his heroes' lives, works, and thought, as working through the ruling "faculty" in each. The theme of Shakespeare's character is "Intellect"; of Dante's, moral "intensity."

> For the *intense* Dante is intense in all things; he has got into the essence of all. His intellectual insight as painter, on occasion too as reasoner, is but the result of all other sorts of intensity. Morally great, above all, we must call him; it is the beginning of all.
>
> ["The Hero as Poet," p. 95]

Another admirer of Carlyle, Garth Wilkinson, had treated Blake's life as the expression of inner vision: Blake, he wrote, was an "Artist . . . in the widest sense," his unconventional "courtship, and marriage, and married life, a series of living designs." [5] Gilchrist's Blake is, in everything, an "enthusiast."

In Carlyle's *The Life of John Sterling,* which he and his wife read with wholehearted admiration soon after it was published in 1851, Gilchrist found the full-scale embodiment of Carlyle's biographical principles.[6] His *Life of William Etty, R. A.* is palpably Carlylean in style. The same (along with the adoption of "hero-worship") is true for the *Life of Blake,*[7] in which Gilchrist indulges in didactic, often sententious animadversions on his subject: "Angels of light . . . handle mere terrestrial weapons of sarcasm . . . in a very clumsy,

5. Wilkinson, p. v.

6. *The Life of John Sterling* [1851], *Works of Carlyle, 11; Anne Gilchrist,* p. 36.

7. One reviewer of the *Life of Blake* wrote that Gilchrist's *Life of Etty* had been "the most perfect imitation of [Carlyle's *Sterling*] . . . we have ever had the ill-fortune to meet with" and that in the *Life of Blake,* Gilchrist repeated his error (*Quarterly Review,* 107 [Jan. 1865], 2).

ineffectual manner" (*1*, 307) or "As if a simple-minded
visionary could advertise, puff, and round the due preparatory
paragraphs for newspaper and magazine, of 'latest fine arts
intelligence'" (*1*, 274). Epithets are common: "A singular
enterprise, for unpractised Blake, was this of vying with
adroit, experienced Cromek!" (*1*, 274). Gilchrist also took
over Carlyle's practice of rendering the setting in exhaustive
detail: the book abounds with tangent biographies and descriptions of streets, buildings, and public events.

Following Carlyle's organization in *Sterling,* Gilchrist arranged the sparse events of Blake's life story into the revelatory
unfolding of character: youth and early visions; earnest courtship and devoted marriage; the soul-trying period spent away
from London in Felpham under the patronage of the minor
poet William Hayley; the Exhibition; Blake's death—every-
where showing his subject's simplicity and "enthusiasm."
Through all the inner man remains unchanged, the same
"Child Angel" who saw angelic figures amid the haymakers:
"If these traits of childish years be remembered, they will help
to elucidate the visits from the spiritual world of later years,
in which the grown man believed as unaffectedly as ever had
a boy of ten" (*Life, 1,* 7). Gilchrist finds complete consistency
between the man and his works. Blake's paintings and poems
are "semi-utterances" of a man whose life was singlemindedly
fixed, with childlike faith, on things "vague and unspeak-
able": "Both [poems and designs] form part in a life and
character as new, romantic, pious—in the deepest natural
sense—as they: romantic, though incident be slight; animated
by the same unbroken simplicity, the same high unity of sentiment" (*1*, 4).

If, in formulating this touchstone of Blake's character, Gilchrist neglected more than one aspect of Blake's personality,
part of the reason is that at the time he was writing, he simply
did not have on hand most of the basic biographical materials.
He did not read the *Note-Book* until 1860 when the biograph-

ical portions were virtually completed. Although Crabb Robinson read Gilchrist his notes he would not "trust him with the manuscript" until 1860, so that these, together with Blake's annotations to Wordsworth's Preface of 1815, appear in a separate chapter. The letters to Thomas Butts were obtained by Mrs. Gilchrist in 1862 and were a last minute supplement in the second volume; the Hayley letters came to light in 1878 and were incorporated into the second edition of the Life in 1880. Moreover, a serious reading of Blake's writings, the most authoritative basis for understanding him, was put off until last; Gilchrist was making notes prior to writing the descriptions of Blake's engraved books at the time of his death. The gaps had to be filled in by his wife and others.[8]

8. Gilchrist's diary for Dec. 1859, notes that he is "giving my MS a last revisal before sending it" to a publisher (*Anne Gilchrist,* p. 74). In the Life he speaks of the biography as having been almost finished, in Jan. 1860 (*1,* 397). Most of the work done in 1860 and 1861 concerned the Selections and the lists and descriptions of designs, paintings, and engraved books—all completed by other hands.

For Crabb Robinson's entries, see *On Books and Their Writers,* June 28, 1855 and Nov. 3, 1860.

When Mrs. Gilchrist began work on her husband's manuscript, she found that "the only grave omission—the only place where dear Alec had left an absolute blank that *must* be filled in—was for some account of Blake's mystic writings, or 'Prophetic Books'." She had returned borrowed copies of the engraved books after his death with the markers for extracts still in some of them (*Jer,* for instance); and she had to reborrow them from Monckton Milnes, and with the aid of Gilchrist's closest friend, William Haines, copy them out. "Then there was to write the account of them" (*Anne Gilchrist,* letters dated August 25, 1862, pp. 125–26; and April 1862, pp. 122–23). In May 1862, she asked William Rossetti for "a brief general description" of *"The Marriage of Heaven and Hell, The Book of Ahania, The Song of Los, Asia,* and *Africa,"* telling him that she had found "blanks left in the MS" where they were to be treated (*Rossetti Papers: 1862–1870,* comp. W. M. Rossetti [London, 1903], p. 6).

There were more blanks than these, but Mrs. Gilchrist was unwilling

Paucity of materials obliged Gilchrist to rely on Linnell and, above all, on Palmer. His hero's ardent and innocent enthusiasm more resembles Samuel Palmer than William Blake. In essence, Gilchrist's Blake is a fleshing out of the portrait sketched in Palmer's memorial letter—never "double-minded," happy, oblivious to worldly concerns.

> He was a man without a mask; his aim single, his path straightforwards, and his wants few; so he was free, noble, and happy. . . . He saw everything through art. . . . He was one of the few to be met with in our passage through life, who are not in some way or other, "double-minded" and inconsistent with themselves; one of the very few who cannot be depressed by neglect, and to whose name rank and station could add no lustre. Moving apart, in a sphere above the attraction of worldly honours, he did not accept greatness, but confer it. He ennobled poverty, and, by his conversation and the influence of his genius, made two small rooms in Fountain Court more attractive than the threshold of princes.

Linnell's Blake was considerably more robust than Palmer's —a "hearty laughder" [9] and a forceful disputant. There is a description by Linnell from an unpublished Memoir of Blake that he wrote in 1855 (probably for Gilchrist) in which Blake

---

to have it altogether known how much her husband had left undone. In 1880 D. G. Rossetti reread the Life before revising his own sections; he writes Mrs. Gilchrist:

> I judged last night that you had probably written the passages in question—with no small effort, doubtless at that time. . . . I fancy your best course might be to admit their authorship in preface or footnote, & quote when desirable from Swinburne as to views.
>
> [A. L., ?March 8, 1880, Thorne Coll.]

For more on the book's assembling, see below; also Chaps. 5 and 6. (It is curious that Gilchrist seems never to have contacted Butts' grandson Captain Butts.)
9. *Life of Linnell, 1,* 161.

appears a much more full-blooded figure than anywhere in the Life. *"Even when unprovoked by controversy,"* Linnell recalled, Blake "said many things tending to the corruption of Christian morals" (italics mine);

> and when opposed by the superstitious, the crafty, or the proud, he outraged all common-sense and rationality by the opinions he advanced, occasionally even indulging in the support of the most lax interpretation of the precepts of the Scriptures.[10]

But Linnell like Palmer scrupled both about Blake and about Christian decency so that together they abetted Gilchrist in suppressing sides of Blake which might be unacceptable to a Victorian public. *The Four Zoas* which Linnell or some member of his family personally censored with an eraser, *An Island in the Moon* owned by Palmer, and several sets of Blake's always vigorous annotations, all available to Gilchrist, were not taken into account.[11] Similarly, Palmer advised Mrs. Gilchrist in 1862 that she ought to remove passages from *The Marriage of Heaven and Hell* on the ground that only a friend could both understand and indulge Blake:

> Blake has said the same kind of thing to me; in fact almost everything contained in the book; and I can understand it in relation to my memory of the whole man, in a way quite different to that roaring lion the "press," or that led lion the British Public.

The Proverbs of Hell left him shuddering "like a child for the first time in Madam Tussaud's 'Chamber of Horrors' ";

10. Ibid., *1,* 247.

11. Among the annotations owned by Linnell and Palmer that were not mentioned by Gilchrist were those to Boyd's commentary on Dante's *Inferno;* Berkeley's *Siris;* Watson's *Apology*—all Palmer's property (Grigson, p. 143). Linnell owned annotated copies of Dr. Robert Thornton's *New Translation of the "Lord's Prayer,"* in which Blake's writing is inked over (see Blake, ed. Keynes, nn.).

do not, he warns, print what would revolt "every drawing-room . . . in England." Mrs. Gilchrist took his advice.[12] Palmer's letter in the Life contains a "regret" that in his writings Blake "should sometimes have suffered fancy to trespass within sacred precincts" (*1,* 347). And Linnell is quoted only as saying

> He was so far from being so absurd in his opinions, or so nearly mad as has been represented, that he always defended Christian truth against the attacks of infidels, and its abuse by the superstitious. . . . It must be confessed, however, he uttered, occasionally, sentiments sadly at variance with sound doctrine.
>
> [*1,* 370–71. Lacunae are Gilchrist's]

This comment is offered in Chapter 35, the apology, where Gilchrist returns an unequivocal "No" to the title-question "Mad or not Mad?" The important issue for Gilchrist is not (as for Palmer and Linnell) Blake's actual beliefs, whether and in what sense he meant what he said—he is inclined to write off these allegedly "unsound" ideas and "false" doctrines, and to concern himself with the more notorious ground for charges of mental unbalance, Blake's matter-of-factness in discussing his "spiritual visitors" (*1,* 362). Linnell had understood very well the positive method in Blake's madness: Blake, Linnell wrote, "could always explain his paradoxes

12. A. H. Palmer, pp. 243–44. Letter dated July 2, 1862. Palmer writes further:

> [Such] very grave suggestions arise in reading *The Proverbs of Hell* that I felt it a duty to give you my opinion about the matter. . . . I speak of what I think will be the prudential proceeding relative to the public, and *reviewers.* . . . I will say *at once* that I think the whole page at the top of which I have made a cross in red chalk would at once exclude the work from every drawing-room table in England.

(For those passages omitted, see Appendix.)

satisfactorily when he pleased, but to many he spoke so that 'hearing they might *not* hear.' " [13]

Blake's more outrageous pronouncements are explained in Gilchrist as an irritable, sometimes deliberate perversity, Blake's unequal defense against temperaments unsympathetic to his own. A person "of scientific turn" remarking on the remoteness of the heavens (possibly Robert Thornton) could provoke him to declare, " 'Tis false! I was walking down a lane the other day, and at the end of it I touched the sky with my stick' " (*1*, 371). And Henry Crabb Robinson, a "friendly but very logical and cool-headed interlocutor," might "ruffle" Blake into "incoherences" or "extreme statements" (*1*, 381). Without intending it Gilchrist thus subverts the force of Blake's brilliant and versatile talk quoted from Crabb Robinson's notes.[14] Such explanations supported by like testimonials from Frances O. Finch, Palmer, Linnell, and Tatham convert the shocking and subtle content of Blake's conversation into at best extravagance of manner.

Applying a commonplace formula, Gilchrist confidently asserts that Blake's "reasoning powers" were "far inferior . . . to his perceptive . . . as are, more or less, those of all artists" (*1*, 372). Blake's opinions on art are given fairly serious attention; his thinking on religion, politics, and morals, however, is either discounted as interesting only because "mentally physiognomic" (*1*, 66–67) or else dispensed with altogether. The polemical annotations to Bacon's sagacious

13. See Linnell's letter to Bernard Barton (Chap. 3, n. 39), dated April 1830.

14. Crabb Robinson's Reminiscences, with Blake's Annotations to the 1815 edition of Wordsworth's poems, appear in Chap. 36. Their placement, following "Mad or not Mad?," is probably strategic on Gilchrist's part.

Gilchrist rewrote Crabb Robinson's notes to some extent, pointing up the extravagance of anecdote or statement. These have been corrected in R. Todd's edition of the *Life of Blake*. See also Symons, *William Blake*, and *Blake, Coleridge, Wordsworth, Lamb, Etc.*

and worldly *Essays* are "characteristic if very unreasonable" sputterings from a "republican spiritualist" (*1*, 315–16). Gilchrist tempers a selection of marginal comments to Lavater's *Aphorisms,* many on religion, with a cautionary reminder that the writer was a painter and no metaphysician (*1*, 66–67). Crabb Robinson's puzzled effort to "reconcile" pronouncements that "seemed to be in conformity with the most opposed abstract systems" (*1*, 383) is rebuked as an intrusion into the sacred precincts of Personality. One cannot and ought not "methodise" Blake; "love" alone and "not . . . the intellect" will grant a "key" to his "wild and strange rhapsodies" (*1*, 383).

Two pages at the end of Chapter 35 touch on Blake's views respecting Christianity, governments, and ethics. (Since the passage either directly quotes or else closely echoes a letter from Palmer to Mrs. Gilchrist written in 1862, it was probably added to compensate for a deficiency sensed in Gilchrist's manuscript.) A "transcendental . . . rather than a literal" Christian, Blake is said to have "believed in a pre-existent state" and "adopted, or thought out . . . many of the ideas of the early Gnostics: and was otherwise so erratic in his religious opinions as to shock orthodox Churchmen." J. T. Smith is cited in evidence of Blake's genuine belief in Christ (*Life,* 1863, *1*, 330). (The quotation from Smith, assuring readers that Blake had daily prayers in his home [see p. 27 above], was dropped from the 1880 edition.) A letter from "Blake's friend" (Palmer) on his republicanism reads: "He loved liberty, and had no affection for statecraft or standing armies, yet no man less resembled the vulgar radical. His sympathies were rather with Milton, Harrington, and Marvel —not with Milton as to his puritanism, but his love of a grand, ideal scheme of republicanism." Lastly, Blake's latitudinarianism is presented together with his practical daily obedience to that "*mere* moral law" which in theory he railed at and abominated:

[In practice, he was] . . . a faithful husband, and temperate in all his habits. . . . His conversation on social topics, his writings, his designs, were equally marked by theoretic license and virtual guilelessness; for he frankly said, described, and drew everything as it arose to his mind.

[1, 374]

Gilchrist does however go beyond negative and oblique partisanship—his positive defense of Blake's sanity turns on an explanation of Blake's "vision." Gilchrist clearly distinguished Blake's "spiritual visitors" from Varleyan ghosts and also from the "gross" and material beings called up by modern spiritists (1, 363). Taken simply as a mode of speaking, Blake's unembarrassed references to his visions and spiritual visitors are consistent with his "naive self-assertion" (1, 278) in all practical dealings, and natural to an "enthusiast." (Crabb Robinson had noted after meeting Gilchrist that he was "desirous to consider Blake an enthusiast, not an *insane* man." [15] Furthermore, as Gilchrist remarks, Blake's visions had no "external, or (in German slang) . . . *objective* existence" (1, 365). Blake saw "subtler realities," to him "a more real kind of fact":

According to his own explanation, Blake saw spiritual appearances by the exercise of a special faculty—that of imagination—using the word in the then unusual, but true sense, of a faculty which busies itself with the subtler realities, not with fictions. . . . He said the things imagination saw were as much realities as were gross and tangible facts.

[1, 364]

There are echoes from Carlyle's discussion of Dante in Gil-

15. Robinson adds, "such question . . . is a mere question of words" (*On Books and Their Writers*, June 28, 1855).

christ's description of Blake's vision. Where Gilchrist writes "In short his [Blake's] belief in what he himself 'saw in vision,' was not as in a material, but a spiritual fact—to his mind a more real kind of fact" (*1*, 364), Carlyle says of *The Divine Comedy*: "we find ourselves in the World of Spirits; and dwell there, as among things palpable, indubitable! To Dante they were so; the real world, as it is called, and its facts, was but the threshold to an infinitely higher Fact of a World. At bottom, the one was as *preter*natural as the other. . . . To the earnest Dante it is all one visible Fact." [16]

The "singular difference in kind between Blake's imaginative work" and that of other imaginative artists is attributed to Blake's more detailed application of vision—the thoroughness of his reliance on his vision for a "revelation of the Invisible" (*1*, 365). Blake is to Gilchrist supremely mystical, the "most spiritual of artists" (*1*, 5). He writes concerning the designs to Blair's *Grave*:

> The unwavering hold (of which his 'Visions' were a result) upon an unseen world, such as in other ways poetry and even science assure us of, and whose revelation is the meaning underlying all religions,—this habitual hold is surely an authentic attainment, *not* an hallucination.
>
> [*1*, 270–71]

The "authentic *attainment*" rests with the strength of Blake's faith not with the designs as such: "whether the particular form in which the faith clothes itself, the language of Blake's mind . . . be adequate or not" (*1*, 271), the fervor of the prophet is always there.

This is the essence of Gilchrist's interpretation, a unified construction of Blake's life and work taken together. His total career in Gilchrist is an emblem for faith in the life of the spirit. And because Gilchrist's claims for Blake are ultimately

16. "The Hero as Poet: Dante; Shakespeare" [1840], *On Heroes and Hero-Worship, Works of Carlyle, 5,* 97.

based on so critically disarming a quality as the exalted character of his spiritual aspiration, the most appropriate way
to appreciate him is through a rather constraining reverence.
Poems, paintings, and ideas go by the board. Readers with
ordinary demands are warned off, while the potential sympa-
thizer is discouraged, gently, from judging Blake's actual out-
put. Readers of the biography would be lastingly impressed
with Blake's uniqueness; he was unclassifiable.

The crudities of Blake's "unsophisticated" technique together with his written strictures on style are considered further expressions of "high spiritual aims" or, in a word, enthusiasm. The violent antipathy seen in Blake's annotations
to the *Discourses* of Joshua Reynolds derives from the note-
writer's "honest contempt . . . for one whose goal . . .
was at [a] widely different . . . altitude" from his own. "Different ends" explain their "wholly different means"; and in
this light Gilchrist would have us view Blake's "slight, inartifi-
cial," and "arbitrary" technique. Once again the manner is
inaccessible to all but "those born" to like it (*1*, 3–5, 314).

In part the lack of finish shows a persistence of the child
in the man, although this was in the very nature of Blake's
singular task.

> For each artist and writer has, in the course of his
> training, to approve in his own person the immaturity
> of expression Art has at recurrent periods to pass through
> as a whole. And Blake in some aspects of his art never
> emerged from infancy. His Drawing . . . the *pose* and
> grouping of his figures . . . [is often] sublime. . . .
> [O]n the other hand [they] range under the category of
> the 'impossible'; are crude, contorted, forced . . .
> though none the less efficient in conveying the visions
> fetched by the guileless man from Heaven.
>
> [*1*, 3]

Similarly, in Blake's behavior, "allowance . . . [must] be
made" for occasional "crudeness and eccentricity." Gilchrist

observes that "In reading . . . [a prospectus for the Chaucer engraving] and similar effusions" one must recognize Blake's "want of early familiarity with the conventions of printed speech, parallel to his want of dexterity with those of the painter's language" (*1*, 278). Thus, eccentricity or appearances of madness on Blake's part are—quite apart from calculated perverseness—accidents of a temperament somewhat unbalanced by a self-fostered, "undisciplined," and "disproportionate" dependence on individual vision.

The natural bent was intensified by a life of solitude "so little interfered with by the ideas of others" (*1*, 365). After the crisis of his Exhibition especially, in the so-called "Years of Deepening Neglect" (Chap. 27), Blake sank more and more into himself. Obscurity, growing solitude, and apparent madness were mutually contingent in Cunningham's version of Blake; Gilchrist took extravagance of expression for a guide in dating some of Blake's writings as in the instance of the bristling annotations to Bacon. These date "I should say during the latter years of Blake's life [because] . . . [we] have frequent indignant comment and execration" (*1*, 315). Typically, Gilchrist's Blake rejects the world arena without resentment: Blake "talked little about 'posterity' "; his "soul turned . . . [to] the invisible world . . . [and there] found refuge amid the slights of the outward vulgar throng" (*1*, 294).

Even with a history so inward and self-contained as Blake's, Gilchrist could not absolutely ignore the realities of time and place; moreover, he was working on the model of Carlylean biography. In the *Life of Sterling* Carlyle exposed the inadequacies of a decadent Romanticism. He conveyed a "confused epoch" (p. 104) which misled and then failed those gifted young men who, like Sterling, wanted strength and steadiness of character to deal with it in a positive way. What Sterling was able to produce—a few essays, a mediocre novel—is of interest to Carlyle chiefly as a glimpse of uncompleted promise. Gilchrist's Blake is also a genius unfortunately situated—in the sterile rationalism that in Gilchrist's day all but defined the age of Johnson.

> In an era of academies, associations, and combined efforts, we have in [Blake] a solitary, self-taught, and as an artist, *semi*-taught Dreamer, 'delivering the burning messages of prophecy by the stammering lips of infancy,' as Mr. Ruskin has said of Cimabue and Giotto.
>
> [*1*, 3]

Though variously interpreted, Blake's separateness and exclusiveness remained for the nineteenth century the most significant impression left by Gilchrist's book. Moreover, the isolation in his age of an imagination such as Blake's is set within a more extensive view of the artist's alienation. Gilchrist speculates in terms that continued to gain force throughout the century:

> [Blake] was, in spirit, a denizen of other and earlier ages of the world than the present mechanical one to which chance had rudely transplanted him. It is within the last century or so, that 'the heavens have gone further off,' as Hazlitt put it. The supernatural world has during that period removed itself further from civilized, cultivated humanity than it was ever before—in all time, heathen or Christian. There is, at this moment, infinitely less practical belief in an invisible world, or even apprehension of it, than at any previous historical era, whether Egyptian, classic, or mediaeval. It is only within the last century and a half, the faculty of seeing visions could have been one to bring a man's sanity into question.
>
> [*1*, 369–70]

This view of Blake derives partly from Gilchrist's knowledge of Cunningham and, especially, of Malkin; it merged congenially with Carlylean conceptions of the autonomous genius

and with Palmer's and Linnell's primitive and pastoral Blake
(Linnell's "ancient pattern or virtue" and Palmer's "primitive
grandeur"). "In such intensity as Blake's," the visionary
imagination "was truly a blissful possession," writes Gilchrist;
"it proved enchanted armour against the world, the flesh,
and the devil, and all their sordid influences" (*1,* 270–71).

Such involvement in the world as Blake's early sympathies
for the French Revolution is deemphasized—perhaps to accord with the received images of a long line of recanting Romantic poets,[17] and also because, as Palmer wrote of Blake,
"In politics a Platonist, he put no trust in demagogues . . .
he might have been a reformer, but after the fashion of
Savonarola . . . [He] rebuked the profanity of Paine" (*Life,*
1, 344–47). Palmer's recollection of Blake saying that the
"Bonaparte of Italy was killed, and . . . another was some-
how substituted . . . who was the Bonaparte of the Empire" (*Life, 1,* 373–74) was submitted by Gilchrist as one
of Blake's "more wilful" utterances; Palmer's comment, "and
a very plausible story he made of it," follows. Even Swinburne at one point finds Blake's association with "Paine and
the ultra-democrats then . . . in London . . . the most
curious episode of those years" (p. 17).

The effect, finally, is to cut Blake off not only from the art,
literature, and thought of his time (or in truth of any time),
but from life itself. From the *Note-Book,* Gilchrist quoted,

> The Angel who presided at my birth
> Said: 'Little creature formed of joy and mirth,
> Go, love without the help of anything on earth.'

remarking, "well might he sweetly and touchingly say [this] of

17. Like "Byron, [Blake] held out 'against the wind'" (Bruce,
William Blake in This World, p. 38). The American publisher Horace
Scudder (1838–1902) attributed the tone of *SE* to Blake's faith in
mankind having been shaken by "the rude shock which the French
Revolution in its development gave to dreams of innocence" ("Review of Gilchrist's *Life,*" *North American Review, 99* [October
1864], 476).

himself" (*Life, 1,* 353). When D. G. Rossetti wrote on "Broken Love" ("My Spectre around me") he observed that it was the only poem in which "Blake has dealt with any of the deeper phases of human passion." He regrets that "the poet did not oftener elect to walk in the ways, not of spirits or children, but of living men" (*Life,* 1863, *2,* 76–77). To "most readers" of Gilchrist's *Life,* remarked a reviewer for the *Eclectic,* "it seems the writer wanted body; he lived so purely and entirely amidst his own volitions and visions." [18]

D. G. Rossetti's contributions to Gilchrist's *Life* tended to Gothicize Gilchrist's already remote hero. Rossetti wrote a "Supplementary" chapter (39) summing up Blake's achievement in art and poetry, an account of the *Inventions to Job,* and short descriptions of the illustrations to *Jerusalem* and *Milton.* For Volume 2 he edited Blake's writings and wrote the introductions—or "Headnotes." [19] Rossetti and his followers drew their medieval Blake from evidences in Gilchrist of an inclination which Gilchrist saw as Blake's proto-Romanticism, namely his appreciation of Gothic art. The years spent drawing from monuments in Westminster Abbey imbued Blake's imagination with the images of Gothic faces. "In Blake's angels and women and, indeed, in most of his figures, we may see the abiding influence of these mediaeval studies in that element of patriarchal quietude which sits meditating among the wildest storms of action," writes James Smetham,

18. "William Blake," *Eclectic Review, N. S.,* 6 (April 1864), 391.
19. The *Job* descriptions are in Chap. 32; *Jer* and *Milt* in Chap. 21. The paragraphs on *Milt* have not hitherto been noted as Rossetti's writing (A MS, Thorne Coll.). There are individual Headnotes to *PS, SIE,* the MS poetry, the prose selections, and the illustrations (2). Rossetti's contributions, taken from the 1880 edition, are reprinted in his *Collected Works,* ed. William Rossetti (2 vols. London, 1886), *1,* 443 ff. (see *Works,* rev. ed., 587 ff.). For Rossetti's editing and literary criticism see Chap. 5 below. His remarks on Blake the man in Vol. 2 accord with Gilchrist's approach (see *2,* 88).

painter, poet, and a friend of Rossetti.[20] Rossetti's followers
noted the testimony to Blake's admiration for Fra Angelico
in Palmer's letter and discerned an air of the cloister in his
taste for mystical writers. Blake, Palmer writes, was "a fitting
companion for Dante."

> He fervently loved the early Christian art, and dwelt
> with peculiar affection on the memory of Fra Angelico,
> often speaking of him as an inspired inventor and as a
> saint. . . .
> He was fond of the works of St. Theresa, and often
> quoted them with other writers on the interior life.
> Among his eccentricities will, no doubt, be numbered
> his preference for ecclesiastical governments. . . . His
> ideal home was with Fra Angelico.

[1, 347]

Rossetti's description of Blake's *Inventions to Job* seizes on
"evidence of Gothic feeling," notably the introduction of a
Gothic cathedral, the "shape in which the very soul of worship is now forever embodied among us" (*1*, 333). Rossetti's
followers, accepting Blake's inner affinities with the medieval,
copied the Gothic ornaments in the borders of the *Inventions*.

This was not to say that "Gothic forms of beauty" are
wedded to asceticism; Blake's women in the *Job* designs appealed to Rossetti because they "are given to us no less noble
in body than in soul; large-eyed, and large-armed also"—
Rossettian, in fact—"such as a man may love with all his
life." Nor are Blake's angels disembodied spirits "drowsing
on featherbed wings, or smothered in draperies" (*1*, 333).
But Rossetti's own sense of the spirituality of nature, his sus-
ceptibility to its power and beauty, and his insistence as a
painter upon the essential inspiration of the living model led
him to regret that Blake had written so vehemently against

20. "William Blake" (1869), *Literary Works of James Smetham,*
ed. William Davies (London, 1893), p. 119. For more on Smetham
see Chap. 7.

nature in his annotations to Wordsworth's 1815 Preface ("Natural objects . . . weaken, deaden, obliterate, imagination" [21]). Recognizing that inspiration "untrammeled by present reference to nature" (*1*, 416) must reign in the conception of any work of art, Rossetti nonetheless asserted:

> But it is equally or still more imperative that immediate study of nature should pervade the whole completed work. Tenderness, the constant unison of wonder and familiarity so mysteriously allied in nature, the sense of fulness and abundance such as we feel in a field, not because we pry into it all, but because it is all there . . . —all this Blake . . . was gifted to have attained, as we may see especially in his works of that smallest size where memory and genius may really almost stand in lieu of immediate consultation of nature.
>
> [*1*, 416]

Gilchrist's reviewers, most of whom favored the ethical, sincere, and natural in life and art, almost unanimously accepted Blake as a Hero. They relinquished mad Blake and took to their hearts the gentle and frugal engraver who chanted hymns on his deathbed and died with his debts paid—so much so that perhaps they felt justified in slighting his paintings and poems. "However we may have spoken of him as a painter, a poet or a . . . thinker, we can only speak of him as a man with praise." The reviewer for *Macmillan's Magazine,* the publisher's own organ, derides the "pre-Raphaelite . . . superlatives" lavished on Blake's poems and paintings; the *Life,* he declares, is primarily about a "most extraordinary man."

---

21. D. G. Rossetti was not in agreement however with Wordsworth's view of nature. He thought him too much "the High Priest of Nature to be her lover . . . [or] to drop to his knees in simple love . . . [or] to thank God that she was beautiful" (Caine, *Recollections of Dante Gabriel Rossetti,* p. 148).

The "purest song" Blake sang according to the first-quoted reviewer was the life he lived. A third, for the *Westminster Review,* saw the beauty of his life in the "fulness of his faith." The *Art Journal's* reviewer rejoiced to find in Gilchrist's *Life* a moral demonstration for the young that poverty might be borne with dignity and that it is inner resources which count.[22]

Independent observations or digressions on Blake's character usually followed through on points made by Gilchrist and sometimes Rossetti.[23] R. H. Hutton's review in the *Spectator* differs from some others in being a more knowledgeable and thoughtful derivation. Hutton's Blake is patriarchal, innocent, simple, remote, and unsusceptible to objective criteria of appreciation. Blake's sensibility is set within a larger perspective; his "essential function," his proper sphere, in a world

22. The five citations in this paragraph, in order of appearance, are from: *New Monthly Mag., 130* (1864), 318; *Macmillan's Mag., 11* (Nov. 1864), 33 and 26; *New Monthly,* 319; *Westminster Review, N. S., 25* (Jan. 1864), 104; and *Art Journal,* pp. 25–26. The writer for *Blackwood's Mag., 97* (Mar. 1865), 291–307, despite serious reservations about Gilchrist's interpretation (see p. 86 below), honors Blake's exemplary "temperate" life, with "one woman" (p. 291).

Other reviews which dwell lovingly on Blake's perfect marriage, the happiness of his life, and the beauty of his death are: *Eclectic,* pp. 387–88; "Pictor Ignotus," *Sharpe's London Magazine, N. S. 31* (1867), 22–23 and 28. Additional points often reiterated are the Cromek-Stothard-Blake dispute, and Blake's supposedly happy stay with Hayley at Felpham (see especially *Eclectic,* pp. 381–82; *Sharpe's,* pp. 27 ff.; and *Westminster,* p. 105). Two propositions became axiomatic: Blake's loss of lucidity and his inability to select or discriminate; the second, reinforced by Swinburne's criticism, became a critical commonplace after 1868 (see *Westminster,* pp. 104 and 110; *Quarterly Review* [see Chap. 2, n. 20]; W. F. Rea, "The Life and Works of William Blake," p. 78; and *Eclectic,* 378).

23. The "Gothic" *Job* replaced the designs to Blair's *Grave* as Blake's acknowledged artistic masterpiece. *Westminster;* [R. H. Hutton], "William Blake," *The Spectator,* No. 1847 (Nov. 21, 1863), pp. 2771–73.

For Rossetti's influence on the valuation of Blake's poetry, see Chaps. 5 and 7.

where "grand" and "free" minds grow "much less common as the world studies and masters its own thoughts," is "to recall by painting—now and then by poetry,—that lost sense described by Wordsworth" in the "Intimations Ode." Hutton quotes the stanza beginning "But there's a Tree" that according to Crabb Robinson had thrown Blake "almost into an hysterical rapture." Blake, Hutton says, mingles at times the "mysterious depth of Wordsworth with the grand symbolism of the primeval world." [24] In effect, Blake is by definition outside the world that is too much with us. His pictures and poems are "very rarely . . . instinct with what we call experience," says Hutton, echoing the *Life*.[25] F. T. Palgrave, for the *Quarterly Review,* writes:

> Blake himself may be said to have lived apart from chronology. In turn he was a philosopher of the early Hellenic world, with Heraclitus, when he uttered his dark sayings; or of the Roman time, in his practical life,

24. Hutton's unsigned review in the *Spectator,* a liberal weekly, was the first to appear in print; he has been identified as the author by R. H. Tener, "More Articles by R. H. Hutton," *Bulletin NYPL, 66* (Jan. 1962), 60. Hutton (1826–97) was an Anglican polemicist, a writer for the *Contemporary Review,* and a respected critic and man of letters.

Hutton terms Blake "a chained visionary" who lived in a time "when there was no open vision," evidencing the letter to Butts in which Blake bitterly confessed the "inadequacy of his own manner to do justice to his character." Hutton is the first writer to allude to anything that suggests "fourfold" meaning (Blake's "hieroglyphic" intelligence errs when his vision becomes "double, treble, and quadruple" instead of remaining "singular"). He does not develop the point or cite examples. Crompton notes this, "Blake's Nineteenth Century Critics," p. 128.

25. The same point is brought up in a number of ways. Oswald Crawfurd (reviewing Swinburne's *William Blake, New Quarterly Magazine,* 2 [April 1874]), 466–501, writes that Blake, like Comte, John Mill, and Bentham, was "unacquainted with ordinary human nature" (p. 478). See also *Westminster,* p. 105; J. Comyns Carr, *The English Poets,* ed. Ward (London, 1880), *3,* 598. Most writers reasserted the primitive, Gothic, or childlike Blake.

with Epictetus; or, again . . . one of the Freemasons
of the Middle Ages, in his passion for Gothic art and
mysticism: or an anchorite in some mountain-cell, in
his realistic belief in the world of dream and vision; or
a poet of the Elizabethan age in his own exquisite lyrics.

[p. 17]

Amid the general agreement there were some few who
found Gilchrist's "hero-worship" excessive or who took exception to his view of Blake's "madness," among them writers
for the *Athenaeum, Blackwood's,* and the *Westminster Review.* The critic for *Blackwood's,* Blake's and Gilchrist's most
unsympathetic reviewer, acknowledges in Blake only a "curiosity" who "invites analysis," a "dreary mystic" behind Gilchrist's "retired poet, singing of his lamb and his tiger";
Blake's visions are a neurotic combination of abnormally distinct imagination and a desire for attention (pp. 291, 307).

The *Athenaeum's* reviewer[26] rejected Gilchrist's Blake on
the ground that "enthusiasm" was a shabby substitute for a
high madness. He appears to be urging the old schema of sublime irregularity, writing that Blake's nature is one "in which
both man's highest aspirations and lowest mistakes (the latter
surprisingly few) were . . . rendered misshapen . . . by an
element akin to 'great wit' yet not therefore part and parcel of
it." "Mr. Gilchrist has failed in his Apotheosis of Incomplete-
ness. . . . He has in no respect explained Blake, but has
rather damaged him by a too vehement distortion of the
facts" (p. 644).

The *Westminster's* reviewer preferred to see in Gilchrist's
work raw material for "psychological studies" (pp. 101–102).
As decisive evidence of Gilchrist's mistaken regard for his

26. *Athenaeum,* No. 1880 (Nov. 7, 1863), pp. 599–601 and No.
1881 (Nov. 14, 1863), pp. 642–44. For evidence that a friend of
Crabb Robinson's, journalist Augustus De Morgan, was the author of
this review, see Chap. 2, n. 26. W. F. Rea (*Fine Arts Quarterly Review*) who follows the *Athenaeum* writer point for point also attacks
Gilchrist's "hero-worship."

subject the story is cited of Mr. Butts chancing on Blake and his wife unclothed in a summerhouse behind their lodgings in London and being hailed by the bard, "It's only Adam and Eve, you know." This apocryphal item, soon to become a dearly cherished Blake story, was told first by Gilchrist who introduced it with enlightened observations about philosophical nudity. Redgrave's *Century of Painters* made it into a family practice with Blake reciting passages of *Paradise Lost* to the scandalized edification of the neighborhood. One reviewer of the *Life* used the story to point out Blake's (and Gilchrist's) naïveté and lack of humor.[27] Nonetheless, even

27. Richard Redgrave, R. A., and Samuel Redgrave, *A Century of Painters* (2 vols. London, 1866), *1*, 441–42, and Crawfurd, Review of Swinburne's *William Blake,* p. 496. Crawfurd wrote that "he had argued himself into thinking *clothlessness* the proper condition of man."

Other writers who seized on the story include the reviewers for the *Fine Arts Quarterly Review:* "Assuredly those who claim to be visionaries indulge in very strange conduct" (p. 67); and for the *New Monthly Magazine,* pp. 309–19. The latter has made studies into cases of insanity and quotes the story as proof that Blake's delusions (including also the Visionary Heads) make him eligible for the madhouse (p. 318).

Linnell remarked that the story

"is so entirely unlike everything I have known of him, so improbable from the impracticability of the thing on account of climate, [!] that I do not think it possible. . . . Blake was very unreserved in his narrations to me of all his thoughts and actions, and . . . if anything like this story had been true, he would have told me of it. I am sure he would have laughed heartily at it if it had been told of him or of anyone else, for he was a hearty laugher at absurdities."

[*Life of Linnell, 1,* 160–61]

Palmer did "not believe it: it is unlike Blake" (A. H. Palmer, p. 256; letter dated June 1864). For William Rossetti's evaluation of the story, see Aldine, pp. xxx–xxxi n.

Rossetti advised Mrs. Gilchrist to cut the anecdote from the 1880 *Life:* the tale "is a great deal too much of a good story" (A. L., Mar. 22, 1880, Thorne Coll.). She deleted only "on more than one oc-

those writers who were skeptical of Gilchrist's defense of
Blake's sanity or condescended to Blake's supposed innocence, admired the earnest life he lived.

So strong was the influence of Gilchrist's portrait, so strong
the conviction of Blake's "sincerity," that many readers were
repelled and outraged by the explications of his poems in
Swinburne's book:

> Blake, who . . . had daily prayers . . . [who was a
> model of] respectability, whose life . . . was as pure
> and blameless as one of the winged messengers . . .
> [of] his daydreams, comes out of Mr. Swinburne's cruci-
> ble with the attributes and aspects of a satyr! [28]

Palmer's letter in Gilchrist's *Life* contains a description
of Blake's "nervous and brilliant" conversation; "brilliant,"
"intent," "susceptible" eyes that "flashed with genius," the
"lips quivering with feeling"—which could well epitomize
Swinburne's picture in the opening pages of *William Blake* of
a Living Sensibility hardly able to contain itself. *William
Blake* begins with a description of the Linnell portrait on
the frontispiece of the *Life*: the "eloquent, excitable mouth,
with a look of nervous fluent power," the countenance wanting "in balance"—the face of a man who never could "be
cured of illusions" (p. 2),[29] a man not unlike the young Swinburne.

---

casion"—referring to the frequency with which the Blakes played
Adam and Eve (see *Life*, 1863, *1*, 115 and *Life*, *1*, 112).

For Butts' own discrediting of the story, see Ada Briggs, "Mr. Butts,
the Friend and Patron of Blake," *Connoisseur, 19* (1907), 92–96.

28. Crawfurd, p. 490. On the reference to daily prayers, see above,
p. 74 (and Chap. 3, p. 27). The interrelating of biography and criticism and the importance put on sincerity in the nineteenth century
was never really absent from Blake criticism despite the efforts of
Swinburne.

29. Swinburne comments on an engraving from Linnell's portrait of
Blake on ivory done in 1827 when Blake was old, sick, and wasted;

Swinburne's *William Blake* was first intended as a commentary on the prophetic books, a sort of supplement to Gilchrist's Life. It was turned into an extended review of the *Life of Blake,* both biography and Selections, when Swinburne learned to his disappointment that William Rossetti was not going to review the book for *Fraser's.* Rossetti's decision was probably taken because his assistance to Mrs. Gilchrist included by this time—November, 1862—writing short passages.[30] The three divisions of Swinburne's study—

---

the face is ultra-refined and sensitive. In 1880 an engraving of Richard Phillips' Academy portrait of Blake appears as the frontispiece to Vol. 2), perhaps because of an observation by James Smetham, in "William Blake":

> Comparing the two so fine and so various portraits, you are able adequately to conceive the man, and in both you feel that this awful *eye,* far-gazing, subduing the unseen to itself, was the most wonderful feature.

[p. 99]

The influence of Palmer's letter may possibly be traced even further; perhaps Yeats's masks had part of the their complex origins in a brooding upon the notion of "a man without a mask" in combination with Blake's "Man is born a Spectre or Satan & is altogether an Evil, & requires a New Selfhood continually, & must continually be changed into his direct Contrary" (*Jer,* pl. 52).

30. For Swinburne's initial project of a "running commentary," see *S. L.,* No. 35, Oct. 6, 1862, *1,* 59–60; and Chap. 6. For William Rossetti and *Fraser's,* see ibid., No. 36, Nov. 3, [1862], *1,* 62 and n. 7.

The contributions actually credited to William Rossetti in Gilchrist's *Life* include an interpretation of "The Mental Traveller" and the Annotated Catalogue of Blake's Paintings and Drawings, in Vol. 2. William Rossetti's part in the book, like most of his life, has been overshadowed by his brother. He served as an intermediary between Mrs. Gilchrist, and his brother and Swinburne, at times (William Rossetti, *Letters Concerning Whitman, Blake, Shelley,* pp. 6–8, letter dated Dec. 8, 1862. For his correspondence on the edition, see pp. 3 ff.). Swinburne dedicated *William Blake* to William Rossetti for having "done more than I to serve and exalt the memory of Blake" (p. iii), seven years before publication of the Aldine edition. His *Reminiscences* reveal that he furnished "several remarks having a

1, Life and Designs; *2,* Lyrical Poems; and *3,* The Prophetic
Books—directly treat Gilchrist's Life; however, the book soon
went beyond the sphere of a review and presented readers
with a new interpretation of Blake as a rebel artist.

William Blake was written, added to, and revised over a
period of some five years during which Swinburne, in his
late twenties, lived a hectic, experimental, and various life.
The book was begun in 1863 when Swinburne was relatively
unknown. By the time it was published, he had become notorious, first as the writer of *Poems and Ballads* (1866), and
then with the publication of *Notes on Poems and Ballads*
(1866) as the leading English polemicist of Art for Art's
Sake. *William Blake* appeared in print in December 1867.
(The date on the title page is 1868.[31]) Also during these

---

critical bearing, which were embodied in the *Life* here and there"
(*Some Reminiscences, 1,* 306). See Chap. 6, n. 4.

31. Most of *William Blake* was written during the summer and
autumn of 1863 and the winter of 1864, while Swinburne was at his
family home, Holmwood, recuperating from a suicidal life in London; its composition may be traced through letters to William
Rossetti. Swinburne worked on Parts *1* and *2* together. By Jan. 31,
1864, he had finished *2,* was nearly through *1,* and had done much
on *3.* In spring 1864, Swinburne traveled on the continent, met Landor, and spoke to Barone Seymour Kirkup, whose recollections of
Blake were added to *William Blake.* See *S. L.,* No. 48; No. 50, Oct.
1863, *1,* 86 and 89; No. 51, Dec. 15, 1863, *1,* 90; and No. 53, Jan. 31,
1864, *1,* 94.

A nearly complete text was finally sent off to Swinburne's publisher,
Moxon, in Jan. 1866 (T. J. Wise, *A Bibliography of Swinburne's
Works, Works of Swinburne* [Bonchurch ed. London, 1927], *20,* 91–
92). Then Swinburne changed to a new publisher after Moxon had
Poems and Ballads removed from circulation. Quickly in the summer
of 1866 Swinburne wrote his defense, *Notes on Poems and Reviews,*
published by J. C. Hotten. *William Blake,* partly in type, was finally
surrendered to Hotten by Moxon; and in late 1866 and in 1867, Swinburne made more changes, added footnotes, and expanded the conclusion. In Feb. 1867 Swinburne writes William Rossetti that the manuscript of *William Blake* has been "twice revised (with additional notes)

years Swinburne began to support actively the movement for Italian independence and broadened his Art for Art's Sake position to embrace all libertarian causes. Almost all his central preoccupations are reflected in this one book on Blake.

Moreover, like many other nineteenth-century Blakeans in writing of Blake, Swinburne is at the same time defining his own critical stance. (Part 2 of *William Blake,* written in 1864, opens with what is probably Swinburne's first aesthetic manifesto; the *Notes on Poems and Ballads* was composed about two years later.) Swinburne wrote, in effect, that he proposed to consider Blake as a type of the true artist prefacing this statement with a discussion of the nature of true art generally:

> Art for art's sake first of all, and afterwards we may suppose all the rest shall be added to her (or if not she need hardly be overmuch concerned); from the man who falls to artistic work with a moral purpose shall be taken away even that which he has. . . . A living critic [Baudelaire] of incomparably delicate insight . . . calls this "the heresy of instruction" . . . one might call it . . . the great moral heresy.
>
> [pp. 91–92]
>
> Thus much it seemed useful to premise, by way of exposition . . . so as once for all to indicate beyond chance of mistake the real point of view taken during life by Blake, and necessary to be taken by those who would appreciate his labours and purposes.
>
> [p. 93]

---

and ought to be all right if trouble and bother can make it" (*S. L.,* No. 180, *1,* 228).

The delay probably helped Blake's cause, since in the period 1864 to 1867, Swinburne had become sufficiently established as poet, polemicist, and enemy to public morality so that many "would read the Essay [on Blake] on your account and some rather fewer, on Blake's." Letter from William Rossetti, *Ashley Library Catalogue,* comp. T. J. Wise, *4* (1923), 172.

Swinburne's "main object" in retracing Blake's life story in
William Blake is "to give the whole a certain dramatic order
by taking each part . . . and examining each detail in the
light given by the personal character." [32] This is not, however,
the Carlylean-Gilchristian approach—the "character" in question is that of the *artist*. Swinburne refocuses Gilchrist's view
of Blake as a saint in life who happened also to be an artist.
Were Blake's productions—incomprehensible as they are to
most men and without moral teaching and uplift, "a heap of
tumbled and tangled relics, verse and prose mainly inexplicable, paintings and engravings mainly unacceptable if not un-
endurable" (p. 85)—to be submitted only to "popular theories of the just aims of life" (p. 85), or to the execrable
Ruskinian "invention of making 'Art the handmaid of Religion' " (p. 90), Blake's life and art should be judged a "de-
plorable waste and failure" (p. 86). "To [Blake] as to others
of his kind, all faith, all virtue, all moral duty or religious
necessity, was not so much abrogated or superseded as
summed up, included and involved, by the one matter of art"
(p. 86).

Swinburne set out to present and discuss Blake's works
apart from questions of individual idiosyncrasy; he meant to
be a critic of Blake's art and not a personal apologist. Nevertheless, Swinburne was more than disposed to recognize the
existence and legitimacy of "artistic personality" in Blake.
Many "singular points and shades of character . . . compose
the vital element and working condition of Blake's art" (p.
39). His so-called conceitedness, his impatience toward
doubters and antagonists, his mode of speaking about his
visions—which worried Gilchrist into pages of explaining
away—are actively justified by Swinburne's view of Blake's
stature and dedication as an artist. "It was no vain or empty
claim that he put forward to especial insight and individual
means of labour. If he spoke strangely, he had great things to

32. *S. L.*, No. 53, Jan. 31 [1864], *1*, 94.

speak. If he acted strangely, he had great things to do" (pp. 46–47).

Swinburne demands that one concede the authority in Blake of what in madmen would be merely madness. Gilchrist saw Blake's seeming madness as defensive, perhaps strategic, or else as hyper-"enthusiasm," the eccentricity of other-worldliness—"Does not prophet or hero always seem 'mad' to the respectable mob, and to polished men of the world, the motives of feeling and action being so alien and incomprehensible?" (*1, 368*). Swinburne stresses that mental unrest is intrinsic to Blake's extreme sensibility and to his earnestness in art.

> To him the veil of outer things seemed always to tremble with some breath behind it: . . . All the void of earth and air seemed to quiver with the passage of sentient wings and palpitate under the pressure of conscious feet. . . . His hardest facts were the vaguest allegories of other men. To him all symbolic things were literal, all literal things symbolic.
>
> . . .
>
> In this spirit he wrought at his day's work, seeing everywhere the image of his own mood, the presence of foes and friends. Nothing to him was neutral; nothing without significance. The labour and strife of soul in which he lived was a thing as earnest as any bodily warfare.
>
> [pp. 41–44]

Swinburne translates Blake's "madness" or "enthusiasm" into a unique combination of aesthetic sensitivity and mystical perception—which was not without danger to the mental composure of the man and, therefore, to the coherence of the work he produced. His visions are seen as emanating from this personality under the stress of outward circumstances. Swinburne ignores anecdotes about Blake's early visions of angels amid the haystacks and God at the window;

he sees the Visionary Heads of Blake's later years as "interesting chiefly for the evidence they give of Blake's power upon his own mind and nerves, and of the strong and subtle mixture of passion with humour in his temperament" (p. 65).

With the Butts letters and, to a lesser extent, the *Note-Book* as his primary sources Swinburne considers the knotty question of Blake's exchange with Spiritual Forms as it is relevant to the Felpham period. He pictures Blake transplanted from smoky London amid human influences hostile to his life as an artist (his years with Hayley and the time of his trial for sedition), his already highly strung senses thrown into near disorder by the headiness of "his first daily communion with the sea" (p. 34). At this time the "mystic" in Blake overcomes the judgment of the artist, and the artist comes closest to unbalancing the man.

> That too much of Blake's written work while at Felpham [Swinburne takes *Jerusalem* and *Milton* as dating from the Felpham years.] is wanting in executive quality, and even in decent coherence of verbal dress, is undeniable. . . . [The] prophetic robe here slips or gapes, there muffles and impedes. . . . Everything now written in the fitful impatient intervals of the day's work bears the stamp of an overheated brain and of nerves too intensely strung. . . . [In] this case did the sudden country life, the taste and savour of the sea, touch sharply and irritate deliciously the more susceptible and intricate organs of mind and nature.
>
> [p. 37]

Swinburne is not advocating any willful *"dérèglement,"* although he does regard a hyperexcitability as all but concomitant with artistic sensitivity. Nevertheless, this is emphatically not to be confused with insanity:

> How far such passive capacity for excitement differs from insanity; how in effect a temperament so sensuous,

so receptive, and so passionate is further off from any risk of turning unsound than hardier natures carrying heavier weight and tougher in the nerves; need scarcely be indicated.

[p. 37]

Swinburne's view of the artist's personality, derived largely from his reading of Baudelaire,[33] finally takes his biography of Blake into a quest for unconventionality, anticonventionality, and even aberration. Reviewing quickly the events of Blake's life as given by Gilchrist, Swinburne bypasses the recollections of Linnell and the Ancients and praises Crabb Robinson's "cautious and vivid transcriptions of Blake's actual speech" (p. 79). He enlarges on Gilchrist's passing mention that Blake once thought of taking a second wife into his house and expands upon whatever evidence he can find of pagan enjoyments. Swinburne and the Rossettis were eager to find sexual license of any sort in art and artists. He also quotes an anecdote from the *Note-Book* (not in Gilchrist), an account of Mrs. Blake's opening Bysshe's *Art of Poetry* (to see her fortune) at an amorous extract by Aphra Behn (p. 130 n.); he coyly describes "When Klopstock . . . ," quoting several lines. Aphra Behn's appearance inspires a tribute to "François Villon and Aphra Behn, the two most inexpressibly non-respectable of male and female Bohemians and poets," whose lyrical gifts have "perhaps borne better fruit for

33. Swinburne read, reviewed, corresponded with, and was deeply influenced by Baudelaire in the late 1850s and early 1860s. For Baudelaire's "practical aestheticism," see W. K. Wimsatt Jr. and Cleanth Brooks, *Literary Criticism* (New York, Knopf, 1957), p. 485. For Swinburne's review of *Les Fleurs du Mal*, written for the *Spectator*, 1861, see "Charles Baudelaire," *Works, 13* (Bonchurch ed., London, 1927), 417–27. For the influence of Baudelaire on Swinburne, Georges Lafourcade, *La Jeunesse de Swinburne (1837–1867)* (2 vols. London, Oxford University Press, 1928), 2, 320–53.
There is a note superadded to *William Blake,* to the passage quoted above (p. 91), in which Swinburne pays tribute to Baudelaire who died Aug. 31, 1867 (p. 91. n.).

us than any gift of moral excellence" (pp. 131–32 n.). The passage was not lost on the aesthetic generation which followed; "Poor dear Aphra . . . She wrote lovely songs which Blake loved," writes Frederick York Powell twenty years later.[34]

Another "inexpressibly non-respectable" writer to whose work Swinburne was introduced in 1862 (by Monckton Milnes) was the Marquis de Sade;[35] he too makes an appearance in *William Blake* as an unnamed "modern pagan philosopher" whose "lay sermon" on the criminal instincts of Nature (p. 158) is quoted in a note: Swinburne concludes "Observe how the mystical evangelist [Blake] and the material humourist [de Sade] meet . . . in their interpretation of the laws ruling the outer body of life." He wrote to William Rossetti in 1867: "I have recently added from an anonymous source a note on Theism which is not yet in type: I expect it will make Urizen [Swinburne's customary word for Morality, in these years] tremble in his bottes éculées à la Robert Macaire!"[36]

Swinburne also tries to suggest affinities in Blake with the criminal. An unusual incident of his early years which Swinburne recounts is a premonition that the engraver Rylands would perish on the gallows. Swinburne includes an account from Blake's later life of "an intimacy not unpleasing to commemorate" between Blake and T. G. Wainewright affixing a brief biography of this artist-criminal and anti-Hero. He traces

34. Oliver Elton, *Frederick York Powell, A Life and A Selection* . . . (2 vols. London, Oxford University Press, 1906), *1*, 271; letter dated Oct. 10, 1889. Powell also absorbed the anecdote (first told by Cunningham) of Blake's having witnessed a "fairy's funeral" in his Felpham garden. In the 1890s, he remarks that "with Blake," he believes "that the fairies exist" (*2*, 320). For Powell's part in Blake research of the 1890s see Chap. 8.

35. For Swinburne's friendship with Monckton Milnes, see *S. L.*, *1*, pp. xlv–xlvii and James Pope-Hennessy, *Monckton Milnes: The Flight of Youth, 1851–1885* (London, Constable, 1951).

36. *S. L.*, No. 180, Feb. 20, 1867, *1*, 228. First identified by Lafourcade, *2*, 354–56.

Wainewright's "organic" career as art critic, painter, writer, and murderer—[37] although the poems never did come up to the murders. Swinburne in the tale of Wainewright parodies the approach to biography in which a subject's accomplishments are applauded, excused, and justified so long as they can be classified as sincere self-expression—in fact, the view implied in Carlyle's "Biography" and embodied in Gilchrist's Life of Blake. Swinburne defends his anti-Hero precisely on grounds of earnestness, satirizing the philistine formulas on life and art:

> Those who would depreciate his [Wainewright's] performance as a simple author must recollect that in accordance with the modern receipt he "lived his poems"; that the age prefers deeds to songs; that to do great things is better than to write; that action is of eternity, fiction of time; and that these poems were doubtless the greater for being 'inarticulate.'
>
> [p. 69]

The last is certainly aimed at Gilchrist on Blake.

Swinburne also develops the theme of the rebellious artist as victim in his treatment of Blake's dealings with Hayley and Cromek. Both encounters show the irreconcilability of

37. For Swinburne on Wainewright, see pp. 67–71. For both Rossetti and Swinburne, Wainewright was a favorite type of the artist-criminal. For Blake's friendship with Wainewright, see Life, 1, Chap. 31. In fact, Swinburne's evaluation of Wainewright's literary and artistic gifts stresses the same points contained in a passage on Wainewright in the 1863 Life, a passage which Rossetti wrote (it has not been identified as his or included in his writings to this date—A MS, Thorne Coll.). This is a combined eulogy and apology comparing Wainewright's essays on art favorably with Ruskin's criticism and noting that despite the man's "great criminality . . . art [demands] a wholly independent verdict . . . which not even the sternest personal censure can annul" (Life, 1863, 1, 281).

In 1880 Rossetti asked Mrs. Gilchrist to drop the passage from the second edition: his estimate had been "founded on mistaken views (as I since find) of W's powers as an artist" (A. L., Mar. 2, 1880, Thorne Coll.).

true art with the lesser aims of lesser men. Hayley's genteel and socially accommodating view of poetry—not to speak of Hayley's poetry itself—provokes from Swinburne a long and vicious lampoon. Going much further than Gilchrist on the strength of the *Note-Book* rhymes and the discontent voiced in the Butts letters, Swinburne describes Hayley as a cock among hens and tame geese, acting the pretentious patron to a naïvely grateful Blake. Gilchrist's innocent is seen as the pure artist exploited, condescended to, and then betrayed by the dilettante-patron (the enemy in artist's clothing). He is then victimized outright by a materialistic culture in the shape of R. H. Cromek. (And to the Cromek-Stothard-Blake affair Swinburne gives much attention, including spilled-over wrath directed at his own former publisher, Moxon.)

Heightening details, to some extent inventing, Swinburne had little concrete fact from Blake's life to support his picture of the deviant artist; mainly he indulges himself. In the end he finds himself, ironically, in the position of Carlyle when writing about Frederick II—his subject does not always co-operate. Swinburne's own quite moralistic obsession with the forbidden, at a time in his life when he was unlikely to be objective, results finally in perceptible disappointment with a *poète maudit manqué;* Swinburne cannot forbear patronizing:

> [There] is a certain unmistakeable innocence which accounts for the practical modesty and peaceable forbear-ance of the man's way of living. The material shape of his speculations never goes beyond a sort of boyish de-fiant complaint, a half-humorous revolt of the will. In-constancy with him is not rooted in satiety, but in the freshness of pure pleasure; he would never cast off the old to put on the new.

[pp. 139–40]

Behind this description of Blake is Swinburne's aesthetic and practical allegiance "Not [to] the luxuries of pleasure in their simple first form, but . . . [to] the sides on which nature looks unnatural" which "go to make up the . . . substance" of *Les Fleurs du Mal*[38]—and indeed, of "Faustine," "Anactoria," "Laus Veneris," and other *Poems and Ballads* written about this time.

Swinburne relishes Blake's attacks on conventional society, compares his visionary theorizing to his beloved Shelley's, but considers his "innocent" and "obscure" ethical idealism (pp. 139–40) naïve. He writes of Blake's *Visions of the Daughters of Albion* (in Part 3): "Blake, as evidently as Shelley, did in all innocence believe that ameliorated humanity would be soon qualified to start afresh . . . after the saving advent of the French and American revolutions" (p. 234). Individual fulfillment for Swinburne is a darker quantity than the Blakes and Shelleys supposed:

> The sinless likeness of his [Blake's] seeming "sins"— mere fancies as it appears they mostly were, mere soft light aspirations of theory without body or flesh on them —has something of the innocent immodesty of a birds' or babies' paradise—or a fool's paradise, too, translated into the practice and language of the untheoretic world. Shelley's "Epipsychidion" scarcely preaches a more bodiless evangel of bodily liberty.
>
> [p. 140]

Moreover, true personal liberation is not subordinate to the reform of society (if the latter is at all relevant). Impatient with Victor Hugo's attacks on society's "artificial hells" that complicate "destiny which is divine," Swinburne left "the question of intention to heaven," suggested an "efficient poor law," and commented that it was "strange that an artist like M. Hugo should believe that . . . any fatality in man's manners . . . can overbear a resolute conception of morality" in a single individual.[39]

38. "Charles Baudelaire," 420–21.
39. "A Study of Victor Hugo's *Les Miserables*" [1862], *Works, 13* (Bonchurch ed., London, 1927), 156–57.

The great Victorian reformers thought that the great Romantic prophet-artists should have led more socially dedicated lives and preached more effectively in their works: Arnold called Shelley an "ineffectual Angel"; Ruskin agonized over Blake's "warped power" and "ineffectual . . . soul"; and Carlyle sneered at a "tragically ineffectual" Coleridge.[40] Swinburne preferred artists to defy more brazenly in their persons and not preach at all in their works. Nevertheless, for his followers and Rossetti's, who felt themselves becoming separated from contemporary experience and therefore tended toward a self-defensive anti-activism and artificiality, Swinburne's picture of Blake as a pure artist, together with Gilchrist's of an other-worldly enthusiast, helped to sanction the aesthete's sensibility—and to sanctify Blake's.

40. "Shelley" [1888], *Essays in Criticism, Second Series, Works of Matthew Arnold* (15 vols. London, Macmillan 1903–04), *4*, 185; Ruskin, "Liberty," *A Cestus of Aglaia, Works, 19*, p. 133; and Thomas Carlyle, *The Life of John Sterling* [1851], *Works of Carlyle* (Centenary ed., London, n.d.) *11*, 60.

Carlyle describes Coleridge (in an influential chapter titled "The Seer of Highgate") as the villain of a chaotic epoch, giving useless directions to confused souls in search of the truth: Coleridge "flabby and irresolute . . . deficient in goal or aim," moved in a "kantean haze-world" (pp. 56–57 and 59).

To Carlyle, Shelley was

> a kind of ghastly object; colourless, pallid, tuneless, without health or warmth or vigour; the sound of him shrieky, frosty, as if a *ghost* were trying to 'sing' to us; the temperament of him, spasmodic, hysterical, instead of strong or robust; with fine affectations and aspirations, gone all such a road:—a man infinitely too *weak* for that solitary scaling of the Alps which he undertook in spite of all the world.

[*Reminiscences*, ed. C. E. Norton (2 vols. London, 1887), *2*, 292–93]

On Victorian criticism of the 1850s and 60s in relation to social reform and humanism, see Buckley, *The Victorian Temper*, especially Chap. 2 ("The Anti-Romantics").

Judgment was seldom passed on Blake; nor was it as harsh on him as on Shelley or even Coleridge because of his comparative obscurity, his biographical image, and the ever hovering ascriptions of insanity.

CHAPTER FIVE

The Mid-Century Revival—Texts and Criticism

Editorial Policy: A General Introduction

With Volume 2 of Gilchrist's *Life,* the Selections, Blake's writings for the first time could readily be bought and read. What this comprised was a liberally rewritten and rearranged, somewhat bowdlerized, not wholly representative selection by many hands. It included prose, lyrics, several poems in blank verse, and only the *Book of Thel* of the prophetic poems (the other prophecies were not part of Blake's "poetry" as his editors defined the term). An "extract" from *The French Revolution* was at first approved for the Selections, but Rossetti decided "on mature deliberation" to omit it—perhaps under Swinburne's influence, since in *William Blake* he calls the poem "mere wind and splutter." [1] Nothing engraved by Blake after 1794 appeared in the volume.

Because the editing was guided largely by a desire to make Blake as "accessible" as possible,[2] the lyrical poetry pre-

1. A. L., Rossetti to Mrs. Gilchrist, written after Jan. 1863, Thorne Coll.; and Swinburne, p. 14. Most of the final decisions for the Selections were made in late 1862 and early 1863.

Chap. 5 is supplemented by the charts in the Appendix showing which of Blake's writings were reprinted and when.

2. A. L., Rossetti to Mrs. Gilchrist, Mar. 2, 1880, Thorne Coll. *Tiriel* also was considered, but Rossetti "said it must be heavy, & would scare readers away from the rest; he would not adventure its perusal himself." He advised cutting it to "make room for everything else of an available kind" (Letter from William Rossetti to Mrs. Gilchrist, dated Dec. 8, 1862, *Letters Concerning Whitman, Blake, Shel-*

dominates, especially the poems of a non-"metaphysical" kind—to use Rossetti's adjective (*Life, 2,* 27). There are, from *Poetical Sketches,* ten shorter lyrics and about three hundred lines of *Edward the Third* put into smooth blank verse; *Thel,* and *Songs of Innocence and of Experience* are complete. In addition there is a large group of manuscript poems collected under the heading "Poems Hitherto Unpublished," which Rossetti culled, revised, and assembled from Blake's *Note-Book* and from what is now known as the *Pickering MS.* For the most part these too are lyrics of an "available kind," but there are exceptions: "Auguries of Innocence," "My Spectre around me" titled "Broken Love"— both freely emended in the interests of presumed clarity,[3] but presenting problems in interpretation nonetheless—"The Crystal Cabinet," "The Golden Net," and "The Mental Traveller" with an explication by William Rossetti. Rossetti had favored omitting a poem as complicated as "The Mental Traveller"; he approved it only after seeing the preponderance of Blake's youthful *Poetical Sketches.*[4] (Once he had entered

---

ley, pp. 6–8). In this same letter, William Rossetti suggested including a note on *Tiriel;* it was never put in. Swinburne, however, described the poem in *William Blake* and quoted three lines (pp. 199–200, n.; see E-B, p. 279, 5: 1–3.)

3. Rossetti sent a much revised text of "Broken Love" to Mrs. Gilchrist with the comment that he thought it "plain enough now," and would comment further in a Headnote (A. L., Feb. or Mar. 1863, Thorne Coll.).

4. A. L. to Mrs. Gilchrist, Dec. 1862, Thorne Coll. As the edition stands, *PS* makes up a fifth of the poetry. Rossetti offered advice to Mrs. Gilchrist on what to include in the Selections soon after Gilchrist's death; the two men had discussed the subject. After Rossetti's wife died, Mrs. Gilchrist wrote to William Rossetti asking "help . . . in those cases in which I do not know my dear husband's intentions" (*Anne Gilchrist,* pp. 112–13 and 122–23; Janet Camp Troxell, ed., *Three Rossettis: Unpublished Letters* . . . [Cambridge, Mass., 1937], p. 15). After reading the first proofs, in summer 1862, D. G. Rossetti at once wrote to Mrs. Gilchrist to cut "The Couch of Death" and "Contemplation" if she had thoughts of printing them: "sad rubbish—

into collaboration Rossetti became final arbiter on the Selections; his brother, who had stepped forward to aid Mrs. Gilchrist when Mrs. Rossetti died, continued as a subordinate adviser.)

The editors were on the whole conservative; nothing previously reprinted was left out.[5] A number of the *Poetical Sketches* and *Songs of Innocence and of Experience* had been read, and the latter had achieved some reputation. What was new, the "Poems Hitherto Unpublished," considerably strengthened Blake's claim to lyrical genius; "The Crystal Cabinet," "The Mental Traveller," and the other larger-scale lyrics gave readers an unmistakable indication of Blake's poetic complexities. This was the essential service to Blake of the mid-century revival and of Rossetti in particular, in recovering and printing the poetry Blake had left in manuscript.

The prose selections were chosen partly with an eye to documenting and supplementing Gilchrist's biography in Volume *1*. The *Descriptive Catalogue* in addition to containing Blake's aesthetic manifesto is part of Gilchrist's record of Blake's unwise venture into competition with Cromek. "On Homer's Poetry" and "On Virgil" (published together under Gilchrist's heading, "Sibylline Leaves," after Coleridge) display Blake's supposedly irrational prejudices; they could also be interpreted to show his Pre-Raphaelite support of Gothic "Living Form" (see "On Virgil"). "[A Public Address]," one of two essays that were edited and assembled from scattered paragraphs in the *Note-Book* (the other is designated "A Vision of the Last Judgment"), is characterized in D. G. Ros-

---

just boyish efforts in the conventional style of the time" (A. L., Thorne Coll.).

5. An exception is "Gwin of Norway" (*PS*), extracted by Cunningham, but not printed in the Selections.

One Blake poem, "The Tyger," had an oral history; Crabb Robinson had often recited it. Linnell remembered Robinson's delivery, and imitated it (*Life of Linnell, 1,* 223–24). Lamb too recalled hearing it recited (probably also by Robinson) (Letter to Barton, see Chap. 2, n. 10).

setti's Headnote as a "fitting and most interesting pendant" to
the *Descriptive Catalogue* (*Life*, 2, 137). It records Blake's
opinions on engraving and on contemporary artists and his
complaints of envy, abuse, and neglect. The title of this piece,
still used though written in brackets, is assumed by Geoffrey
Keynes to derive from a phrase that Blake uses in the text
(*Note-Book*, p. 58; Blake, ed. Keynes, p. 914), but it may
have been taken from J. T. Smith's brief account of the
Exhibition in which he recalls an "address to the public" by
Blake on the subject of the painting "Chaucer's Pilgrims"
(p. 475).[6]

6. Of Blake's engraved and published prose only *DC* was reprinted
before Gilchrist's *Life*. Extracts appeared in Cunningham and Robert
Southey, *The Doctor* (7 vols. London, 1847), and in articles on Blake
based on Cunningham's biography. *There is no Natural Religion* appeared in facsimile (London, 1886). *All Religions are One* first appeared in print in EY. For *MHH*, see Appendix.

None of Blake's prose in manuscript was printed before 1863. Gilchrist included emended passages from Blake's annotations to Reynolds's *Discourses*, Bacon's *Essays*, Lavater's *Aphorisms*, and Wordsworth's *Poems* (1826) and Preface of 1815 in Vol. *1* of the *Life of
Blake*.

The two compilations of *Note-Book* prose in the Selections, "VLJ"
and "PA," include everything in Blake, ed. Keynes (which E-B follow
[see pp. 797 and 798]), except for the following omissions:

Page in *Note-Book*	Page in E-B	Page in Blake, ed. Keynes
56	560	591
78	567	598
17	567	598
18	569	600
38		602 (in "Additional Passages")
44		603 (in "Additional Passages")

Also omitted from the Selections are the verses on *Note-Book* pages
60–62 and 66 (see E-B, pp. 496, 783 and 798). These appear in
Chap. 29 of the Life.

The arrangements in Blake, ed. Keynes and the Selections are very
different; both are conjectural, as would be any coherent essay put
together from such scattered fragments. However both editions include the same passages in each individual essay with these excep-

"[A Vision of the Last Judgment]," titled after a projected painting of the Last Judgment which it describes, presents an aspect of Blake's thought hardly touched upon by Gilchrist— his interpretation of salvation and judgment in terms of art. It is a difficult essay, one which D. G. Rossetti introduces somewhat diffidently:

> The *Vision* is almost as much a manifesto of opinion as either the *Catalogue* or *Address*. But this work is in a wider field, and one which, where it stretches beyond our own clear view, may not necessarily therefore have been a lost road to Blake himself. Certainly its grandeur and the sudden great things greatly said in it, as in all Blake's prose, constitute it an addition to our opportunities of communing with him, and one which we may prize highly.
>
> [*Life, 2,* 137–38]

Rossetti gathered a number of lively short pieces from the *Note-Book* into a group of "Epigrams and Satirical Pieces on Art and Artists." These help to relieve the saintliness of Gilchrist's hero and convey something of the character censored from the Life and other writings. They also voice some of Rossetti's own opinions on art, particularly such lines as

---

tions: the Selections prints a passage on p. 86 of the *Note-Book* in "VLJ" which Blake, ed. Keynes places in "PA" (p. 598; E-B, p. 567). There are four sections that are listed as "Additional Passages" to "PA" in Blake, ed. Keynes, pp. 602–03, two of which are incorporated into the text in the Selections.

The text of "VLJ" contains an interesting concession to censorship: paragraph seven reads, "All things are comprehended in their Eternal Forms in the Divine body of the Saviour the True Vine of Eternity . . . who appeared to Me" (*Life, 2,* 187). The anacalouthon (almost never used in the Selections) is for "The Human Imagination" (*Note-Book,* pp. 69–70; E-B, p. 545). In *William Blake,* Swinburne writes: "Compare . . . in the *Vision of the Last Judgment* (V. 2, p. 163), that definition of the "Divine body of the Saviour, the true Vine of Eternity," as "the Human Imagination, who appeared" (p. 123 n.).

"the taught savage Englishman spends his whole fortune/ On a smear or a squall" or "Seeing a Rembrandt or Correggio/ Of crippled Harry I think and slobbering Joe." Even in these fragments, Rossetti changed readings: Blake wrote, "I think of *the* Crippled Harry" (E-B, p. 506). Also, Rossetti prints, "The greater the fool, in the *Art* [for "Pencil"] the more blest" (italics indicate Emendations[7]).

Rossetti's policy of freely editing Blake's text might have claimed the sanction of Gilchrist who himself made changes in Blake's prose in the Life. Gilchrist had read D. G. Rossetti's transcriptions of some of the *Note-Book* poems when he borrowed the volume. He admired them and perhaps in this way encouraged Rossetti's subsequent procedure. Rossetti writes to Gilchrist, in the summer of 1861, "I am glad you approve of my rather unceremonious shaking up of Blake's rhymes. I really believe that is what ought to be done—perhaps with a word of general explanation." [8] Gilchrist also consulted with Rossetti about selections from the *Pickering MS;* in August 1861 he writes that he is "obliged . . . for your version of *Auguries of Innocence* which I think a real amendment. By your transpositions you have very much brought out the general coherence and pertinence of the thing." [9]

7. See Epigrams 3 and 4, "Poems Hitherto Unpublished," Appendix. I indicate emendations in Blake's writings made by his nineteenth-century editors by italicizing the changes. The correct—that is Blake's reading (here shown in brackets) is based on E-B's texts.

Generally, I have indicated only the changes relevant to my discussion. There are minor changes which I usually do not supply in punctuation, capitalization, and contractions (e.g., the universal practice of expanding Blake's "&" and disregarding his distinctions between "'d" and "ed").

8. *Anne Gilchrist,* p. 94. Letter dated July 1861. After the word "rhymes," H. H. Gilchrist notes in brackets, "The editing of the poems, i.e. the corrections of Blake's grammar." Clearly, however, Rossetti means rewriting and not grammatical corrections. I follow Keynes in taking Rossetti's letter to refer to his old transcriptions of Blake's poems (*Blake Bibliography*).

9. Troxell, p. 15. Letter dated Aug. 31.

Justifications for rewriting Blake's poetry and prose date back to the Reverend A. S. Mathew's short preface to the *Poetical Sketches,* which apologized for the "irregularities and defects . . . in almost every page," due to Blake's youth and his failure to revise. (Smith, in reprinting the preface, perpetuated the apologies [p. 463].) Blake's second editor, Malkin, introduced not the boyhood poems but the *Songs of Innocence and of Experience* as "several irregular and unfinished attempts" by an "untutored proficient" (p. xxv). Cunningham spoke of the fine thoughts and rough meters in *Poetical Sketches,* citing *Edward the Third* and "The Tyger" (sic) as examples (pp. 144–45). The poems of Blake's adolescence and the poems of his thirties were indiscriminately labeled as rude and unfinished, hence requiring improvement.

Cunningham's revised texts were doubtless the strongest precedent for later emendators.[10] They show "unauthorized readings" in nearly every line, writes John Sampson who, in 1905, edited the first genuinely critical edition of Blake's *Poetical Works* of any scope; he continues, "it is plain that Cunningham treated Blake's text with the same freedom which he would have thought himself entitled to use in an old Scots ballad."[11] Some of Cunningham's changes do actually

10. Malkin's emendations are perfunctory (spelling changes, corrections of grammar, and so forth); there is only one interesting variant among his texts. His version of "The Tyger" has "What dread hand *forged thy* dread feet?" for Blake's "What dread hand? & what dread feet?" Smith printed only a few lines of Blake's poetry. Cunningham, however, smoothed meter and changed words.

After Cunningham, editor Garth Wilkinson in 1839 deplored Blake's "utter want of elaboration . . . [and his] inattention to the ordinary rules of grammar" (p. xxi). His texts are discussed below.

11. Sampson's edition of Blake's *Poetical Works* (1905) is subtitled "A New and Verbatim Text"; it restores Blake's original texts of *PS, SIE, GP,* and of the songs and verse fragments in Blake's letters, *IM,* the *Pick MS,* the *Note-Book,* and in Blake's annotated copy of Reynolds' *Discourses.* (It also includes a few short extracts from the prophetic books.)

Sampson's footnotes to the lyrical poetry (in which he includes

suggest the conventions of folk ballad: the fourth "weep!" of
line 3 of "The Chimney Sweeper" is eliminated leaving the
triple repetition, more common to the sung ballad:

And my father sold me	
while yet my tongue	
Could scarcely cry—	weep weep weep
weep! weep! weep!	weep
[p. 151]	[E-B, p. 10]

Another poem is introduced as an autobiographical love ballad from Blake's courtship. "I love the jocund dance" is supposed to evidence Blake's affection for his wife (in fact, he
met her long after the poem was written). Cunningham
changed "Kitty" in the last stanza to "Kate." [12]

Blake's singular personal reputation also made him a subject for editorial liberties. The problems in Shelley's manuscript poems were complex, and there were biographical com-
plications there too; but Shelley did not labor under the double
disadvantage of self-education and alleged insanity. When
F. T. Palgrave wrote to William Rossetti about the latter's

---

the epigrams, fragments, and doggerel in the *Note-Book*) document
the most important emendations made by Blake's nineteenth-century
editors, including Malkin, Smith, Cunningham, Gilchrist (in *Life, 1*),
the Rossettis, Swinburne, R. H. Shepherd (see pp. 110 ff., 122), and
Ellis and Yeats. These footnotes, as well as the "Bibliographical
Prefaces" form the basis of much of the criticism in this chapter:
unless specified, the emendations Sampson records are the ones here
treated. His texts have been checked against E-B; and the references
to Blake's texts are to page numbers in E-B's (not in Sampson's)
edition.

12. Cunningham had composed several volumes of "genuine" Scots
ballads on commission (*Life, 1*, Chap. 26). Another change that
suggests the diction of the popular ballad, is *"brown bread,"* a homely
substitution for Blake's "white and brown" ("I love the jocund dance,"
l. 21; see Cunningham, p. 186. Not in Sampson [1905]). Cunningham's
text of "The Chimney Sweeper" shows another change: Tom is sweet-
ened to *"Tommy"* (l. 23).

projected edition of Shelley's poems he indicated the difference quite clearly:

> No one can admire more . . . the taste and skill your brother showed in his corrections of Blake; but (even in that case) I still desiderate notes showing the original, and I also think that similar amount of correction in Shelley is not so admissible as it really was for Blake, who was "super grammaticum" as well as *super* many other things.[13]

Of course, the editors' zeal to make the best possible case for Blake should not be overlooked. Theirs was a frankly partisan, even missionary, labor on Blake's behalf, not a merely scholarly endeavor. As the revivers, indeed first real editors of Blake's poems, and perhaps also as proprietors of the *Note-Book,* they felt specially privileged, even bound, to print texts to which readers would be drawn.

There were three immediate models for Rossetti's texts: Wilkinson's edition of *Songs of Innocence and of Experience* (for mechanical and grammatical corrections), his own earlier transcription of "The Tyger" (based in turn on Cunningham's version), and Southey's *Doctor* (for a line in *Poetical Sketches*). Wilkinson had corrected errors in tense, agreement, and principal parts; he had changed and supplied punctuation. Most of these emendations were adopted by Rossetti. Southey's text for "Mad Song" has "rustling birds of dawn" for "rustling beds of dawn" in the 1783 printing; Rossetti (or perhaps it was Gilchrist) followed Southey's reading.[14] "The Tyger" is a unique instance of Rossetti's reprinting one of his *Note-Book* transcriptions.

13. G. F. Palgrave, p. 116; letter dated Feb. 1869.
14. The reading "birds" has since been found, written in, in two copies of *PS.* On the strength of this, Keynes prints "birds" ("Poetical Sketches," *Blake Studies,* pp. 23–39). All nineteenth-century editors, except R. H. Shepherd, followed Rossetti, printing "birds.")

The changes that Rossetti made ultimately extended through the whole range of represented poetry, not only *Note-Book* poems. (The manuscript includes drafts for eighteen of the poems of *Experience*.) His work was supported and imitated by Swinburne and also to some extent by William Rossetti; it represents a unified editorial policy on the part of the major mid-century Blakeans.

Describing emendations to *Edward the Third* in his Head-note to *Poetical Sketches,* Rossetti maintains that he has in no way altered Blake's intention:

> In the original edition, however, these [lines] are marred by frequent imperfections in the metre (partly real and partly dependent on careless printing), which I have thought it best to remove, as I found it possible to do so without once, in the slightest degree, affecting the originality of the text. The same has been done in a few similar instances.

[2, 1]

When Swinburne reviewed the Selections (in Part 2 of *William Blake*) he paid warm tribute to Rossetti's improvements upon Blake. In the engraved poems roughnesses due to the "curiously reckless and helpless neglect of form which was natural to Blake when his main work was done" have been "smoothed off," and the "shapeless chaos of unmanageable MSS" has been subdued and shaped through the "arrangement and selection" of a "sure and strong hand." "Nor can any one thoroughly enter into the value and excellence of the thing here achieved who has not in himself the impulsive instinct of form—the exquisite desire of just and perfect work" (pp. 109–10).

There was a dissenting voice. Blake's only mid-century editor not of the Rossetti-Gilchrist-Swinburne circle was R. H. Shepherd (termed by Swinburne a "literary . . . drudge of all work" [15]), who edited three quite reliable and accurate edi-

15. *S. L.,* No. 586, Jan. 1875, 2, 367–68.

tions of Blake's poetry: the *Songs of Innocence and Experience* containing also the *Pickering MS* poems, 1866; *Poetical Sketches,* 1868; and a volume of the *Poems of Blake,* 1874, incorporating the contents of the two earlier books. These were commissioned by an interested publisher, B. M. Pickering (who acquired the *Pickering MS* in 1866).[16] Shepherd prefaced each of these editions with serious appeals for editorial fidelity and vigorous protests against printed texts rewritten as Blake's editors "considered they should have been written." [17] It was probably Shepherd's first appeal in 1866 that provoked Swinburne, in a jeering footnote to *William Blake,* to excoriate those who touch verse "merely with eyelash and fingertip in the manner of sandblind students," slavish editors who disdain to correct (p. 120 n.). Despite this outburst, there are other footnotes in Swinburne's book, especially in Part 2, which perform conscientious editorial offices such as supplying stanzas Rossetti had omitted or giving alternate (unchanged) lines from Blake's manuscripts; Swinburne appears to have taken heed after all.

Shepherd's second Blake volume, published later in the

16. Before 1864 the *Pick MS* was apparently owned by Tatham who lent it to the Gilchrists. (In 1864, Mrs. Gilchrist held the copyrights to the *Pick MS* texts in the Selections.) In 1864 or 1865 it was in the hands of a bookseller; and in 1866 Pickering bought it. See Geoffrey Keynes, "Blake's Library," *TLS* (Nov. 6, 1959), p. 648.

17. *Poems of Blake,* ed. R. H. Shepherd (London, 1874), p. xiii. Shepherd's Preface to *Songs of Innocence and Experience* (London, 1866) stressed that his editing consisted solely in grammatical corrections and the modernization of spelling. The only liberty is the suppression (marked by asterisks) "in one poem [of] a stanza, and in another [of] a couplet . . . for sufficient reasons" (pp. vii–viii). The omissions are lines 17–20 of "Mary" and 113–14 of "Auguries of Innocence" where the word "whore" occurs.

Designations of "accurate" or "inaccurate" are comparative in speaking of texts that date from before about 1905 or 1910; from the standpoint of a modern editor a genuinely accurate text probably does not exist. Considerations of spelling, capitalization, and punctuation do not figure in evaluating nineteenth-century texts.

same year as Swinburne's Essay, openly and strongly restates the arguments for textual fidelity; in fact, his preface is a manifesto in the spirit of the scholarly movement which had begun early in his century with the first restoration of Renaissance texts. He recommends faithfulness to his poet's incontrovertible "ruggedness of metre and crudeness of expression" on the basis of a desire to preserve "the historical value of the poems. . . . Mr. Rossetti (though sanctioned by Mr. Swinburne) has no more right to alter William Blake's poems than Mr. Millais would have to paint out some obnoxious detail of mediaevalism in a work of Giotto or Cimabue" (pp. vii–xi).

The last of the Pickering Blakes, Shepherd's edition of the *Poems of Blake,* appeared some months before the publication of the Aldine edition which was edited by William Rossetti; it claimed to be the first complete collection of Blake's lyrics except for the *Note-Book* poems which Rossetti's copyright prevented Pickering from printing. (Pickering's copyright, on the other hand, prevented William Rossetti from restoring certain of Blake's texts in the Aldine edition.[18]) Between the appearance of Shepherd's edition and the publication of the Aldine Blake in the autumn of 1874, Pickering issued a pamphlet challenging the Rossettis' editing practices; William Rossetti answered him in the pages of the *Academy* (at that time a Pre-Raphaelite organ) with several highhanded and evasive columns defending himself and his brother. The bickering subsided, and the Aldine Blake became the definitive edition of Blake's lyric poems for the next twenty years.[19]

18. See a letter from William Rossetti to Mrs. Gilchrist, *Letters Concerning Whitman, Blake, Shelley,* pp. 86–87.

In 1880 D. G. Rossetti wrote to Mrs. Gilchrist that "Mr. P[ickering] has an edition of his own which cannot be interfered with" (A. L., Mar. 2, Thorne Coll.).

19. See William Rossetti, "Review of Blake's *Poems,* ed. R. H. Shepherd (Pickering, 1874)," *Academy, N. S.,* No. 122 (Sept. 5, 1874), p. 255; B. M. Pickering, *Blake and His Editors* (1874)—a fly-sheet, described by William Rossetti in *D. G. Rossetti: His Family Letters,* 2, 314; two letters from D. G. Rossetti to his brother sug-

In one province alone had Shepherd's campaign been completely effective: William Rossetti felt obliged to print the *Poetical Sketches* as written by Blake.[20] He did so grudgingly.

> I thus forego certain emendations . . . introduced by my brother . . . [which] were indeed great improvements. . . . At any rate, as the compositions in question have been already reproduced . . . in their original shape . . . I have not felt justified in recurring to another form of the same poems, which if better, as it assuredly is, is also less absolutely exact.
>
> [pp. cxxxi–cxxxii]

Although Rossetti did not renounce his emendations in the 1880 edition of the Selections,[21] it can be said that, thanks to Shepherd, the nineteenth century did have a uniform, estab-

---

gesting answers to Pickering's attack but declining to have anything to do with the business himself, dated Oct. 6 and Oct. 9, 1874, ibid., pp. 314–15; William Rossetti, "Correspondence," *Academy, N. S.,* No. 127 (Oct. 10, 1874).

20. There are two exceptions: "Prologue to King John" and "Samson" are put into loose blank verse. William Rossetti did not print the prose pieces "The Couch of Death" or "Contemplation," from *PS.*

21. A distinction should be made between the public and private position of the Rossettis on the subject of Rossetti's texts. William Rossetti from the beginning had misgivings about extensive emendation; but in print, especially in the Aldine-Pickering controversy, he steadfastly defended his brother's work, and often alluded to "manuscript authority" (see pp. 121 below for his defense of his brother's version of "The Tyger"; see, too, G. F. Palgrave, p. 116).

Publicly he never admitted during his brother's lifetime that either one of them had second thoughts; but in 1895 he recalled that Rossetti had confessed (in 1874) that he would not "now have adopted . . . that [method] of treatment . . . to the same extent," and that "I could not but concur with him" (*D. G. Rossetti: His Family Letters, 2,* 314; see, too, Notes for 1874, in William Michael Rossetti, *Dante Gabriel Rossetti as Designer and Writer* [London, 1889], p. 165).

lished, accurate text for the poems of Blake's adolescence, if for no others.

It was inevitable that Shepherd's texts, in particular his edition of 1874, should have had considerably less circulation than the Rossettis'. The Aldine edition contained more poems than did Shepherd's edition; it also bore the authority and sanction of both Rossettis, Swinburne, and Mrs. Gilchrist. In criticism and in point of general prestige Shepherd could not hope to compete with any one of them; moreover, the closely guarded and copyrighted *Note-Book* gave them a sort of monopoly on an important group of Blake's poems. The Aldine texts became the ones which most editors reprinted (even after the Ellis-Yeats edition) until Sampson's collection appeared in 1905.

Poetical Sketches

Stressing Blake's affinities with the early Romantic movement, Gilchrist associated *Poetical Sketches* and the *Songs of Innocence* with Percy's *Reliques of Ancient Poesy;* he saw in them the "homely subjects" and "familiar manner" of Wordsworth's experiments in the *Lyrical Ballads*—the "virtues of simplicity and directness the new poets began [to bring] once more into the foreground" (*1,* 23, 74).

> 'Tis hard to believe these poems were written in the author's teens, harder still to realize how some of them, in their unforced simplicity, their bold and careless freedom of sentiment and expression, came to be written at all in the third quarter of the eighteenth century.
>
> [*1,* 23]

Later writers echoed Gilchrist and went even further, completely neglecting Blake's relationships with contemporary eighteenth-century literature. Shepherd accepted Blake as a Wordsworthian poet and in 1866 introduced the *Songs of Innocence and Experience,* remarking the "resemblance in tone and style, the similarities of subject and metre . . . [with] such pieces as the Idiot Boy, Goody Blake and Harry Gill, Poor Susan, The Two Thieves, Rural Architecture, and all that class" (pp. ix–x). (As late as 1885 an edition of Blake's lyrical *Poems* edited by Joseph Skipsey, a coal miner poet of rustic verse, introduced Blake as an early nature poet.) Swinburne speaks of Blake's genius as "straight ahead of the times," whether the "pseudo-Hellenic" eighteenth century of Mason *or* the "pseudo-Hibernian" nineteenth of Moore (pp. 132–33). Neither he nor Rossetti was to follow Gilchrist in comparing Blake and Wordsworth, but they did accept the complete isolation of Blake from the poetry of his time.[22]

Gilchrist's criteria of "simplicity and directness" inclined him toward Blake's early poems. The amount and type of attention given *Songs of Innocence* (considered as "early") and the youthful *Poetical Sketches* points to their preeminence in the case for Blake as a poet. Still, Gilchrist repeatedly patronizes "technical blemishes" in *Poetical Sketches,* contrasting "poetic power" and "imperfect form"—"occasional hackneyed rhyme, awkward construction, and verbal repetition" (these "any poetical reader may by ten minutes' manipulation mend") (*1,* 41). The only poems not flawed are "My silks and fine array" and the "Mad Song" (*1,* 24–25).

Rossetti's Headnote to *Poetical Sketches* contains a direct refutation:

> These Songs . . . deserve no less than very high admiration in a quite positive sense, which cannot be even qualified by the . . . imperfections of execution to be met with in some of them, though by no means in all.
>
> [2, 1]

22. Gilchrist noted that Blake's *Edward the Third* might have been influenced by Chatterton's work. He preferred however to stress Blake's imitation of Shakespeare. Ossian is mentioned by both Gilchrist and Swinburne as an unfortunate influence (*Life, 1,* Chap. 4). For contemporary influences on *PS,* see Margaret Lowery, *Windows of the Morning* (London, Oxford University Press, 1940).

To Rossetti, and to Swinburne in a more qualified way,[23] poetry was to be defined, evaluated, and defended if necessary on formal grounds, not on the basis of its subject matter. They therefore submitted the Songs in *Poetical Sketches* which Gilchrist praises mainly for directness or simplicity to more specifically poetic criteria. In this way they hoped to disarm condescensions to "immature form" and to demonstrate that a number of the *Sketches* would stand on poetical merits alone, without reference to their precociousness or to their anticipation of *Lyrical Ballads*. Swinburne terms comparison with Wordsworth "needless" and specifically contradicts Gilchrist to show that the lyrics "are evidence of [a] rare . . . gift of poetical judgment." Gilchrist alluded to "imperfect" form in "To the Evening Star." Swinburne cites lines 9 and 10 of the same poem ("speak silence with thy glimmering eyes,/ And wash the dusk with silver") as being of "quite incomparable grandeur"; he also compares them with the best of Tennyson "for vigorous grace" as well as for "subtle strength of interpretation that transfigures the external nature it explains"—this to discourage the sort of analogy with simple pastoral poetry which Gilchrist's criticism might promote.

Both Swinburne and Rossetti were lyrical and dramatic poets committed to the poems of Shelley, Coleridge, Tennyson, and Blake[24] as their models of English lyric, experimenters in sound, meter, and form; their intense and peculiar appreciation of Blake was allied with their appreciation of lyrical and dramatic values in poetry above all others. Gilchrist was urging acceptance of Blake within the bounds of an established taste; Rossetti and Swinburne were themselves actively

23. Swinburne deals with *PS* on pp. 8–14 of *William Blake*. For a fuller account of his critical criteria see below.

24. Hall Caine recalled Rossetti more than once claiming that the "three greatest English imaginations . . . are Shakespeare, Coleridge, and Shelley," and that he would sometimes add a fourth name, "Blake." Also, preferring Coleridge, Rossetti "grudge[d] Wordsworth every vote he gets" (*Recollections of Dante Gabriel Rossetti*, p. 148).

engaged in shaping a new poetry and a new audience for it.

However they may have operated to promote the *Poetical Sketches,* these formalist criteria had a negative effect on appreciation of the prophetic books. Nominating "To the Muses" for a place among the greatest lyrics written in English, Swinburne writes: "So beautiful indeed is its structure and choice of language that its author's . . . later vagaries and erratic indulgences in the most lax or bombastic habits of speech become hopelessly inexplicable" (p. 10). And Rossetti notes:

> It is singular that, for formed style and purely literary qualities, Blake, perhaps, never afterwards equalled the best things in this youthful volume, though he often did so in melody and feeling, and more than did so in depth of thought.
>
> [2, 1]

These passages, each epitomizing its author's apprehension of Blake, indicate how Swinburne's and Rossetti's approach led some later critics to maintain that *Poetical Sketches* were Blake's best poems. To the totally committed adherents of Art for Art's Sake (whose taste Rossetti in large part formed) there could be no question about the superiority of "purely literary qualities" to "depth of thought."

Although Swinburne and Rossetti both revered Blake's "gift . . . for the writing of short sweet songs" (Swinburne, p. 132), they felt no compunctions about correcting him when he defected from their ideal. Consequently, among their tributes to a "sweet facility for being right" (Swinburne, p. 134), are corrections of very Blakean lines in the general interests of form and poetic decorum—Rossetti even struck out one line from *Edward the Third* because he felt it was a "triumph of unconscious comedy." [25] The omission is made

---

25. A. L. to Mrs. Gilchrist, summer 1862, Thorne Coll. In addition to metrical and grammatical changes, Rossetti altered words. For

at a point where Blake seems to violate the logic of personification. The line to which Rossetti is referring is probably "and vales in rich array/ Shall laugh, whose fruitful laps bend down with fulness" (sc. 6, ll. 47–48).[26] In "To Summer" D. G. Rossetti changed lines 11–12 from Blake's "throw thy/ Silk draperies off" to "throw *all*/ Thy draperies off"—perhaps on the dual grounds that silk is nonnatural and that it seems unsuited to a masculine deity, and also to smooth an awkward enjambment. There is an echo of Spenser in the image that Rossetti did not note.[27]

---

example, where Blake has "We sit us down, and view our former joys/ With distaste and dislike." Rossetti substitutes "We . . . joys/ *As worthless*" (Sc. 3, ll. 260–61).

After seeing *Edward* in proof for the first time, Rossetti remarked approvingly that there were cuts "as I seem to remember even worse things than are here"; he was tempted to "recast it" all into "true measure"—and ultimately did so, after first cutting it further (A. L., summer 1862, Thorne Coll.).

26. It has been argued that for Blake this is not personification, not a trope, but vision (or mythopoeic perception). Swinburne recognizes in Blake what he terms "the habit of direct mythical metaphor" (p. 101).

Rossetti also cut from *Edward* lines in which Blake's imagery becomes extravagant, proliferating, and rather Shakespearean (see sc. [6], ll. 3–6 and 31–33).

27. Swinburne, Rossetti, and Gilchrist would be unlikely to note resemblances to Spenser. Rossetti knew Italian Renaissance literature better than he did literature of the English Renaissance. Swinburne followed Lamb in preferring drama and lyric to the Spenserian-Miltonic tradition. Spenser was less widely read at this time than Shakespeare certainly or even Marlowe among the Elizabethans; generally it was the dramatists who interested the later nineteenth century. And the eighteenth-century strain of poetry that derived from Spenser and the minor poems of Milton was to Rossetti or to those who saw Blake as herald of *Lyrical Ballads,* dead letter.

Swinburne objected to Spenser's excessive allegorization: "Give Dante a moral image, he will make of it a living man: show Spenser a living man, he will make of him a moral image." William Rossetti concurred although he was not as vehement in his expression. Swinburne's feeling was doubtless reinforced by the fact that Spenser's

In a poem praised highly by both Swinburne and Rossetti, "To the Evening Star," Blake wrote:

> Smile on our loves: and, while thou drawest the
> Blue curtains of the sky, scatter thy silver dew
> On every flower that shuts its sweet eyes
> In timely sleep.
>
> [E-B, ll. 5–8]

Rossetti changed the lines to read

> Smile on our loves; and *whilst thou drawest round*
> *The curtains of the sky, scatter thy dew*
> On every flower that *closes* its sweet eyes
> In timely sleep.
>
> [*Life, 2*, 10]

In *William Blake*, Swinburne again revised them.

> Smile on our loves; and while thou drawest *round*
> *The sky's blue curtains, scatter silver dew*
> On every flower that *closes* its sweet eyes
> In timely sleep.
>
> [p. 11]

Besides regularizing the meter Swinburne's change shifts attention from drawing blue curtains to the night sky; Rossetti's

---

enthusiastic admirers included Scott, Southey, Ruskin, and Leigh Hunt; and that Landor positively disliked Spenser (see Swinburne's "Short Notes on English Poets," [1880] *Miscellanies, Works* [Bonchurch ed., London, 1927], *14*, 102–03; William Rossetti, *Lives of Famous Poets* [London, 1878]).

Blake's "Imitation of Spenser" was not one of the poems from *PS* reprinted in the Selections; nor does Gilchrist allude to Spenser as one of Blake's early models—as he cites Shakespeare, in Chap. 4 of the Life. The first nineteenth-century scholar to note an echo of Spenser in "To Summer," or to relate Blake at all to Spenser was Henry G. Hewlett ("Imperfect Genius," *Contemporary Review, 28* [Oct. 1876], 765). For more on Hewlett see Chap. 7. For Spenser and *PS*, see Lowery, *Windows of the Morning*.

eliminates a more arresting literal image. Both changes, particularly Rossetti's, suggest an objection not to literalism as such but to making the intrinsically poetic evening sky prosaic. A related kind of change is Swinburne's adjustment of a line in *Songs of Innocence,* lines 15–16 of "The Little Black Boy":

> And these black bodies and this sun-burnt face
> Is but a cloud and like a shady grove

Swinburne smooths "Is but" to *"Are like"*; "like," however, blurs Blake's distinction between an identity and a resemblance. Objection to the overleaping of the natural goes back farther than Coleridge's epistolary comments on *Songs of Innocence and of Experience* (see Chap. 2, pp. 20 ff.). Malkin complained that "my golden wing" in the last stanza of "How sweet I roam'd" had neither literal justification nor tradition (the rights of classical metaphor) to recommend it. As one of Wilkinson's emendations shows, the objection may reside ultimately in an uneasiness toward the merging of divine and human that often underlies Blake's license with natural fact.[28] In "A Cradle Song," Wilkinson prints the last lines:

Infant smiles, *like H*is own *smile*	are his own smiles.
Heaven and earth to peace *beguile*	beguiles
[Sampson (1905), p. 93]	[E-B, l. 32]

Cunningham's changes were also aimed at removing offenses to literal meaning: two lines from "The Chimney Sweeper" (*SI*), "Then down a green plain leaping laughing they run/ And wash in a river and shine in the Sun" (ll. 15–16), are changed to "a green *vale*" where the boys "shine *like* the sun"

---

28. Wilkinson's only other interesting emendation, in "On Another's Sorrow," has the effect of suggesting hymn tune diction:

Think not thou canst sigh a sigh,	
And thy maker is not *nigh*	by.
[Sampson (1905), p. 102]	[E-B, ll. 29–30]

(p. 151). In another emendation (to *Edward the Third*), "joy, and love, and calm content,/ Sit singing *on* the azure clouds" (p. 147) like proper allegorical personages, and not "in" them (E-B, [sc. 5], l. 31).

Songs of Innocence and of Experience

The most important changes Rossetti made in *Songs of Innocence and of Experience* are in the poems of Experience. He added a second "Cradle Song" that Blake never engraved, which he took from the *Note-Book* (advising of the addition in a note). He added two opening stanzas to "The Garden of Love," again taking them from the *Note-Book*; these are not from an early draft of the poem, but from another poem clearly separated from the draft by a line in the manuscript. The title "Christian Forbearance," instead of Blake's "A Poison Tree," comes from the *Note-Book* version of that poem and may reflect Swinburne's antinomian preoccupations. Emendations to "The Tyger" are based on Cunningham's version rather than on either of the two drafts of the poem that appear in the *Note-Book,* although William Rossetti claimed in the Aldine Blake that Rossetti's "Tyger" had manuscript authority. William Rossetti restored Blake's text; the so-called "Second Version" with his brother's "improvements" (Aldine, p. 120 n.) was appended to the *Songs.* The same was done for the *Note-Book* "Cradle Song." Otherwise William Rossetti follows the 1863 texts for the *Songs*— "Christian Forbearance," the same "Garden of Love," and so forth—without making clear that there are changes from Blake's engraved texts. Most subsequent editors followed William Rossetti's practice. W. B. Yeats restored the title "A Poison Tree" and the text of "The Garden of Love" but preferred to be guided by the Rossettis for the second "Cradle Song." [29]

29. See Sampson (1905), pp. 79, 267–68, and 269 ff. nn. and W. B. Yeats, ed., *The Poems of William Blake* (London, 1893), p. 241.

Shepherd's edition, based on the Tulk copy of the *Songs,* was accurate as nineteenth-century texts go; still, he added a poem never included by Blake among the *Songs.* "A Divine Image" appears in two sets of the *Songs* printed after Blake's death, by Tatham probably, one of which was acquired by the British Museum in 1864. "A Divine Image" was silently included to follow "A Little Girl Lost" in *Songs of Experience* after 1866 by all Blake's editors beginning with William Rossetti. Sampson was the first to move the poem out of the *Songs.*[30]

J. J. Garth Wilkinson was the first critic to contrast the *Songs of Innocence* and the *Songs of Experience.* As poetry he thought one "as well and wonderfully sung" as the other, although thematically he preferred the *Songs of Innocence.* Indeed he apologized for including *Songs of Experience* in his edition; for him they were spiritually marred by "darker themes" and "dark becloudment," which neglect and disappointment had wrought into Blake's understanding (pp. xxi–xxii).[31] (After Wilkinson *Innocence* stood opposed to *Experience,* much as Shakespeare's "light" comedies to his "dark" period.)

Gilchrist accepted the contrast, presenting the two sets (Chaps. 9 and 13) as evidence of a change in Blake's personal awareness:

> The first series, quite in keeping with its name, had been of far the more heavenly temper. The second, produced during an interval of another five years, bears internal evidence of later origin, though in the same rank as to

30. See Sampson (1905), pp. 135–36; and *SIE,* ed. Shepherd, pp. viii and 73. Gilchrist and Rossetti probably never saw "A Divine Image" until it appeared in Shepherd's edition.

31. The fact is, that the period in which many of the *SE* were composed (the early 1790s) was one of relative prosperity and rising renown for Blake (see Chap. 2; and Paul Miner, "William Blake's London Residences," *Bulletin, NYPL, 62* [Nov. 1958], 535–50).

poetic excellence. As the title fitly shadows, it is of grander, sterner calibre, of gloomier wisdom.

[*Life, 1,* 116]

Furthermore, the *Songs of Experience* are trenchant intuitions, products of a "bold" but also "careless freedom"; compared with *Songs of Innocence* they are "unfinished" poems (*1,* 118). (Gilchrist's phrases recall B. H. Malkin's view of Blake.) Taken up and repeated, Gilchrist's analysis became oversimplified into a view that the poems of Experience were composed when Blake was—as Northrop Frye has put it— "no longer a child of thirty-two but a grown man of thirty-seven." [32] Moreover, Gilchrist allows that Blake's darkening temper could still achieve excellence in the *Songs of Experience,* though not after: "Blake never again sang to like angelic tunes; nor even with the same approach to technical accuracy. His poetry was the blossom of youth and early manhood" (*1,* 119).

Nineteen years after the publication of the *Lyrical Ballads,* Coleridge concluded his defense of Wordsworth by attacking

the strange mistake, so slightly grounded, yet so widely and industriously propagated, of Mr. Wordsworth's turn for SIMPLICITY! I am not half so much irritated by hearing his enemies abuse him for vulgarity of style, subject, and conception; as I am disgusted with the gilded side of the same meaning, as displayed by some affected admirers, with whom he is, forsooth, a *sweet, simple poet!* and *so* natural, that little master Charles and his younger sister are *so* charmed with them that they play at "Goody Blake," or at "Johnny and Betty Foy!" [33]

32. *Fearful Symmetry* (Princeton University Press, 1947), p. 4. Four poems in *SIE* appear in either *SI* or *SE,* in different copies of *SIE:* of these, "The Little Girl Lost," "The Little Girl Found," and "The Schoolboy" may have been composed at the same time as *SI.* E-B date the *Songs* 1784–1805.

33. *Biographia Literaria,* ed. J. Shawcross (2 vols. London, Oxford University Press, 1949), *2,* 131. See, too, *2,* 7.

It was a great deal longer before the ideas of "sweet" and "simple" were detached from Blake, and longer even, because of the great influence of Gilchrist's *Life,* before they were pried loose from the *Songs of Innocence.* In the early years neither Coleridge nor Hazlitt, who called them "too deep for the vulgar," thought the *Songs* were either lucid or particularly childlike. Yet Crabb Robinson, a relatively astute Wordsworthian, brought the same charges against Blake as were commonly made against Wordsworth: the *Songs of Innocence* are "childlike songs of great beauty and simplicity: . . . many of which, nevertheless, are excessively childish." [34]

Garth Wilkinson did not term the *Songs of Innocence* naïve or simple; he held rather that they portrayed simplicity, a state —to him an ideal state—of childhood perception. Gilchrist shifted the *Songs'* viewpoint from that of childhood perception to that of the simple enthusiast who is the perceiver and who frequently speaks in the guise of a child. The *Songs,* in no way regarded as provisional or as interacting with *Experience,* are fixed images from the Innocence world of Blake's (as well as Palmer's and Calvert's) woodcuts seen through the eyes of a gentle-hearted mystic:

34. [Hazlitt] was much struck with [some of Blake's poems] and expressed himself with his usual strength and singularity. "They are beautiful," he said, "and only too deep for the vulgar. He has no sense of the ludicrous, and, as to a God, a worm crawling in a privy is as worthy an object as any other, all being to him indifferent. So to Blake the Chimney Sweeper, etc. He is ruined by vain struggles to get rid of what presses on his brain—he attempts impossibles. . . . W. Hazlitt preferred the *Chimney Sweeper.*

[*On Books and Their Writers,* Mar. 10, 1811]

For Robinson on *SIE,* see Esdaile, p. 245.

Blake's "freshness and spontaneity," his "extraordinary simplicity," his "sweet" songs are cited by George Saintsbury. He notes that these are concomitant with Blake's "childish" and irrational critical opinions, in particular his dislike of Rembrandt ("Review of the Aldine Edition . . . ," *Academy, N. S.* No. 135 (Dec. 5, 1874), pp. 600–01). For more on Saintsbury, see Chap. 7.

The Golden Age independent of Space or Time, object of vague sighs and dreams from many generations of struggling humanity—an Eden such as childhood sees, is brought nearer than ever poet brought it before. For this poet was in assured possession of the Golden Age within the chambers of his own mind.

[*Life, 1,* 71]

Blake in the *Songs of Innocence* is a "child Angel" wearing a "brow of thought"; however, the point elaborated and stressed by Gilchrist is that often in these poems Blake imagines himself a child. At times, he becomes a child.

From addressing the child, the poet, by a transition not infrequent with him, passes out of himself into the child's person, showing a chameleon sympathy with childlike feelings. Can we not see the little three-year-old prattler [in "Spring"] stroking the white lamb, her feelings made articulate for her? . . . In *The Lamb* the poet again changes person to that of a child.

[*1,* 72–73]

The poet James Thomson (writing in 1866) totally identified the subject of the poems with the personality of the poet: Blake was a child. Spiritually, he walked in the steps of the great mystics:

[When] Blake was thirty-two, the "Songs of Innocence" appeared; and we learn from them the strange fact that he who was mature in his childhood and youth became in his manhood a little child. A little child, pure in soul as the serenest light of the morning, happy and innocent as a lamb leaping in the meadows, singing all its joy in the sweetest voice with that exquisite infantine lisp which thrills the adult heart with yearning tenderness.[35]

35. "The Poems of William Blake," *Biographical and Critical Studies* (London, 1896), p. 251. For more on James Thomson, see Chap. 7.

To Swinburne Blake was certainly no child. Observing that of all Blake's works only *Songs of Innocence and of Experience* escaped being "thrown into Lethe," he writes: "Perhaps on some accounts this preference has been not unreasonable. What was written for children can hardly offend men" (p. 144). To stress that the singer of the *Songs* (both sets) is not to be simply identified with Blake, he adds: "and the obscurities and audacities of the prophet would here have been clearly out of place" (p. 144). Further, Swinburne points out that the childlikeness of these poems "is so to speak kept fresh by some graver sense of faithful and mysterious love, explained and vivified by a conscience and purpose in the artist's hand and mind" (p. 113). In the *Songs* themselves "the singing is done by clear children's voices to the briefest and least complex tunes" (p. 114). They are "poems of childhood" (p. 123) sung by children, "written for children" (p. 114).

In another place, however, Swinburne terms these poems, not "songs for children," but studies "of childish music" (p. 135). Whether or not he is actually saying that children are the poems' intended audience, his idea of childhood and the childlike is unusual if not perverse for his time. Remarking on Blake's delight in Mrs. Blake's opening a book to Aphra Behn, Swinburne observes that "Nothing is ever so cynical as innocence, whether it be a child's or a mystic's" (p. 131 n.). He neither looks for nor expects to find purity and goodness in childhood utterances: "Infant Joy" is a "little bodily melody of soulless and painless laughter" (p. 116). Glossing the lines to *Gates of Paradise,* he writes: "They were done 'for children,' because, in Blake's mind, the wise innocence of children was likeliest to appreciate and accept the message involved in them" (p. 27). Swinburne freely applauds something that Coleridge in the letter to Tulk perhaps had acknowledged, though not approvingly, when he said that he would have omitted "A Little Girl Lost" from the *Songs,* "not for the want of innocence in the poem, but by the probable want of it in many readers."

Nonetheless, a great many readers of Swinburne's time, swayed by the biographical criticism applied to the *Songs, did* take them to be simply "songs for children," sung by a child. And "namby-pamby" "Willy Blake" who "foundered on sweet cake," according to John Crowe Ransom, proceeded to father numbers of special children's editions of *Songs of Innocence.* While old-fashioned children still played at Johnny and Betty Foy the aesthetic moppets were lambs, tigers, and blossoms. Appropriately on the eve of the Blake revival, Lewis Carroll "got [Macmillan] to print me some" of Blake's poems of Innocence on large paper.[36]

Rossetti's short note to *Songs of Innocence and of Experience* treats them as poems about childhood and repeats Gilchrist's biographical explanation of their contrast. Rossetti also follows earlier editors, preferring *Songs of Innocence* to *Songs of Experience.* His reasons, however, are those of the aesthete:

> The first series is incomparably the more beautiful of the two, being indeed almost flawless in essential respects; while in the second series, the five years intervening between the two had proved sufficient for obscurity and the darker mental phases of Blake's writings to set in and greatly mar its poetic value. . . . For instance, there can be no comparison between the first *Chimney Sweeper,*

36. *The Diaries of Lewis Carroll,* ed. Roger L. Green (2 vols. London, Oxford University Press, 1954), *1,* 205; journal entry for Oct. 19, 1863.

See *Blake Bibliography* for children's editions. References to namby-pambyism occur in Saintsbury, "Review of the Aldine Edition," p. 600 and Hewlett, "Imperfect Genius," p. 770. Hewlett's comment is typical: "There is but one step between the simple and the puerile, and that step Blake is apt to take, straying here into the swamp of namby-pamby." See, too, the preface to W. G. Robertson's edition of Gilchrist's *Life of Blake* (London, 1906).

Oswald Crawfurd (*New Quarterly Magazine*) thought *Thel* verged on "goody-goodiness" as well as "namby-pamby-ism" (pp. 489–90).

which touches with such perfect simplicity the true
pathetic chord of its subject, and the second, tinged
somewhat with the commonplaces, if also with the truths,
of social discontent.

[*Life, 2,* 27]

Swinburne appreciated fully the "impeccable simplicity,"
"pure clear cadence of verse," and "sweet and direct choice of
the just word and figure" (p. 114) in *Songs of Innocence*—
as he did also in *Songs of Experience.* He felt that without the
gift of song no man could be deemed a poet. This was not the
sole measure, however, nor was lyricism the highest element
even of lyric poetry.[37] "Against all articulate authority" Swinburne therefore classed some of the poems of Experience
"higher for the greater qualities of verse" (p. 116). Considering them primarily as vehicles of Blake's thought, "profound
and perfect lyrics," which by virtue of their deeper themes
would naturally "rise higher and dive deeper in point of mere
words" (p. 116) than the *Songs of Innocence,* Swinburne
fashioned an appreciation for Blake's difficult lyrics which
D. G. Rossetti had published primarily on the basis of their
lyrical beauties—and thus an access to the prophecies. When
he affirmed their appropriate values he departed from the
almost purely formalist approach he had taken with D. G.
Rossetti toward *Poetical Sketches.* In positive terms he in-

37. In the last pages of *William Blake,* he asserts:

> [Blake's poetry] partakes the powers and the faults of elemental
> and eternal things . . . and is in the main fruitful and delightful
> and noble. . . . Any work of art of which this cannot be said is
> superfluous and perishable, whatever of grace or charm it may
> possess or assume.

[p. 303]

See also E. K. Brown, "Swinburne: A Centenary Estimate," in *Victorian Literature,* ed. Austin Wright (New York, Galaxy Books, 1961),
pp. 296–97.

It will appear that Swinburne's criteria tend to be less formalistic
as his criticism progresses from early to late poems.

stituted new standards of judgment and placed greater demands upon the readers of Blake's poems. "The simpler
poems claim only praise. . . . Those of a subtler kind (often,
. . . the best worth study) claim more than this if they are to
have fair play" (p. 127).

D. G. Rossetti's sway over Swinburne's early view of Blake
is discernible in a letter that Swinburne wrote in the summer of
1862 before he began his independent commentary; he is addressing Milnes, who had recently consented to lend him the
works of the Marquis de Sade. A lyric from de Sade's *Aline et
Valcour,* says Swinburne, is "sweet and perfect and unlike any
contemporary work—medieval rather in grace and quietness
of beauty," reminding him of Blake's poems of the same
period—"both of them sweet and perfect." [38] In the course
of critical remarks on the poems of Experience Swinburne
makes particular departures from Rossetti's criticism. He
specifically praises the second "Chimney Sweeper" for its
"passionate grace and pity," and he relates it to a number of
poems in which Blake speaks out against social injustice, dis-
playing a

> fiery pity for all that suffer wrong; something of Hugo's
> or Shelley's passionate compassion for those who lie open
> to 'all the oppression that is done under the sun'; some-
> thing of the anguish and labour, the fever-heat of sleep-
> less mercy and love incurable which is common to those
> two great poets.
>
> [p. 126 n.]

Swinburne completely disregards the principle of a biographical contrast in the two sets of poems; he sees *Songs of
Innocence* and *Songs of Experience* as the self-expression and
judgment of a wise innocence. Poems of Experience take up
"from the opposite point of view matters already handled to
such splendid effect in the *Songs of Innocence*" (p. 126 n.).

38. *S. L.,* no. 34, *1,* 59.

Swinburne does not think so much of "contrary states of the
soul" as of unself-conscious indulgence versus deliberate and
purposeful indulgence—both opposed to self-denial. Thus he
defines "Innocence" in semi-Rousseauistic terms as "the
quality of beasts and children." The first set of poems pictures for us the world of Innocence, a natural paradise in
which the lion lies down with the lamb, a "heaven of sinless
animal life." It is the world "conceived so intensely and
sweetly" by Blake in the "hymn of *Night*" (p. 115). Innocence, that "natural impulse of delight" found only in those to
whom the dualism of body and soul is unknown, Swinburne
notes, is for Blake a direct opposite of that ignorance or denial
of the body which defines the term for society in general:
their "natural depravity" would be Blake's "innocence." Swinburne simply glosses; he does not (as yet) explain Blake's
paradoxical usages as a technique; moreover, he begins to use
Blake's unorthodox definitions in contexts that suggest his
personal revolt against the society of Victorian England in
the 1860s.

Blake's "Experience" according to Swinburne implies a
necessary and willful expression, or perhaps submersion, of
the whole self in what is generally thought to be sinful. Though
to the world at large they might suggest evil, impure and simple, the tactics of Experience to Swinburne's Blake are a
necessary good:

> Experience must do the work of innocence as soon as
> conscience begins to take the place of instinct, reflection
> of perception; but the moment experience begins upon
> this work, men raise against her the conventional clamour
> of envy and stupidity. She teaches how to entrap and
> retain such fugitive delights as children and animals en-
> joy without seeking to catch or cage them; but this
> teaching the world calls sin.

[pp. 124–25]

Insofar as Experience frees man from restraints of moral law
Swinburne takes the side of the devil and is much more personally engaged than when speaking of Innocence. Generally
he regards "actual" experience as the proper theme of the
artist. The world of the *Songs of Innocence* is one of "outer
forms"; the poems of Experience lay bare "the actual mysteries of experience." In the vocabulary of Swinburne's hierarchy this means that the poems of Innocence are merely
"buds"; *Songs of Experience* are "fire" and the "sea." Swinburne focuses on their broader and deeper conception of the
human soul—not simply the tender flower, but "the distilled
perfume and extracted blood of the veins in the rose-leaf, the
sharp, liquid, intense spirit crushed out of the broken kernel
in the fruit" (p. 116).

It is mainly in the definition of "Experience" that Swinburne imposes upon Blake's thought the aura of masochism
and fleshly self-mortification with which his own sexual libertarianism is often associated. Later, when he speaks of poems
by Blake that advocate free love, he notes that Blake's "desire
is towards the freedom of the dawn of things—not towards the
'dark, secret hour' " (p. 140). For the most part Swinburne's
exposition of *Songs of Experience* insists that Blake is not
merely a crude advocate of license, that he does not believe
in simply banishing restraints: "always, the cry is as much for
light as for license, the appeal not more against prohibition
than against obscurity" (p. 119).

In "The Voice of the Ancient Bard," which Swinburne
understands as a preface to *Songs of Experience,*[39] the poet
"summons to judgment" the "young and single-spirited" (the
wise innocents) that they may "give sentence against the
preachers of convention and assumption" (p. 117) who
would strangle liberty. These preachers are the representatives

39. The Forster copy, supposed to have been Blake's "own copy"
of *SIE* on which the text of the Selections is based has "The Voice of
the Ancient Bard" at the end of *SI*.

of a morality and religion which have made nature and human
nature something separate from the soul, something gross and
material. The "two fetters of life" for Blake in the poems
of Experience are "Nature and Religion" (p. 119). Nature
remains a "fetter," says Swinburne, only insofar as it is "mere
separate and human nature" (p. 122), a creation of organized
religions and of all preachers of abstinence for the soul's sake.
The world of Experience is then a blighted world,

> an obscure material force on this hand [Nature], and on
> that a mournful imperious law [Religion]: the law of
> divine jealousy, the government of a God who . . .
> rules by forbidding and dividing: the "Urizen" of the
> prophetic books, clothed with the coldness and the grief
> of remote sky and jealous cloud.

[p. 119]

Once both innocent and fallen nature are defined, Swinburne
discusses the poems of Experience as prophetic calls for the
deliverance of natural desire. For closer analysis he chooses
"Introduction," "Earth's Answer," "The Human Abstract,"
and "To Tirzah," both for their beauty and for their thought.[40]
"Introduction" to *Songs of Experience* is a plea to earth to
free herself from the shackles and the shadow "of a jealous
law." The poem speaks in the "same 'voice of the bard' " as
the summons of the innocents to exercise judgment; Swinburne comments that "by faithful following of instinct and
divine liberal impulse, earth and man shall obtain deliverance." Swinburne quoted the opening stanzas, making two
changes:

40. For the texts of these poems in Swinburne, see: "Introduction,"
two stanzas on p. 117, the rest on p. 118; "Earth's Answer," ll. 6–10
on p. 118, ll. 18–20 on p. 119; "The Human Abstract," ll. 13–20 on
p. 121; "To Tirzah," ll. 9–12 on p. 125.

The poems from *SI* most praised by Swinburne are poems that gave
Coleridge pleasure "in the highest degree" (letter to C. A. Tulk);
"The Little Black Boy" and "Night." Swinburne terms them "of
loftiest loveliness" (p. 115).

Hear the voice of the bard!
  Who present, past, and future sees:
  Whose ears have heard
  The *ancient* Word   Holy
    That walked among the *silent* trees: ancient
                 [p. 117]   [E-B, ll. 3–4]

The effect of the changes is to give the poem, and the bard of
Experience, a plainly pagan aspect—to remove the poet entirely from suggestions of "Holy" inspiration—in effect to re-
duce the density of paradox in an already anti-conventional
poem. Perhaps Swinburne is trying to avoid the difficulty of
distinguishing (before speaking of Blake's inversions as such)
between a "Holy Word" of freedom and the Word of restriction for readers to whom Blake was a "gentle-hearted mystic"
and to whom faith and "Holy Word" were now even more
closely associated with ethical and moral codes than in Blake's
time. Swinburne suppresses another paradox quoting from
"To Tirzah." Tirzah's "false self-deceiving tears" (l. 11) are
altered to "self-deceiving *fears*" (Swinburne, p. 125) which
bind the "nostrils, eyes, and ears." Possibly "fears" are as-
similated more easily into Swinburne's exposition of themes of
Urizenic restraint. The place of the oppressor's tears or pity
requires more complex explication.

    The last stanza of "Introduction" contains a transposition
which may have been determined by Swinburne's stress on
"divine liberal impulse":

  Why wilt thou turn away?
The starry *shore*   floor
The wat*ery floor*   wat'ry shore
  Are given thee till the break of day.   Is
       [Swinburne, p. 118]   [E-B, ll. 18–20]

Blake's lines seem to remind earth that she is condemned in
her nature (or so long as the sky *appears* a floor); Swinburne's
suggest a more material consolation, especially when he com-

ments: "During the night of law and oppression of material form, the divine evidences hidden under sky and sea are left her" (p. 118). (This comment suggests why he titled his most important book of poems *Songs Before Sunrise.*) Swinburne's explication of "To Tirzah," the last of the *Songs,* contained the first non-apologetic description of Blake's "spiritual creed" that Christ is the human imagination: "how intense [is] the reliance on redemption from . . . [natural] law by the grace of imaginative insight and spiritual freedom, typified in the "death of Jesus" (pp. 122–23).

The Manuscript Poetry

Rossetti's Headnote to the Selections described the *Pickering MS* only as "a small autograph collection of different matter, somewhat more fairly copied" than the *Note-Book (Life, 2, 85).* ("Pickering" is Sampson's designation.) The manuscript consists of apparently finished poems which Blake copied but never engraved. They date from the years 1800 to 1804 according to Sampson and Keynes and contain very few corrections. Revision is not in order here as with half-written or abandoned poems; nonetheless Rossetti introduced alternate readings from drafts in the *Note-Book* and made independent changes. Nor was there ever a record in print in the nineteenth century of the ways in which the nameless "autograph collection" differs from the *Note-Book.* Rossetti's Headnote to "Poems Hitherto Unpublished" tells that he occasionally "resorted to" omission, transpositions, and combination in the "somewhat more fairly copied . . . autograph collection," that is to say, in the *Pickering MS.* The *Note-Book* was subject to these drastic reclamation measures as a matter of course (2, 85). Swinburne considered all Blake's manuscript poems under a single title taken from the *Note-Book,* "Ideas of Good and Evil," which he adopted "for purposes of readier reference" (p. 112). In the 1880 edition of Gilchrist's *Life* Rossetti replaced "Poems Hitherto Un-published" with "Ideas of Good and Evil"; W. B. Yeats re-printed it because he liked it, so much so that he used it for the title of a volume of his critical essays. It became in time the heading for an increasing number of poems.[41]

Another point left unclear was whether Shepherd's or Ros-setti's Pickering texts were the authoritative ones. William Rossetti's account of the manuscript poetry in the Aldine Blake obscured the fact that Shepherd had had manuscript authority for the Pickering poems and had printed *all* of them (p. cxxx). Margin for confusion increased when the manu-script dropped from sight after it was sold by Pickering. Samp-son was fortunate to have it turn up just as his edition was going to press in 1905. Yeats and Ellis never saw the *Picker-ing MS,* which was buried during the 1890s in collector Fred-erick Locker-Lampson's Rowfant Library. They did not know Shepherd had had access to it and reposed their confi-dence in the Rossettis.[42]

Everyone knew where the *Note-Book* was until 1882 when it was sold after Rossetti's death, but no one outside the Ros-setti circle had been granted reference to it. Indeed, since Ellis and Yeats worked substantially from a copied version and not the *Note-Book* itself, the only nineteenth-century edi-tors to use the manuscript were Gilchrist, Swinburne, and the Rossettis.

41. Swinburne mistakenly notes that "Ideas of Good and Evil" was meant by Blake to "serve as a general title" in the *Note-Book* (p. 112); this would mean that all the manuscript poetry, written over all the years in which Blake used the book is legitimately to be con-sidered "Ideas of Good and Evil." (W. B. Yeats repeats Swinburne's statement.)

In the second edition of Gilchrist's *Life,* Rossetti, in introducing the section, wrote a short explanatory note on the title.

42. See notes to the *Note-Book* and *Pick MS* poems in Blake, ed. Keynes; also *Blake Bibliography;* and Sampson (1905).

William Rossetti's Aldine texts for the manuscript poems follow his brother's in nearly all important respects (see Sampson [1905]).

The set of texts Rossetti produced from the *Note-Book* and
the *Pickering MS* (see Appendix) demonstrates his critical
preference for Blake's "exquisite metrical gift and rightness
in point of form" (*Life, 2,* 88). Wherever he saw an opportunity, Rossetti exercised his ingenuity in conjoining fragments
and rounding off longer pieces, to construct neatly made poems—even where Blake had left clearly marked self-contained
units. For instance, Rossetti put two congenial quatrains together to make an aphoristic poem which he called "Opportunity." The title provides interpretation, and the quatrains
appear to illuminate one another. However, the effect is gained
at the intellectual expense of each, especially the first, entitled
"Eternity" in the *Note-Book* (E-B, p. 461).

Opportunity

He who bends to himself a joy
Does the winged life destroy;
But he who kisses the joy as
            it flies
Lives in eternity's sunrise.

If you trap the moment before
            it's ripe,
The tears of repentance you'll
            certainly wipe;
But if once you let the ripe
            moment go
You can never wipe off the tears
            of woe.

[*Life, 2,* 126]

(Rossetti assembled a poem titled "Riches" in a similar manner [see Appendix, p. 242].)
    We can see Rossetti sacrificing complexity in a number of
instances. For example, he reassembled Blake's series of
couplets entitled "Auguries of Innocence" (*Pickering MS*)
into seven loosely unified passages, moving to a coherent and

unified poetic statement. He introduced them with the lines, "To see a World in a Grain of Sand/ And a Heaven in a Wild Flower/ Hold Infinity in the palm of your hand/ And Eternity in an hour" (E-B, p. 431), printed in italics so that they served as a motto. These prophecies, with increasing grimness, move in an emotional straight line to an unalloyed resolution —not so much by seeing "through" the eye as by mystically apprehending that "a joy runs under every grief." Rossetti has taken all the passages that promise culmination (ll. 53–62, 119–32) and rearranged them so that the lines "It is right . . ." (ll. 55–58), instead of following the ways of "mutual fear" within and between nature and man as they do in the manuscript, are made into the epiphany upon "Under every grief . . ./ Runs a joy . . ." (ll. 61–62).

Every night and every morn	119	
Some to misery are born;	120	
Every morn and every night	121	
Some are born to sweet delight;	122	
Some are born to sweet delight,	123	
Some are born to endless night.	124	
Joy and woe are woven fine,	59	
A clothing for the soul divine;	60	
Under every grief and pine	61	
Runs a joy with silken twine.	62	
It is right it should be so;	55	
Man was made for joy and woe;	56	
And when this we rightly know,	57	
Safely through the world we go.	58	Thro' the World we safely go,
We are led to believe a lie	125	
When we see *with* not through the eye	126	see ["With" deleted] not through
Which was born in a night to perish in a night	127	

When the soul slept in beams of
   light.   128
God appears and God is light   129
To those poor souls who dwell in
   night;   130
Both *doth* a human form display   131 does
To those who dwell in realms of
   day.   132

              [*Life, 2,* 110–11]   [E-B]

Apart from the violation done in trying to turn "Auguries of
Innocence" into a dramatic lyric, Rossetti's individual sections
are sometimes effective—so effective that editors still accept
the principle of rearranging this poem.[43] One passage builds
scattered couplets on social institutions into a prophecy of
England's ruin. (This is section 5 of Rossetti's "Auguries.")

Nought can deform the human race   99
Like to the *armourer's* iron brace;   100 Armour's
The soldier armed with sword and gun   77
Palsied strikes the summer's sun;   78
When gold and gems adorn the plough,   101
To peaceful arts shall envy bow;   102
The beggar's rags fluttering in air   75
Do to rags the heavens tear;   76 Does
The prince's robes and beggar's rags   51
Are toadstools on the miser's bags;   52

    43. Sampson (1905) rearranged the poem, speculating that Blake
"either wrote down the couplets in the order of composition or tran-
scribed them as loose jottings, referring rearrangement for future
consideration" (p. 287). Keynes's note to the poem says Sampson's
arrangement, "in which each theme treated by Blake is followed to
its conclusion instead of being woven in one with another . . . is to
be preferred to those made by other editors" (Blake, ed. Keynes,
p. 907). And see Erdman's "Editorial Arrangement," E-B, pp. 484 ff.
    According to Swinburne, the "Auguries" was Rossetti's favorite
poem by Blake (*S. L.,* No. 1582, Nov. 23, 1891, *6,* 23).

One mite wrung from the labourer's hands	81
Shall buy and sell the miser's lands,	82
Or, if protected from on high,	83
Shall that whole nation sell and buy;	84 Does
The poor man's farthing is worth more	79
Than all the gold on Afric's shore.	80
The whore and gambler, by the state	113
Licensed, build that nation's fate;	114
The harlot's cry from street to street	115
Shall weave old England's winding-sheet;	116
The winner's shout, the loser's curse,	117
Shall dance before dead England's hearse.	118 Dance

[*Life*, 2, 109]   [E-B]

In "Cupid" Rossetti printed the first sixteen lines and cut out the last four ("Twas the Greeks love of war/ Turnd Love into a Boy/ And Woman into a Statue of Stone/ And away fled every Joy"). The speaker in Rossetti's "Cupid" is wholly tuned to the bitterness of the single moment; the *Note-Book* speaker assimilates his own simple vehemence into a larger view. Swinburne's review supplied the last stanza for readers but incorrectly said that Blake had rejected it (p. 144).[44]

The emendation to "Cupid" is one of a number of changes which reflect Rossetti's personal poetic absorption with "intense moments," vignettes of emotional experience, and his sensitivity to the psychological give and take of romantic love. His text of "My Spectre around me," entitled "Broken Love," leaves out entirely stanzas in which the speaker would "agree

44. Swinburne printed the actual last lines to show Blake's antipathy to Roman violence and Greek "mathematic form," remarking that "To his half-trained apprehension Rome seemed mere violence and Greece mere philosophy" (p. 144; see E-B, p. 470).

to give up Love," "root up the Infernal grove," and "annihilate" love "on the rocks"; in his Headnote Rossetti describes "Broken Love" with intimate sympathy as a psychomachy of shame and false pride, ever in need of being resolved anew within the love relationship, in a kind of perpetual agony of suffering and forgiveness:

> Never perhaps have the agony and perversity of sundered affection been more powerfully (however singularly) expressed than here. The speaker is one whose soul has been intensified by pain to be his only world, among the scenes, figures, and events of which he moves as in a new state of being. The emotions have been quickened and isolated by conflicting torment, till each is a separate companion. There is his 'spectre,' the jealous pride which scents in the snow the footsteps of the beloved rejected woman, but is a wild beast to guard his way from reaching her; his 'emanation' which silently weeps within him, for has not he also sinned? So they wander together in 'a fathomless and boundless deep,' the morn full of tempests and the night of tears. Let her weep, he says, not for his sins only, but for her own.
>
> [*Life*, 2, 86] [45]

What he says is illuminating, as Swinburne remarks, although the illumination is "external . . . and none of the author's

45. Rossetti describes the "stately imagery" of woe, that is the seven loves, of stanzas 10, 11, 12, 13:

> some that still watch around his bed, bright sometimes with ecstatic passion of melancholy and crowning his mournful head with vine. . . . Has she not pity to give for pardon: nay, does he not heed her pardon too? He cannot seek her, but oh! if she would return! Surely her place is ready for her, and bread and wine of forgiveness of sins.
>
> [*Life*, 2, 86]

For the text and subsequent editorial career of "Broken Love," see Appendix.

[Blake's] kindling" (p. 279 n.). Rossetti's version of Blake's
lyric "I told my love I told my love," which he titled "Love's
Secret," is a Rossettian poem:

Love's Secret

NEVER *seek* to tell thy love,	1	[Never pain (seek del.) to tell thy love
Love that never told can be!	2	Love that never told can be
For the gentle wind *doth* move	3	For the gentle wind does move
Silently, invisibly.	4	Silently invisibly (del. st.)]
I told my love, I told my love,	5	I told my love I told my love
I told her all my heart,	6	I told her all my heart.
Trembling, cold, in ghastly fears.	7	Trembling cold in ghastly fears,
Ah! she *did* depart.	8	Ah she doth depart
Soon *after* she was gone from me	9	Soon as she was gone from me
A traveller came by,	10	A traveller came by
Silently, invisibly:	11	Silently invisibly
He took her with a sigh.	12	(Del. line)
	13	O was no deny

[*Life, 2,* 98]   [E-B, pp. 458, 768]

(The punctuation added in lines 6 and 7 is that of editors
after Sampson.) Rossetti's punctuation has assigned the
tremblings and "ghastly fears" to the speaker, not to his
beloved. Ironic possibilities are effectively suppressed by
his title; the changes in tense and conjunction can be said
almost to provide the lady with a decent interval between
lovers. Rossetti's emended three-stanza poem is a lover's
complaint, akin to the translations of courtly love poems he
published in 1861; Blake's two-stanza poem is an ironic observation and satire on the conventions of the genre). As in

"Cupid," Rossetti erased the distance between the speaker and the subject.

In these and other poems where Rossetti has tended either to sentimentalize Blake or to alter intellectual grasp into purely emotional response, Swinburne often tries to readjust Rossetti's product. His corrections are seldom direct. "Broken Love," he says, is "akin in form and manner" to "The Golden Net" (p. 148), one of Blake's poems on destructive "female will." Rossetti had effectively edited this theme out of "Broken Love." Swinburne quotes the two lines "Are not the joys of morning sweeter/ Than the joys of night?" in a context that nullifies completely the title "Young Love" by which Rossetti had accommodated them to his own poetic vision of youth and beauty. Rossetti saw Mary (in the poem "Mary") as an embodiment of poetic sensibility or perhaps ideal feminine beauty; Swinburne sees her as the victim of hypocritical morality, the poem as an expression of Blake's sexual libertarianism (p. 177). Swinburne singles out a "much better and more solid version *of the same fancy* than the one given in the 'Selections' under the head of 'Love's Secret'; which is rather weakly and lax" (p. 141, italics mine), a poem not published by Rossetti: "I asked a thief to steal me a peach." He entitles it "The Will and the Way," praising its "sweet and rapid daring" and "angelically puerile impudence." In addition Swinburne prints a line Blake deleted, preferring it to "Blake's own amended reading; in which otherwise the main salt of the poem is considerably diluted by tepid water: the angel (one might say) has his sting blunted" (pp. 141–42 n.).

The Will and the Way

"I askèd a thief to steal me a
    peach;
  He turned up his eyes;
I *askèd* a lithe lady to lie her
    down   ask'd
  Holy *and* meek, she cries.   &

As soon as I went   5 As soon . . . came: [One
                                            line]
  An angel came;
He *winked* at the thief   6 wink'd
And *smiled* at the dame;   7 smil'd
                                        [One stanza]

And   without   one   word
    spoke   8

Had a peach from the
    tree;   9
And 'twixt earnest *and* joke   10 [Deleted line] &
  Enjoyed the lady."   11 And still as a maid
                                    12 Enjoy'd the lady

    [Swinburne, p. 141]   [E-B, pp. 460, 769]

Swinburne's emendations and criticism of "The Will and
the Way" reflect the Victorian immoralist; Rossetti's of
"Love's Secret," the sensibility immersed in *Vita Nuova* and
the poems of the *dolce stil nuovo*. Both Rossetti and Swinburne saw the *Note-Book* largely as diary— Swinburne calls
it a repository of "points of personal faith and feeling"; each
draws from it poems that enforce his view of Blake. Swinburne neither alludes to nor quotes the Epigrams on Art that
Rossetti printed for their Pre-Raphaelite sentiments. When
he came to print as yet unpublished writings (mainly out of
the *Note-Book*), Swinburne chose lines, stanzas, and epigrams on repressive morality or else those that conveyed the
range of Blake's thought. More for its "convenience of explanation" in furnishing a definition of "Experience" than
for its poetic virtues, Swinburne quoted the *Note-Book*
"Motto to the Songs of Innocence and Experience" (p. 123).
He prints "The Fairy," preferring to call it "The Marriage
Ring" (Blake's deleted title). "A fairy leapt [sic; "skipt," see
E-B, p. 473] upon my knee" is a "dim and slight sketch," but
it indicates "Blake's views of the apparent and substantial

form of things, the primary and the derivative life" (p. 144 n.). A quatrain beginning "There souls of men are bought and sold" is an illustration of Blake's sensitivity to social wrongs (p. 127).

Swinburne's commentary often indulges his own delight in the witty, sometimes ribald, and irreverent Blake; ultimately it is the combined lyricist and rebel that his review exalts. He singles out a group of poems which he terms songs of "melodious revolt" (p. 136): "I walked abroad on a snowy day," "Are not the joys of morning sweeter," "I laid me down upon a bank," "Abstinence sows sand all over." These expose most exactly and passionately the ways of Urizen: hypocrisy, jealousy, and abstinence; organized religion and the moral law. Concerning the first poem, Swinburne writes that against "the 'winter' of ascetic law and moral prescription Blake never slackens in his fiery animosity; never did a bright hot wind of March make such war upon the cruel inertness of February." He has underscored his point with a change in Blake's lines. (It is difficult to see what obvious purpose is served in the first change from "snowy" to *"sunny."*)

I walked abroad on a *sunny* day;   snowy
I *wooed* the soft snow with me to play.   askd
She played and she melted in all her prime;
And the winter called it a dreadful crime.

                              [p. 135]   [E-B, p. 464]

In a footnote Swinburne gives an alternative reading of the last line, "Ah! that sweet love should be thought a crime," only to reject its "simple lyrical sweetness" for the "pungent and brilliant effect" of the other (pp. 135–36 n.).

Swinburne's twenty-eight page exposition of *The Everlasting Gospel* further develops the idea of Blake's antagonism to organized religion and moral law; the line "Moral virtues do not exist" is his theme. In the course of his discussion, Swinburne prints a total of 253 lines (about five times the length of Rossetti's excerpt) from the scattered *Note-Book* fragments that compose the poem. *The Everlasting Gospel* interested Blake's three mid-century editors: the section beginning "Was Jesus Chaste or did he/ Give any Lessons of Chastity/ The morning blushd fiery red/ Mary was found in Adulterous bed" (E-B., p. 512, ll. 1–4), which Swinburne called the "greatest passage" in the poem and one of the greatest in all Blake, was printed in 1863 over the objections of the publisher, Alexander Macmillan, at the particular insistence of Rossetti. He wrote to Mrs. Gilchrist, "If there is anything to shock ordinary readers, it is merely the opening, which could be omitted, and the poem made to begin with 'Jesus sat in Moses' chair,' etc." This was done and the passage entitled "The Woman Taken in Adultery." Swinburne restored the opening and other lines, lifting, as he put it, the editorial fig leaves from the "Woman Taken in Adultery" (pp. 152–53).[46]

As it is near the end of Part 2, the exposition of the *Everlasting Gospel* serves both as summary and also as an introduction to the commentary on the prophetic books. It cites, illustrates, and defines Blake's "passion of contradiction" (William Rossetti's phrase [Aldine, p. cxvii]). Moreover, trying to explain to the nineteenth-century Christian how Blake uses "Jesus Christ" in the poem, Swinburne draws a distinction between and at the same time connects Blake's "mysticism" and his poetic intelligence. Although his vision

46. For Rossetti's letter, dated Jan. 1863, see *Anne Gilchrist*, p. 139. William Rossetti printed 313 lines (as a consecutive poem) in the Aldine Blake. He follows Swinburne, citing the poems "importance in scale and purport" (p. cxiv), Also, compare Aldine, p. cxvii with Swinburne, pp. 148 and 152. William Rossetti's new contribution, besides printing *EG* as a poem, is to indicate its fragmentary state in the *Note-Book* and admit doubt about its date (p. 144 n.). For further editorial information, see Aldine, pp. 244–45. For passages printed in the *Life*, Swinburne, the Aldine Blake, see Appendix.

trembled always on the inner meanings of things, Blake was
no "minor mystic." He was a poet and therefore "prone to
beat out into human shape even the most indefinite features
of his vision" (p. 149).

> [In Blake's] detestation of deism and its "impersonal
> God," he must needs embody his vision of a deity or
> more perfect humanity in the personal Christian type
> [that is, Christ]: a purely poetical tendency, which if
> justly apprehended will serve to account for the wildest
> bodily forms in which he drew his visions from the
> mould of prophecy.
>
> [pp. 150–51]

Finally, Swinburne reviewed the Selections from the standpoint of their place in an as yet unpublished canon of Blake's
work, taking into account their relation to the prophecies:

> Future editions may be, and in effect will have to be,
> altered and enlarged: it is as well for people to be aware
> that they have not yet a final edition of Blake; that will
> have to be some day completed on a due scale.
>
> [p. 112]

CHAPTER SIX

The Mid-Century Revival—The Prophetic Books

In his chapter "Mad or not Mad?" Gilchrist dismissed the allegations of insanity that were based on "wild passages in [Blake's] writings" (*1*, 366). To keep Blake's "professedly mystical writings" (*1*, 368) in the background would simplify his defense of Blake's sanity. Early in the autumn of 1862 Swinburne considered writing a short exposition of Blake's major ideas to append to the Life but was discouraged by the work as it then stood: "To . . . stick on a supplement at the end would be absurd, even if the addition could be made . . . to look as if it fitted on." Apparently (and Rossetti confirmed this) nothing "like a comprehensive critical 'exposition' or summary . . . [had ever been] designed" for the prophecies.[1] Moreover, it is clear that neither Rossetti nor his brother would ever have produced an extended analysis and commentary; he writes:

> S. is however a downright enthusiast through thick & thin; and thick is the Jrusalem [sic] at any rate, whatever the Heaven & Hell may be. My brother, who has as analytical a mind as I know for such purposes (and an absolutely safe one) admits the continual & inscrutable incoherence of the Jerusalem. I only heard him say so

1. Swinburne's comments in this and the following paragraphs occur in the letter to William Rossetti dated Oct. 6, 1862 (*S. L.*, No. 35, *1*, 59–60).

the other day. I myself cannot tackle such a book at all.[2]

Gilchrist's less than sanguine "half-handling"[3] was not the only obstacle as it turned out. There was also obstinate propriety, represented by the publisher Macmillan, and the "virtuous editor"—Swinburne's word for Mrs. Gilchrist. "Mr. Macmillan is far more inexorable against any shade of heterodoxy in morals, than in religion. . . . It might be well perhaps to mention to Mr. Swinburne, if he is so kind as to do what was proposed, that it would be perfectly useless to attempt to handle this side of Blake's writings," Mrs. Gilchrist writes. In the same letter she apologizes to William Rossetti for having censored the exposition of *Visions of the Daughters of Albion* which he had written for her.[4] Three

2. A. L. to Mrs. Gilchrist, ?Mar. 8, 1880, Thorne Coll.

3. The word is applied specifically to the criticism of *GP,* but it reflects Swinburne's view of criticism in the Life generally (see *S. L.,* No. 51, Dec. 15, 1863, *1,* 90).

4. *Anne Gilchrist,* p. 128; dated Oct. 3, 1862. William Rossetti had written to Mrs. Gilchrist, in a letter dated Sept. 1862:

> The pervading idea of the 'Daughters of Albion' is one which was continually seething in Blake's mind, and flustering Propriety in his writings; or rather *would have* flustered Propriety, if she had either troubled herself to read the oracles, or succeeded in understanding them. It is the idea of the unnatural and terrible result in which, in modern society, ascetic doctrines in theology and morals have involved the relations of the sexes. A great deal of his most powerful, appealing, incisive, odd, provoking, and enigmatic writing is expended upon this formidable question, in whose cause he is never tired of up-rearing the banner of heresy and non-conformity.
>
> [Ibid., p. 127]

She shrank from trying to get this exposition past Macmillan who "reads all the proofs"; and apologized, "I would have tried it . . . but as that sheet has been twice set up . . . I therefore 'reduced the subject' still less." Only this short account appeared:

> Formidable moral questions are in an enigmatic way, occasionally opened up through the medium of this allegory [that is, of

days later Swinburne wrote to William Rossetti that he would begin within the next year an independent "distinct small commentary of a running kind":

> Not that one need be over-explanatory of Blake's extreme crotchets or in the least prurient, but just fair and careful and rational, going as much to the heart of the matter handled as possible . . . [this not to] jar with the Life.

The commentary on the prophecies which did appear in the Life was composed chiefly of vague or apologetic generalities written by Mrs. Gilchrist. *Milton,* she says, is "very like *Jerusalem* in style: it would seem . . . to be a sort of a continuation. . . . [It] equals its predecessor [sic: *Milton* was finished before *Jerusalem*] in obscurity. . . . the same religious fervour, the same high, devout aim" (*1,* 241–42). *The Visions of the Daughters of Albion* is a "dreamy" poem like *Thel,* in which "Formidable moral questions are, in an enigmatic way, occasionally opened up . . . [which] we will not enter on . . . here." *America* is a "retrospect, in its mystic way (*Life,* 1863, *1,* 108).[5] Of the actual texts quoted in the Life, *Gates of Paradise* alone was given in full; of the longer prophecies only *The Marriage of Heaven and Hell* was sub-

---

VDA], and in many another of Blake's writings: questions on which he had his own views, and gave fearless and glowing expression to them,—as the exemplary man had good right to do. But we will not enter on them here.

[*Life,* 1863, *1,* 108]

The passage was cut entirely in 1880. For more on the circumstances which governed the two editions of Gilchrist's *Life,* see Dorfman, "Blake in 1863 and 1880: The Gilchrist *Life,*" *BNYPL,* 71 (April 1967), 216–38.

5. Mrs. Gilchrist wrote the accounts of *MHH* in Chap. 10; *GP* and *VDA* in Chap. 12; *Amer. Eur, SLos,* and *Ahan* in Chap. 14; and *Jer* and *Milt* in Chap. 21. Her interpretation of *MHH* was probably influenced by comments on Blake and on *MHH* in particular in Palmer's letters to her. See *Life,* 1863, *1,* 78, and A. H. Palmer, p. 244; also Chap. 4, n. 11 above.

stantially quoted. However, this was compromised by Mrs. Gilchrist's comment that "any endeavour to trace out any kind of system, any coherent or consistent philosophy in this or any other of Blake's writings" appeared nearly hopeless. Blake, she wrote, "laid to heart very zealously and practically his favorite doctrine, that 'the man who never alters his opinion is like standing water, and breeds reptiles of the mind.' Hence antagonistic assertions may be found almost side by side" (*Life,* 1863, *1,* 78).

Not wanting to "jar with the Life," Swinburne decided against including a set of texts with his criticism; he did extract longer, as yet unpublished, passages from the prophetic books and printed one complete work, *The Ghost of Abel.* Swinburne's criticism did not, however, just tactfully ignore the Life. He prefaced his remarks by dismissing everything in Gilchrist on the prophecies except the criticism of the "illustrative parts," which he deemed "final and faultless, nothing missed and nothing wrong" (p. 186);[6] he observed that "to excuse and to explain are different offices" (p. 209).

(With the exception of four relatively minor works, the texts of Blake's prophecies did not appear without exegetic commentary prior to the twentieth century. The four are *Tiriel, Thel, Gates of Paradise,* and *The Ghost of Abel* (in Swinburne); the Aldine edition included *Tiriel* and the previously printed *Gates* and *Thel.*)

To Swinburne Blake's greatest and most important book

6. The description of the designs to *MHH,* beginning at "A strip of azure" and going to "good and evil" (*Life, 1,* 86–88) is taken verbatim from Palmer's letter to Mrs. Gilchrist dated June 27, 1862 (A. H. Palmer, pp. 242–43), although neither Swinburne nor Rossetti knew this. In 1880, Rossetti wrote to Mrs. Gilchrist: "I was reading last night the description [of *MHH*] which you now tell me are [sic] by Palmer with the highest admiration. It is strange he has not been impelled to literature" (A. L., Mar. 8, 1880, Thorne Coll.).

was *The Marriage of Heaven and Hell,* a "work indeed which we rank as about the greatest produced by the eighteenth century in the line of high poetry and spiritual speculation," and the "high-water mark of [Blake's] intellect" (p. 204). Swinburne's exposition of this book—so diffidently handled by Mrs. Gilchrist in that "insufficient but painstaking and well-meant chapter" (p. 187)—sharpens the image which he had drawn in his readings of the *Everlasting Gospel* and the *Songs of Experience*: Blake the arch-rebel. Swinburne explicitly shows what he had implied for "Innocence" and "Experience," that the Blakean usages of "Hell," "Heaven," "Angel," "Devil," and so forth are prophetic inversions of their accepted applications.

> That impulsive energy and energetic faith are the only means, whether used as tools of peace or as weapons of war, to pave or fight our way toward the realities of things was plainly the creed of Blake; as also that these realities, once well in sight, will reverse appearance and overthrow tradition: hell will appear as heaven, and heaven as hell. The abyss once entered with due trust and courage appears a place of green pastures and gracious springs: the paradise of resignation once beheld with undisturbed eyes appears a place of emptiness or bondage, delusion or cruelty.
>
> [p. 220]

The *Marriage* then is seen as a "transvaluation of values," a reversing of meanings serving to emphasize a reversing of conventional valuations. (Reviewing Swinburne's book M. D. Conway [see pp. 180 f.] speaks of inversion in Blake "amounting almost to a method." [7]) Twenty years later H. P. Horne compares *The Marriage of Heaven and Hell* with Matthew

7. Moncure D. Conway, Review of Swinburne's *William Blake, Fortnightly Review, N. S., 3* (Feb. 1868), 216–20.

Arnold's *Literature and Dogma,* the aim of both being "to
recast religion." [8]

Paradox and apparent contradiction are necessary tools for
the Satanic prophet envisaged by Swinburne in the *Marriage.*
Blake's use of "current terms of religion, now as types of his
own peculiar faith, now in the sense of ordinary preachers,"
his "impugning therefore at one time what at another he will
seem to vindicate" (p. 212) are anything but the signs of a
confused intelligence Mrs. Gilchrist took them for. Allowing
that Blake's "material forms," his wrenching of words and
meanings, are "inadequate and obscure" at the opening of
the *Marriage* (but there only), Swinburne maintains that
despite appearances there is essential unity. Where later critics
have spoken of Blake's ironic and dialectical devices, Swinburne holds that "The expression shifts perpetually, the types
blunder into new forms, the meaning tumbles into new types;
the purpose remains, and the faith keeps its hold" (p. 188).

Swinburne's exposition of Blake's method in the *Marriage*
is part of his overall argument in "The Prophetic Books": to
show that Blake's thought is basically consistent. His reading
bequeathed to later writers on Blake a core of concepts and
doctrines which constituted the "evangel" or "faith" of a man
whom Swinburne termed both a prophet and a poet, the
fashioner of a "fierce apocalypse" (p. 195):

> He believed in redemption by Christ, and in the incarna-
> tion of Satan as Jehovah. He believed that by self-sacri-
> fice the soul should attain freedom and victorious de-
> liverance from bodily bondage and sexual servitude; and
> also that the extremest fullness of indulgence in such
> desire and such delight as the senses can aim at or attain

8. "William Blake's *Marriage of Heaven and Hell,*" *The Century
Guild Hobby Horse,* 2 (1887), 136.
    Arthur Symons, *William Blake,* opens with the statement that *MHH*
"anticipates Nietzsche in his most significant paradoxes" (pp. 1–2).

was absolutely good, eternally just, and universally requisite.

[p. 190]

Swinburne's commentaries on the earlier prophecies, though qualified as he proceeds, place the doctrine of "indulgence"—always "indulgence bracketed to faith" (p. 212)—at the center of Blake's vision. The doctrine is reiterated with considerable vehemence: the "one matter of marriage laws is still beaten upon, still hammered at" (p. 232) in the *Visions of the Daughters of Albion.* Swinburne often adds his own invective to Blake's; *The Marriage of Heaven and Hell* was meant "to blow dust in the eyes of the sand-blind," that is, Philistia; since it could not help but offend it was meant "to offend much" (pp. 205–06). In his exposition of the *Visions, America,* and the *Marriage*—as in his previous allusions to Blake's sexual libertarianism—Swinburne insists, however, that there is "no prurience of porcine appetite for rotten apples" in this "sensual doctrine." The senses as " 'the chief inlets of the soul,' " says Swinburne quoting the *Marriage,* "are worthy only as parts of the soul" (p. 212).

For many (G. B. Shaw for one) who based their views on Swinburne's reading of the *Marriage,* Blake became the teacher of a "dysangel" (p. 106), the Satanic "exponent of the 'Romantic agony.' " [9] Examining the reversed definitions

9. Northrop Frye, "William Blake," *The English Romantic Poets and Essayists: A Review of Research* (New York, 1957), pp. 11–12; Mario Praz, *The Romantic Agony,* trans. Angus Davidson (sec. ed. London, Oxford University Press, 1954), p. 278, n. 50.

Shaw writes, "A century ago William Blake was, like Dick Dudgeon, an avowed Diabolonian: he called his angels devils and his devils angels" (Preface to *The Devil's Disciple* [1897], in *Three Plays for Puritans, Collected Works of George Bernard Shaw, 9* [Ayot St. Lawrence Ed., 30 vols. New York, W. H. Wise & Co., 1930–32], p. xxviii). See also Shaw's "Epistle Dedicatory to Arthur Bingham Walkley" *Man and Superman* [1903], *Collected Works, 10,* and "The Quintessence of Ibsenism" [1890], *Major Critical Essays, Collected Works, 19.*

of "Heaven" and "Hell" Swinburne shows little interest in
seeing how Blake's contraries are mutually qualifying. To
explore such interaction—as in Blake's statement "Reason
and Energy . . . are necessary to Human existence" (*MHH*,
pl. 3)—would run counter to his temperamental conviction
that the forces of liberty and the forces of restraint must by
nature remain opposed, and to his unqualified partisanship
of "Energy."

This antinomian posture which Swinburne saw in the *Marriage* became absorbed within his broader philosophy, "mystical pantheism"—which he also reads into Blake, especially
Blake's later prophecies. Rooted in the doctrine of sensual indulgence, Pantheism is a belief in the essential divinity of the
whole man. Swinburne quotes as evidence from the *Marriage*:
"Man has no Body distinct from his Soul," "the five Senses
[are] the chief inlets of Soul in this age," "All deities reside in
the human breast"; and from "A Song of Liberty," "For every
thing that lives is Holy" (pls. 4, 11, 27). In exposition of
Jerusalem and *Milton,* and in a long note that seems to have
been added to the *Marriage* later (pp. 225–26), Swinburne
asserts that the (Blakean-Swinburnean) "pantheistic evangel"
is founded on the insight that all faiths preaching the separation of body and soul are mistaken. All such dualistic beliefs
are versions of the error of "Theism." The religion of Jehovah
is a particularly vicious instance of Theism; the religion of
Christ is redemptive and pantheistic. On *Milton,* Swinburne
notes that Blake "represents Monotheism" with its separated
God, "its stringent law and sacred creed, Jewish or Christian,
as opposed to Pantheism whereby man and God are one, and
by culture and perfection of humanity man makes himself
God" (p. 263). Hence in Blake's "evangel" Christ is the
archetypal Pantheist: "[A]nd as Satan (under "names divine" . . .) is the incarnate type of Monotheism, so is Jesus
the incarnate type of Pantheism" (p. 263). Swinburne has
it that for Blake Theism and ("absorbing") Pantheism (not
"Heaven" and "Hell") are the crucial contraries.

> On the right hand, let us say (employing the old figure
> of speech), is the Theist—the 'man of God' . . . the
> believer in a separate or divisible deity, capable of exist-
> ence apart from ours who conceive it; a conscious and
> absolute Creator. On the left hand is the Pantheist. . . .
> His creed is or should be much like that of your prophet
> here [that is, of Swinburne's Blake].[10]

[p. 226]

Blake's term of opprobrium is of course "Deism."

Swinburne's own faith, his way of resolving opposites, en-
visions universal evolution toward Pantheism through the
agency of sensual liberty. The "mystic, atheistic democratic
anthropologic poem" called "Hertha," begun in 1869,[11] is
Swinburne's full poetic statement of man's natural, spiritual,
and also political liberation and progression toward his own
divinity. Expounding on Blake's Pantheism, Swinburne wrote:
"God appears to a Theist as the root, to a Pantheist as the
flower of things" (p. 226 n.). The central metaphor in
"Hertha" is the Tree of Life, which is also a leading motif in

10. Swinburne quotes a note of "pure and simple exposition" from
a mythical "correspondent," which summarizes the overall teaching
of the prophecies, pp. 225–26 n. It has been supposed that he wrote it
himself.
There is a playful veiled acknowledgment that the interpretations of
Blake are a means to preach a personal gospel:

> (I must observe in passing that my correspondent seems so
> unable to conceive of a comment apart from the text, an ex-
> ponent who is not an evangelist,—so inclined to confuse the
> various functions of critic and of disciple, and assume that you
> must mean to preach or teach whatever doctrine you may have
> to explain.)

11. *S. L.*, No. 316, Oct. 26 [1869], *2*, 45. On Jan. 8 [1870], Swinburne writes that "I have just discharged the most formidable piece
of artillery yet cast or launched in [Urizen's] direction—the best
stanzas written of 'Hertha' strike such a blow at the very root of
Theism" (*S. L.*, No. 336, *2*, 79; and see No. 337, *2*, 85). "Hertha,"
quoted below, was published in *Songs Before Sunrise* [1871] (*Works*,
2 [Bonchurch ed., London, 1927], 137–45).

Blake; the poem is spoken in the voice of vital, organic nature,
"The life-tree am I" (l. 99).

> A creed is a rod,
>   And a crown is of night;
> But this thing is God,
>   To be man with thy might,
>
>   .   .   .
>
> And the lives of my children made perfect with freedom
>   of soul were my fruits.
>
> I bid you but be;
>   I have need not of prayer;
> I have need of you free
>
>   .   .   .
>
> Thought made him and breaks him,
>   Truth slays and forgives;
> But to you, as time takes him,
>   This new thing it gives,
> Even love, the beloved Republic, that feeds upon free-
>   dom and lives.
>
>   .   .   .
>
> One birth of my bosom;
>   One beam of mine eye;
> One topmost blossom
>   That scales the sky;
> Man, equal and one with me, man that is made of me,
>   man that is I.
>
>   [ll. 71–74, 155, 156–58, 186–90, and 196–200]

Except for the comprehensive natural metaphor of growth
all the ideas and attitudes contained within the poem appear
as well in Swinburne's book on Blake. Through an evolution-
ary vision (a Darwinesque interpretation of Blake's Tree of
Life) Swinburne synthesizes and reconciles two persistently
contradictory views about nature held throughout most of

the nineteenth century. Swinburne, provoked to his synthesis by Blake, went further than Coleridge, whose reading of the *Songs* resulted in an expression of contrary objections to Blake's indefensible liberties with nature on the one hand and to his acceptance of all of human nature on the other.

In light of his own sense of the unity of the human spirit with external nature—his Pantheism is "rooted in nature and respect for it" (p. 226 n.)—Swinburne must encounter the difficulty of explaining Blake's apparent rejection of "Nature" in *Jerusalem* and *Milton*. He argues that the "Nature" upheld in the *Marriage* and that condemned in the later works are two different, in fact, opposite things.

> [W]hen, as throughout the *Marriage of Heaven and Hell,* he uses ["Nature"] in the simple sense of human or physical condition as opposed to some artificial state of soul or belief, he takes it as the contrary of conventional ideas and habits (of religion and morality as vulgarly conceived or practiced); but when, as throughout the *Milton* and *Jerusalem,* he speaks of nature as opposed to inspiration, it must be taken as the contrary of that higher and subtler religious faith which he is bent on inculcating, and which itself is the only perfect opposite and efficient antagonist to the conventional faith and (to use another of his quasi-technical terms) the "deistical virtue" which he is bent on denying.
>
> [p. 281]

The deists were seen as those "who select this and reject that, assume and presume according to moral law and custom." Swinburne is silent about the possible connection between Blake's two senses of Nature; he opposes the deists' mistaken vision to what he considers Blake's teaching: "the Pantheistic revelation which consecrates all things and absorbs all contraries" (p. 289 n.). Swinburne is anti-natural only as this implies anti-conventional; he is satisfied to rest at the "Pantheistic revelation" and to remove only one of Blake's ap-

parent contradictions—between the doctrine of bodily release
and contempt for nature.

Elaborating on Blake's Pantheism, Swinburne suggests affinities beween Blake's myths and teachings and Oriental
thought. The myth of the horse and harrow of Palamabron
(in *Milton*) is "Asiatic in tone" and "full of the vast pro-
portion and formless fervour of Hindoo legends" (p. 262).
Swinburne describes the mode of "culture and perfection of
humanity" as "self-abnegation"—probably a substitute for
Blake's "self-annihilation"—which he wants clearly to dis-
tinguish from the Christian "self-denial":

> The point of difference here between Blake and many
> other western Pantheists is that in his creed self-abnega-
> tion (in the mystic sense, not the ascetic—the Oriental,
> not the Catholic) is the highest and only perfect form
> of self-culture.
>
> [p. 263]

Swinburne tended to interpret "sensual indulgence" in terms
of Eastern doctrines of nonascetic self-effacement and higher
tolerance in which personal salvation is submerged. Blake's
view that "everything that lives is Holy," taken with his mythmaking imagination—which sees "in things inanimate or in
the several limbs and divisions of one thing, separate forms of
active and symbolic life" (p. 197)—suggested a further affinity with the Eastern doctrine of transmigration of souls.
Such mystical doctrines permeated Swinburne's political views
as they did those of many transcendental and politically radical thinkers of the time—proponents of ideal democracy,
followers and admirers of the work of Emerson and Whitman, and, especially in Swinburne's circle, supporters of
Italian independence. Through William Rossetti, Swinburne
met American Whitmanians; they corresponded in detail
about Rossetti's English edition of Whitman's poems (to be
published in 1869). In these years Swinburne identified him-

self with three great exiled libertarians: Landor, Hugo, and Mazzini. "[I]t is nice to have something to love and believe in as I do in Italy. It was only Gabriel and his followers in art (l'art pour l'art) who for a time frightened me from speaking out." [12] With Mazzini's encouragement Swinburne began his "book of songs of the European revolution," which was modeled on Hugo's *Châtiments* and Whitman's *Drum Taps*.[13] (*Songs Before Sunrise* appeared in 1871.)

Although Swinburne dismissed *The French Revolution* (Blake's "most Swinburnian" poem Northrop Frye notes[14]) in Part *1* of *William Blake* (written in 1863), in 1866 he rejoiced to write to Moncure D. Conway, an American Unitarian minister at Finsbury who promoted Whitman's reputation in England, that Blake was a "republican under the very shadow of the gibbet . . . a lover of America, of freedom, and of France from the first and to the last"; he identifies Blake with Walt Whitman the transcendental Natural Man. Blake's books, Swinburne says,

> preach almost exactly the same gospel. . . . In the original 'Prophecies' there are passages quite as broad (and perhaps more offensive) as any in the *Leaves of Grass*. These I have not quoted . . . but the gist of

12. *S. L.* No. 149, Oct. 9, [1866], *1*, 195. Swinburne of course never deserted aesthetic criteria; in 1870 he writes Rossetti that he hopes *Songs Before Sunrise* are poems and not sermons, despite their themes. (*S. L.*, No. 343, Feb. 19, *2*, 97).

For Swinburne's interest in Whitman (he had read *Leaves of Grass* in 1859), see *ibid.*, *1*, 28; *1*, 58; and letters, 1866–68, passim. For his interest in William Rossetti's edition, see *1*, 266–70. The essay in which Swinburne ultimately denounced Whitman, "Whitmania," was published in 1887, *Studies in Prose and Poetry, Works, 15* (Bonchurch ed. London, 1927), 307 ff.

13. *S. L.*, No. 222, Oct. 6, [1867], *1*, 268. For Swinburne on *Drum Taps,* see a letter to Monckton Milnes, Lord Houghton, dated Nov. 2, 1866 (*S. L.*, No. 156, *1*, 204).

14. *Fearful Symmetry*, p. 205.

them is . . . Whitman's . . . healthy, natural, and anti-natural.[15]

Toward the close of his study, Swinburne introduces a comparison between Blake and Whitman. Despite its brevity (it is only three pages) this probably affected Blake's later reputation as much as did the Satanic Blake of the rest of the book, particularly for American and English admirers of Whitman. He writes:

> I can remember one poet only whose work seems to me the same or similar in kind; a poet as vast in aim, as daring in detail, as unlike others, as coherent to himself, as strange without and as sane within. . . . The great American [Walt Whitman] is not a more passionate preacher of sexual or political freedom than the English artist. To each the imperishable form of a possible and universal Republic is equally requisite and adorable as the temporal and spiritual queen of ages of men. To each all sides and shapes of life are alike acceptable or endurable. . . . Both are spiritual and both democratic; both by their works recall, even to so untaught and tentative a student as I am, the fragments vouchsafed to us of the Pantheistic poetry of the East. . . . Their outlooks and theories are evidently the same on all points of intellectual and social life.

> [pp. 300–01]

By providing a ready analogy with a more available poet, Swinburne confirmed his portrait of the prophet of sensual

15. *S. L.,* No. 160, Nov. 7, 1866, *1,* 209. Three days before the letter to Conway, Swinburne asked Hotten to send him the "last few sheets" of *William Blake;* "I think of enlarging the final paragraph, which was rather hurried through" (*S. L.,* No. 159 [Nov. 4, 1866], *1,* 206). His comparison between Whitman and Blake is doubtless a product of later rather than first thoughts on Blake.

liberty and of the Pantheist akin to Oriental mystical writers.[16]

Though he was convinced of an underlying consistency in the man and in the entire range of Blake's thought and writings,[17] Swinburne was undecided whether each individual prophecy had its own internal coherence or even any graspable continuity; he vacillated in his overall critical estimate of Blake. *The Marriage of Heaven and Hell* was certainly a unified work in itself, but in *Jerusalem,* although the "main symbols are of a monotonous consistency, . . . no accurate sequence of symbolic detail is to be looked for" (p. 286). Swinburne's appraisal of all the prophetic books that lie between these two, both in time of composition and range of difficulty, is mixed. He sees them as gorgeous and uneven terrain, worth groping through the prevalent "dimness and violence of expression" for the clear stretches of brilliant lyric and lucid epic narrative or for arresting displays of prophetic intensity, "passages . . . full of fate and fear" (pp. 194–95). Swinburne's choice of extracts bears out his critical opinions: he selects from the lyrical parts mainly and as a rule gives little space to mythic quotation. From *Milton* there is the "pure," "lovely," and lyrical passage beginning, "Thou hearest the nightingale begin the song of spring" (pp. 273–74, from pl. 31[18]). And from *America* a passionate image of "melodious revolt": "For the female spirits of the dead pining in bonds of religion/ Run from their fetters reddening and in long-drawn arches sitting/ They feel the nerves of youth renew, and de-

16. Whitman himself found "Swinburne's ["wild"] idea of resemblance . . . quite funny" (Walt Whitman, *The Correspondence* [*1868–1875*], ed. Edwin Haviland Miller [New York University Press, 1961], pp. 48–49; letter dated Sept. 27, 1868).

17. Swinburne observes that Blake's "main myth," which he takes to be the story of Urizen, was "afterwards assumed as the admitted groundwork of later and larger myths" (p. 249).

18. For plate, line, and page references to Swinburne's extracts, see Appendix. I list here only the plate number.

sires of ancient times" (p. 237, from pl. 15). A rare citation
of myth is the lush and rich Spenserian passage from *America*
on the "Atalantean hills," so-called "Because from their
bright summits you may pass to the golden world,/ An ancient
palace, archetype of mighty emperies/ Rears its immortal pin-
nacles, built in the forest of God/ By Ariston the king of
beauty for his stolen bride" (p. 236, from pl. 10)—one of the
less hermetic and more self-contained of Blake's mythologies.
A more typical mythic passage, which Swinburne plucked
from the "weedy waters" (p. 273) of *Milton* later became
centrally significant for W. B. Yeats in reading Blake (and in
his own system)—the lines from plate 28 on the duration of
time which begin "And every moment has a couch of gold for
soft repose/ (A moment equals a pulsation of the artery)"
(pp. 272–73).

Early in his book Swinburne regarded Blake's mythmaking
imagination closely and with sympathetic insight. His descriptions are at times so vivid and florid in fact as to be re-
creations. He writes that to Blake "all symbolic things
were literal, all literal things symbolic" (p. 41); vision might
be two-, three-, and at its most exalted, fourfold (pp. 41–42).
In Swinburne's individual analyses of the prophetic books
Blake's persons are understood and presented as types—Orc
"a stronger Vulcan or Satan" (p. 193). Throughout his exposition Swinburne conveys the moral import of natural attributes. (Ellis and Yeats will treat these later on as occult
symbols.)

> Urizen, God of cloud and star, "Father of jealousy,"
> clothed with a splendour of shadow, strong and sad and
> cruel; his planet faintly glimmers and slowly revolves, a
> horror in heaven; the night is a part of his thought, rain
> and wind are in the passage of his feet. . . . Star and
> cloud, the types of mystery and distance, of cold aliena-
> tion and heavenly jealousy, belong of right to the God
> who grudges and forbids: even as the spirit of revolt is

made manifest in fiery incarnation—pure prolific fire, "the cold loins of Urizen dividing."

[pp. 192–93]

When it came to a practical assessment of Blake's mythopoeic faculty, Swinburne was quick to denounce extravagance and blundering. Because it is frequently pushed too far, Blake's "habit" of animating natural phenomena leads to animating "limbs and divisions" of things and to introducing "absurdly familiar" London streets into the poems; too much is "obscure" and grotesque, even "hideous" (pp. 196–97). The catalogues of names, the "windy" mythologies (p. 196) "break the metres of the stars" (p. 197). This is the verdict on *Jerusalem* in particular, the only prophecy which could confound Swinburne's sympathy with the more recondite in Blake. Swinburne reminds his reader of the difference between "attempts at gospel" (p. 194) and poems: "For metrical oratory the plea . . . [at the beginning of *Jerusalem*] against ordinary metre may be allowed to have some effective significance; however futile if applied to purer and more essential forms of poetry" (p. 285). Nevertheless, he finds Blake culpable of disrespecting his art:

And unfortunately [Blake] had not by training, perhaps not by nature, the conscience which would have reminded him that whether or not an artist may allowably play with all other things in heaven and earth, one thing he must certainly not play with, the material forms of art: that levity and violence are here prohibited under grave penalties.

[p. 198]

The tone of reproof here is in accord with Swinburne's (and Gilchrist's) assumption that Blake wanted intellectual discipline. He was "as far from being critical as from being orthodox. Thus his ecstasy of study was neither on the one

side tempered and watered down by faith in established forms
and external creeds, nor on the other side modified and directed by analytic judgment and the lust of facts" (p. 189).
William Rossetti followed Swinburne, writing that Blake possessed "Power of thought," but "not of analytic or reasoning
thought": his work must be apprehended "intuitively" or not
at all (Aldine, pp. ciii and lxxiv).

Swinburne, however, had reservations about the prophecies
on grounds more essential than mannerism and obscurity.
When he wrote about Baudelaire, he declared allegory—for
him allegory meant teaching—"the dullest game and the most
profitless taskwork imaginable"; as a critic he is loath to wring
"elaborate meanings" from poetry.[19] He explicates with careful selectivity and refuses to be exhaustive: "more words,"
Swinburne writes, "would possibly not bring with them more
light" (p. 198). Hence Blake's "quasi-technical terms" (p.
281) in the prophecies are probed only as they are needed for
general exposition. In one of his rare glosses Swinburne connects the "seven houses of brick" in the *Marriage* to a "reminiscence of the seven churches of St. John," suggesting that in
Blake one continually finds traces of other prophets. These he
declines to track down, commenting wryly, "Lest however
we be found unawares on the side of these hapless angels and
baboons, we will abstain with all due care from any not in-
dispensable analysis" (p. 200). His book leaves a reader not

19. "Charles Baudelaire," *Works, 13,* 424. See, too, Swinburne's
reaction to William Rossetti's "too reasonable" and "ingenious" suggestions about the roots of Blake's names. [*S. L.,* No. 509, Mar. 5,
[1874], *2,* 286]. For Rossetti on "Los," "Enitharmon," and "Orc,"
see Aldine, p. cxxi.
Swinburne is inconsistent on the subject of Blake's myths. He
praises *Amer* and *Eur* because they contain "more fable and less
allegory"; but he also notes that though divine, the poetry in them
is "divine babble" (p. 196). At another point, he remarks that "of
allegory pure and simple [as opposed to myth] there is scarcely a
trace in Blake" (p. 265).

so much with the sense that exegesis is pedantic and unpoetical
as with the feeling that Blake was unpoetical in writing poems
which need it. The prophetic books emerge from *William
Blake* not really poems; "Formless" and "singular," "sonorous" and "eloquent," and conveying a "floating final impression of power" (pp. 288, 249), they are would-be Scriptures.[20]

The final comprehensive study of the mid-century movement is William Rossetti's long Prefatory Memoir to the
popular Aldine edition; it is a judicious extrapolation from
the work of Gilchrist, Swinburne, and D. G. Rossetti. Mainly,
however, Rossetti follows and substantiates Swinburne's view
of Blake as visionary mystic, "daring speculator in religion and
morals, and enemy of kings and of war," and "inspired seer"
(pp. xxiv–xxv). Rossetti also terms Blake a Pantheist, under-
lines the doctrine of "sensual indulgence," and more exactly
relates Blake to a mystical tradition than did Swinburne,
bringing in analogies to "metempsychosis" (glossing Blake's
remark to Crabb Robinson, "I was Socrates or a sort of
brother") and *"nirvana":* "Rapt in a passionate yearning, he
realized, even on this earth and in his mortal body, a species
of *nirvana*" (pp. lix–xi). Rossetti speculates independently
that Blake may have read "some of the mystical cabalistic

20. These judgments are supported in individual estimates: *Ahan*
is a "fine and sonorous piece of wind-music" (p. 249); *SLos* has "a
contagious power of excitement in the musical passion of its speech."
Meanings aside, "it is impossible to read continuously [all the prophetic books] and not imbibe a certain half-nervous enjoyment from
their long cadences and tempestuous undulations of melody" (p. 257).
On p. 194 he terms them "attempts at gospel."
    Swinburne, followed closely by William Rossetti, characterizes the
form of the books as "regular though quasi-lyrical blank verse" (p.
227; Aldine, p. cxxv); for Rossetti they are "scriptures" (p. cxiii)—
"not exactly prose, nor yet exactly poetry" (p. cxxv).

writers—Paracelsus, Jacob Behmen, Cornelius Agrippa—
and carries out an extended comparison between the doctrines
of Blake and those of the Manichaean mystic Marcion (pp.
lxx–lxxxii).[21]

William Rossetti's literary judgments of the lyrics follow his
brother's; his judgments on *The Marriage of Heaven and Hell*
and *The French Revolution* follow Swinburne's. For the
other prophecies he refers readers to *William Blake;* Rossetti
himself is reluctant to grant that they are either sane or even
potentially consistent.

To the chronic question "Was he mad?" William Rossetti
says "Yes and no." Such an answer to such a question tends
to mean yes:

> it may, I think, be allowable to say that he was a sublime
> genius, often perfectly sane, often visionary and *exalté*
> without precisely losing his hold upon sanity, and some-
> times exhibiting an insane taint.
>
> [p. lxxxix]

Essentially, Rossetti redefines Gilchrist's epithet "enthusiast,"
which in the *Life* carries pure approbation. Blake, says William Rossetti, is an "enthusiast" also in the "older" application
of the word, "a person of morbid spiritual and religious self-
consciousness, a fanatic partly insane," although he is *more
usually* ("in his accustomed moods") "an enthusiast in the
modern sense" of being divinely carried away ("visionary and
exalté") (p. xc). Rossetti's estimate stands as the mid-century
movement's summary word. It met with the approval of Swinburne, who wrote to his friend:

> What you say of his sanity seems to me the sanest thing
> ever said on the certainly difficult subject—but . . . our

21. Palmer had written of Blake's Manichaeanism; Mrs. Gilchrist
was convinced that Swedenborg and Behmen would open up *Jer;* and
both M. D. Conway and James Thomson suggested further investigation into Swedenborgian thought (see Chap. 7).

[Gilchrist, D. G. Rossetti, and Swinburne's] first object (and duty) was to combat with all our might the prevalent lying tradition that Blake was mad in the vulgar sense, a view which of course you agree . . . [is] much further from the truth than the doubtless untenable opposite view that he was always wholly sane, or sound in mind, in the equally vulgar sense.[22]

22. *S. L.*, No. 567, Oct. 30, 1874, *2*, 348.

CHAPTER SEVEN

Legacy of the Revival—Minor Critics

In the preface to their edition of Blake's writings Ellis and
Yeats list Swinburne, the Rossettis, Thomson, and Smetham
as the most important Blake critics to date. The Aldine Prefatory Memoir quoted Thomson and Smetham; it cited and referred readers to Swinburne's criticism (pp. lxvii, cxviii, and
passim). In 1879 Thomson complimented Swinburne; the
1880 edition of Gilchrist's *Life* reprinted Smetham's review,
quoted extensively from Swinburne, and cited Thomson's
work. The mutual support and reinforcement of the mid-
century Blake critics in part reflects personal connections. The
only important writer on Blake at this time who was not an
intimate of anyone in the group was James Thomson. More
important, however, despite their differences, Blakeans and
Blake worshippers of the period shared a common ground as
members of the Culture of the Opposition; their impulse was
less to expand and sharpen interpretation through mutual debate than to use Blake to reinforce the solidarity of a coterie
position. Their immediate collective accomplishment was to
transform Blake into the hero of a religion of beauty who
was consequently rejected or ignored by the Victorian intellectual establishment.

James Smetham, an acquaintance of Linnell and a close
friend of Rossetti, was a poet and a painter of religious subjects; he was an admirer of Ruskin, by whom his work was
held in high regard, and a deeply religious Methodist.
Smetham's life was too inward and retired for him to be regarded as a full-fledged member of the gregarious circle of
poet-painters and painters who worshipped Rossetti and Blake

and who formed Blake's most clearly defined audience; however, between 1863 and 1868 he was in regular communication with Rossetti. His "William Blake," an extended essay appearing as a review of Gilchrist's *Life* (1869),[1] takes as its base Gilchrist's and Rossetti's picture of Blake in the *Life*; Smetham is not, however, much indebted to Rossetti's literary opinions. Nor has he any use for Swinburne's efforts: "And yet an unconquerable indifference to his transcendental philosophy does not in the least interfere with our veneration of the artist, as such" (p. 144).

Smetham presented his readers with a full-fledged cult of beauty with Blake as its patron saint; there is no question that Blake is anything but a specialized taste. The essay is suffused with medievalism and the atmosphere of esoterica, conjuring paneled rooms in a still twilight among rare and precious books. Blake is envisioned as an aesthetic saint, his shrine a combination secret society and Pre-Raphaelite cathedral to which carefully screened members would hold "life-tickets" (p. 191). The "sacred precincts"—"a strong, enduring, greystone, simple building of one long chamber . . . divided into niches"—would contain the *Inventions to Job* "inlaid in a broad gold flat," with the text in "deep brown," something like a Burne-Jones canvas:

> They [i.e. the designs to *Job*] should be executed by men
> . . . like G. F. Watts and D. G. Rossetti, and Madox
> Brown and Burne-Jones, and W. B. Scott. At the inner

1. "William Blake," *Literary Works of James Smetham*, ed. William Davies, pp. 98–194; reprinted from "Gilchrist's *Life of William Blake*," *London Quarterly Review, 31* (Jan. 1869), 265–311. For Smetham's life, see "Memoir of Smetham" [1821–89] by William Davies, *The Letters of James Smetham*, eds. Sarah Smetham and William Davies (London, 1892), pp. 1–45. For Smetham and Rossetti, see *D. G. Rossetti: His Family Letters, 1,* 192–93 and 351. On Smetham's acquaintance with Gilchrist see "Journal for 1861," *Letters of Smetham*, p. 110, and *Anne Gilchrist*, p. 57. Smetham's essay was extracted in the *Life* at the suggestion of Rossetti (A. L. to Mrs. Gilchrist, Apr. 26, 1880, Thorne Coll.).

end of this hall of power there should be a marble statue
of Blake by Woolner. . . . He should be standing on a
rock . . . overlapped by pale, marmoreal flames.

[p. 191]

Twenty-five years later Andrew Lang wrote, "To admire
Blake is the mark of a clique"; Laurence Housman recalled
how in the 1890s he copied and worshipped two painter-poets,
D. G. Rossetti and William Blake.[2]

Smetham is mainly interested in Blake as a graphic artist;
he deals with Blake's literary work as accessory to or else
intertwined with the illustrations. Moreover, he refuses to
proceed further into the poetry than *Songs of Innocence*; beyond this he finds Blake's statement dim and insane.[3] Blake's
thought is dismissed without investigation; Smetham regrets
that it should have existed at all:

> As to any serious consideration of Blake's vocation to
> teach aught of morals; of theology, or non-theology; of
> Christian Atheism, or Atheistic Christianity; we . . .
> "calmly, but firmly and finally," on a general glance at
> the tone and tenor of these portentous scrolls of *Thel,*
> and *Urizen,* these *Marriages of Heaven and Hell,* which
> would look blasphemous if we did not tenderly recollect

2. Laurence Housman, *The Unexpected Years* (New York, Bobbs-
Merrill Co., 1936), pp. 98, 100, and 109. Others associated with the
Rossetti circle who participated in the Blake revival were W. B. Scott
and F. J. Shields. Shields, an "ardent worshipper" (A. L., Rossetti to
Mrs. Gilchrist, Mar. 3, 1880, Thorne Coll.), supplied "Descriptive
Notes" to *NT* and copied three of Blake's pencil sketches for the
1880 *Life;* he also designed the cover (see Ernestine Mills, *The Life
and Letters of Frederick James Shields,* 1833–1911 [London, John
Castle, 1925], pp. 254–57).

3. "If we say . . . at once that . . . he was 'slightly touched,'
we shall save ourselves the necessity of attempting to defend certain
phases of his work, while maintaining an unqualified admiration for
the mass and manner of the thoughts" (pp. 121–22).

by whom they were written, refuse any serious further
investigation of their claims, and must dismiss them, not
scornfully, though it may be sorrowfully. We regard
them as we regard the gentle or exalted incoherences of a
dear friend's delirium.

[p. 145]

Smetham's approach to the problem of Blake's vision is
surprisingly commonsensical, if ingenious. He reconstructs
the angelic visions described in Gilchrist so as to render them
neither supernatural nor experientially absurd:

It was in no green-topped suburban tree that he saw
the heavenly visitants; we must rather suppose him re-
turning after the oxygen of the Surrey hill winds had
exalted his nerves, among the orchards of some vale into
which the last rays of the sun shine with their setting
splendours. Here he pauses, leans over a gate, looks at a
large, blossom-loaded tree in which the threads of sun-
light are entangled like gossamers, which "twinkle into
green and gold." A zephyr stirs the cloud of sun-stricken
bloom, where white commingled with sparkling red
flushes over leaves of emerald. Tears of boyish delight
"rise from his heart, and gather to his eyes" as he gazes
on it. The *rays* which kindle the blossoms *turn his
gathered tears to prisms,* through which snow-white and
ruby blooms, shaken along with the leaf-emeralds,
quiver and dance. The impressible brain, already filled
with thoughts of the "might of stars and angels," kindles
suddenly into a dream-like creative energy and the sunny
orchard becomes a Mahanaim, even *to his outward eye.*

[pp. 111–12. Italics mine]

The exalted and delicate pitch of Blake's sensibility is his chief
value in Smetham's view. In his illustrations, primarily, Blake
is a source of religious inspiration, of "winged and fiery
imagery which will be useful to us in our attempts to realise

things invisible, in so far as the elements of matter may bridge
over for our conceptive faculties the gap between the seen
and the unseen" (p. 146).

Smetham similarly insists, despite Blake's protestations that
natural objects and the natural model were a hindrance to
imaginative art, the artist could never dispense utterly with
outer forms: even for the lineaments of the "Ghost of a Flea,"
the work in which Blake carried "realistic idealism" to its
"utmost verge," he is indebted to the human skull.

> The solemn boundaries of form become ridiculous when
> they wander without enclosing some expressive fact
> visible to the eye either in heaven above or in earth
> beneath, and the question only remains, *How much* of
> this array of fact is needful adequately to convey the
> *given idea?*
>
> [pp. 125–26]

Smetham, in fact, regrets Blake's failure to augment his
"mighty faculty of conception" with "that scientific appre-
hensiveness which, when so conjoined, never fails to issue in
an absolute and permanent greatness" (p. 103). Nevertheless, Blake's genuine inspiration is so sacred to Smetham
that he hastens to advise:

> let us not spoil one of the most original and charming of
> the many joys to be found "in stray gifts to be claimed
> by whoever shall find" along the meads of art, by hanker-
> ing after what will not be found, or quarrelling with what
> we cannot mend.
>
> [p. 103]

Blake is made a touchstone for the purest taste in works of
imagination—for appreciation of inspiration unadorned, in-
artificial, without affectation: "If we wished by a single question to sound the depth of a man's mind and capacity for the

judgment of works of pure imagination, we know of none we should be so content to put as this one, 'What think you of William Blake?' " (pp. 100–01).[4]

It is not Blake's recorded personality which Smetham values—in fact, he finds the man "difficult and repulsive" on close contact (p. 142). What he reveres is the inspired religious soul, capable of transcendence, which is manifested in the works in which Blake is faithful to his highest genius. Moreover, where this is in evidence, as in Blake's woodcuts to Thornton's edition of the *Pastorals* and in the designs to *Job*, Smetham almost seems to find the works more sacred by virtue of their technical imperfections. It is his profound and solemn concentration upon the inward person that distinguishes Smetham's Blake-worship from that of the other "medieval" Blakeans. Smetham has transformed Gilchrist's "enthusiast" into a religious-aesthetic monk, thereby making Blake even more remote: an almost entirely disembodied image for contemplation; a figure who never was and never could be centrally relevant in any age.

When young George Saintsbury reviewed the Aldine Blake, he warned of the danger of "wilfully seeing beauty where there is mere deformity and sense where there is nonsense." He had read eagerly the *Poems and Ballads* at Oxford,[5] felt himself liberated by Swinburne's generation from self-contradictions and restraints, and took for granted an autonomous art. His review, a revaluation of Blake's accomplishment, synthesizes the criticism of Swinburne and the Rossettis. But he applies a more rigid aestheticism than his mentors: Blake, he says, was a poet only until he was blighted by the "heresy of instruction." Both here and in his *History of Nineteenth Cen-*

4. He also wrote "If a man can see and feel that which makes Blake what he is, he can see and feel anything" (*Letters of Smetham*, p. 336; dated 1874).

5. "Review of the Aldine Blake"; see Chap. 5, n. 46. Unless specified, quotations from Saintsbury are from this article (pp. 599–601). On Saintsbury's reading, see Wimsatt and Brooks, p. 485.

tury Literature Saintsbury finds error in everything after *Poetical Sketches.* Even in *Songs of Innocence and of Experience,* "The poet is no longer a poet pure and simple; he has got purposes and messages, and these partly strangle and partly render turbid the clear and spontaneous jets of poetry." [6] Dismissing the *Everlasting Gospel* as an overpraised piece of "controversial versification" Saintsbury takes his teachers to task for their poetic tone-deafness and their weakness for "purposes and messages": "Its inward heterodoxy will not be very shocking to people who have got over being easily shocked, but its outward huskiness cannot be acceptable to any who prefer good prose to doubtful verse."

Saintsbury also brushes aside the question of madness or oddity: "The man is dead, the work lives." Although he is rigorous on its irrelevance to aesthetics, Saintsbury nonetheless takes Swinburne's argument further and defends Blake's type of insanity. Admit that Blake was both "superior" and mad, he recommends, instead of insisting that he was sane; conclude that "some madness does not of necessity imply inferiority." No intrinsic connection, however, is demonstrated between poetic obscurity, madness, and greatness. Ultra-aesthete that he is, Saintsbury appears as a forerunner of the doctrine of "pure" poetry by going so far as to argue the positive value of obscurity. He defends the use of ambiguity[7]

6. *A History of Nineteenth Century Literature* (*1780–1895*) [1896] (New York, 1931), p. 12. In all points Saintsbury here reaffirms his 1874 estimate. He discusses Blake in a chapter on pre-Romantic poets (Chap. 1, "The End of the Eighteenth Century"), as critics generally did prior to the twentieth century—reflecting Gilchrist's classification of Blake as a precursor of Wordsworth, and the nineteenth-century practice of reading and regarding as poetry chiefly those works by Blake written (or dated) before about 1793. (To this Swinburne is of course an exception.)

7. A long passage by Saintsbury on the "Mad Song" justifies William Rossetti's (really Shepherd's) restoration of "beds of dawn" (which Southey and Gilchrist print as "birds of dawn" [see Chap. 5]) on the grounds that "beds" is appropriate to a poem where the

and praises "Long John Brown and Little Mary Bell" because it leaves scope for conjectural interpretations. The stricture that had made it a difficult exercise to affirm Blake's greatness as a poet (or painter)—that artistic genius must communicate clearly[8]—gives way here to a position that has no need to make allowances for a "special case." As art itself grows more autonomous and more special in theory and practice, Blake becomes less exceptional within the general extreme.

For the poet and radical journalist James Thomson, reviewing Gilchrist's *Life* in 1866,[9] poetry by definition meant esotericism. "Indeed, I doubt whether it would be an exag-

---

"whole imagery . . . is atmospheric and daemonic, ordinary things being nowhere introduced."

A revival of debate about Blake's sanity did not discourage the Blakeans of the 1870s. J. Beavington Atkinson remarked that in the East, "men of a certain twist of intellect are gifted with insight into the world of spirits" ("Exhibition of Works of William Blake, Burlington Club," *Portfolio*, 7 [May 1876], 67). On the Burlington Club show of Blake's works, see pp. 183 ff. below. For the debate on Blake's sanity, see Wilson, *Life of William Blake*, Chap. 3; and Chap. 3, n. 21.

8. The *Athenaeum*'s reviewer in 1863 (see Chap. 2, n. 26), classed Blake with the world's greatest artists, writers, and thinkers in innate "genius"; and then exempted him, on the basis of execution, from art, literature, and philosophy: Shakespeare, Spenser, Milton, Michelangelo, and others of "great wit," he asserts, were "clear." Another critic spoke of Blake's "tone of thought" as superior to his "power of embodying it" (*New Monthly Magazine* [see Chap. 4, n. 22], p. 316.)

9. "The Poems of William Blake," *Biographical and Critical Studies* (see Chap. 5, n. 35), pp. 240–69; reprinted from a review signed with Thomson's pseudonym "B. V." (Bysshe Vanolis for Shelley and Novalis), *National Reformer, N. S.,* 7 (Jan. 14, 21, and 28; and Feb. 4, 1866), 22–23; 42–43; 54–55; and 70–71.

Thomson introduced himself to William Rossetti with suggestions about editing Shelley. Rossetti's commendation in the Aldine Prefatory Memoir and Thomson's own reputation as a poet advanced recognition of his essay, which was reprinted with Thomson's *Shelley: A Poem* (London, 1884).

geration to assert that for a very large majority of those who
are accounted educated and intelligent people, poetry in itself is essentially an unknown tongue" (p. 259). This is because the language of poetry in Thomson's theory has its
origin in a condition of alienation:

> Every man living in seclusion and developing an intense
> interior life, gradually comes to give a quite peculiar
> significance to certain words and phrases and emblems.
> . . . His writings must thus appear, to any one reading
> them for the first time, very obscure, and often very
> ludicrous.

[p. 258]

On this basis, though he had not read them, Thomson defended the probable significance of the prophetic books
against doubts and equivocal descriptions in Gilchrist's Life.

In the Aldine Blake William Rossetti quoted Thomson's
defense of Blake's obscurity; it became part of a general
apology for obscure art when in 1879 Thomson quoted himself.[10] However when he speaks here (in 1866) of an "intense interior life," Thomson is speaking primarily of the
language of mysticism, which may or may not express itself
in poetry. He read Gilchrist's *Life* with a knowledge of Emerson and *The Human Body and Its Connection With Man,* a
book in which Garth Wilkinson tries to reconcile scientific
method with Swedenborgian correspondences. Wilkinson cited
Blake's "The Divine Image" together with George Herbert's

10. In 1879 Thomson wrote an essay on J. J. Garth Wilkinson's
Improvisations from the Spirit (1856), entitled "A Strange Book," *The
Liberal* (Sept., Oct., Nov., and Dec. 1879); it appears in *Biographical
and Critical Studies,* pp. 289–371. It deals in great part with Blake,
whose method of writing Wilkinson claimed to have imitated in his
"Improvisations," or automatic poems. Pages 321–23 and 326–32
contain an account of poetic inspiration as a divine afflatus in which
Thomson, quoting from Plato's *Ion* and Shelley's "Defense of Poetry,"
argues the interrelatedness of divine inspiration, poetic inspiration,
obscurity, and madness.

"On Man" as "two glorious scientific songs." [11] Thomson applied the principle of correspondences to *Songs of Innocence and of Experience,* adopting Rossetti's view of them and of Blake (and Wilkinson's as well), and concluded that the *Songs* were a psychical analogue to childhood breathing; they came from a man who had become, spiritually, a child [12] (see Chap. 5). Blake "did not *act* the infantine, for he *was* infantine, by a regeneration as real while as mysterious as ever purest saint experienced in the religious life" (p. 252 n.).

Blake, to Thomson, is not the mystic of systems: "more purely a mystic than Swedenborg, he does not condescend to dialectics and scholastic divinity" (p. 252 n.); but Thomson's account of Blake's mode of perception draws on Swedenborg as well as on the poetry of Vaughan and later seventeenth-century religious meditations.

> It [this spirit of mysticism] sees, and is continually rapturous with seeing, everywhere correspondences, kindred, identity, not only in the things and creatures of earth, but in all things and creatures and beings of hell and earth and heaven, up to the one father (or interiorly to the soul) of all. . . . And the whole universe being the volume of the Scriptures of the living word of God.
>
> [p. 261]

The tendency of this mysticism, "passionately and profoundly religious, contemplating and treating every subject religiously" and admitting the "beings of hell" (p. 252 n.), accords with Swinburne's "pantheistic evangel" in a common and widely contemporary impulse to consecrate the secular, if not the

11. Garth Wilkinson, *The Human Body* . . . (Philadelphia, 1851), pp. 319–20.

12. "What is true of common breathing is true more conspicuously of breathing idealised and harmonised, of the breathing of songs in which psychical have superseded the physical rhythms. The adult cannot sing like a child; but Blake in these Songs does so" (p. 252 n.). See pp. 251–53 n.

sacrilegious. Writing two years before the appearance of Swinburne's exposition of Blake, Thomson finds this spirit "by no means strict in its theology, being Swedenborgian in one man and Pantheistic in another" (p. 262).

For all his sympathy with those whom he saw as true mystics, Thomson never abandoned scientific values and a secular attitude; he held that some day physiology would be able to explain what is unique about the perceptions of "Blake and Swedenborg and other true mystics (Jesus among them)" who "undoubtedly had senses other than ours." His assurances of a material cause reflected the views of many Victorians seriously concerned with psychical phenomena. In the more influential essay of 1866 Thomson wrote only that "it is as futile to argue against the reality of their perceptions [those of mystics] as it would be false in us to pretend that our perceptions are the same" (p. 253 n.). (Later writers saw such senses as Blake's unreservedly in the light of the supernatural.)

Thomson also reflects mid-Victorian thought when he tries to assimilate evolutionist thinking into a developmental history of the spirit. As did D. G. Rossetti, he saw in Blake the poetic seeds of that trait of mystical simplicity growing in his own time which eventually would bear fruit:

> [It is] in this second childhood and boyhood and youth [Thomson means here *SI, SE,* and the MS poems, respectively], when he was withdrawn from common life into mysticism, when moonlight was his sunlight, and water was his wine, and the roses red as blood were become all white as snow, in the "Songs of Innocence," (always Innocence, mark, not *Virtue*) that the seeds may be traced of much which is now half-consciously struggling towards organic perfection, and which in two or three generations may be crowned with foliage and blossoms and fruit as the Tree of Life for one epoch.

[pp. 260–61]

The poets who are part of this growth are not the more popularly accepted idols such as Tennyson, Wordsworth, Scott, and Byron, but rather Coleridge, Keats (potentially), Browning, Mrs. Browning, Shelley "to the uttermost," and finally Ralph Waldo Emerson, who "stands closest of all in relation to Blake" (p. 267).[13]

After Thomson read Swinburne's *William Blake,* in his 1879 article he harmonized the Blake of the *Marriage* and the *Visions of the Daughters of Albion* with the mystical innocent of his early review, welcoming Blake into the company of political and social rebels:

> I perceive much likeness between Blake and Shelley
> . . . (as Swinburne does in several places) certain rare and conspicuous identical traits: their dauntless devotion to political and religious liberty; their impassioned and yet more daring advocacy of sexual freedom; their reanimation and ardent propagation of the great doctrine . . . that in the appalling and unintermitted struggle between the spirits of good and evil, the evil has hitherto prevailed.
>
> [p. 317]

A new note in the essay is Thomson's placement of Blake in a genealogy of mystical writers; this appears in the context of Wilkinson's theory of automatic writing. Wilkinson's "theory of Divine inspiration," "allowing your faculties to be directed to ends they know not of," is no other than "the fundamental principle of all mysticism,"

> from the most ancient Indian gymnosophists to the Hebrew prophets and poets, to Christian apostles, as Paul and John, to Plato and Plotinus, to Mohammed

13. For Thomson's early admiration of Carlyle and Emerson, see his essays on Shelley (*Biographical and Critical Studies*, pp. 270–82 and 283–88). In "A Strange Book," he quotes *English Traits and Representative Men* to show Emerson's admiration for Wilkinson.

and the Sufis, to early and mediaeval Christian eremites
and saints with their trances and ecstasies, to George Fox
and his Quakers, walking by the interior light and waiting to be moved by the Spirit, to Behmen and Law, to
Swedenborg and Blake, to Shelley with his opening of
"Alastor," his "Hymn to Intellectual Beauty," his "De-
fence of Poetry," his "Ode to Liberty."

[pp. 325–27]

Moncure Conway, who reviewed Swinburne's book from
the standpoint of an American transcendentalist and political
liberal, took up the interpretation of *America*.[14] On the basis
of this work he sees Blake as an early prophet of transcendental democracy. Blake inaugurated an "era of rebound"
against the "prevalent and inadequate materialism" of Thomas
Paine against which he pitted his own vision of a "heavenly
Jerusalem" on the American continent. Conway wrote that
Paine's ideal was being "transcendentalized" along Blakean
lines "in the re-ascent of mystical beliefs which have taken
the form of transcendentalism among the cultivated and
spiritism with the vulgar." Blake was an early voice crying,
"All deities reside in the human breast." Religious mysticism
had come more and more to admit nature (by which Conway
and other mid-century Blakeans mean not only human but
external nature) and to simplify its traditional symbols to
accord with the "extension of civil liberty" in an ever-growing
"emancipation from the letter." Finally, in an amalgam of
nature-worship, mysticism, and radical politics which is
uniquely of the time and which spells out in detail the sugges-

14. *Fortnightly Review* (see Chap. 6, n. 7); quotations are from
pp. 217 and 218. Conway, a Unitarian minister, was more secular
religionist than religious secularist as Swinburne and Thomson; he
is dubious about Blake's antinomianism.

For another discussion of Blake as a prophet of release, see W. A.
Cram's review of Swinburne, "William Blake," *The Radical, 3* ([Bos-
ton], Feb. 1868), 378–82.

tions in Swinburne, Conway says that Whitman has come to
fulfill what Blake had only prophesied in the wilderness.

> With Blake the soul of the current theology which still
> haunted Swedenborg is utterly dead and trampled on;
> but he has not been able to rid himself of its body of
> language and images, however he may force these to
> strange and for them suicidal services. Nature, without
> and within, with all her powers and passions, is vindi-
> cated and worshipped; but these claim to be baptized and
> struggle for Christian shrines, and to supersede church
> saints in the same niches. . . . This strange fire . . .
> has burst forth again in the large and free genius of Walt
> Whitman, by whom the traditional and theological lan-
> guages and form are entirely ignored.
>
> [pp. 217–18]

If Blake was a prophet, and many believed that he was,
where did his prophecies come from? It was inevitable, given
the experimentalistic bent of the time, that Blakeans should
search all the nooks and crannies of scientific and pseudo-
scientific doctrine to find the source of Blake's visions, if not
his vision. Mrs. Gilchrist was struck in the 1860s by how
remarkable it was that "the latest views of science corroborate
Blake and the mystics in regarding everything as Force
Power." Swinburne encouraged the search into the occult
when he pictured Blake's "twofold" vision in the language of
the spiritist—the "veil of outer things seemed always to tremble with some breath behind it" (p. 41)—or else into Eastern
thought when he concluded that Blake's concurrences with
Whitman were "so many and so grave, as to afford some
ground of reason to those who preach the transition of souls
or transfusion of spirits" (p. 300). Conway acknowledged
the connection when he noted that the mysticism in "Plotinus,

Behmen, Swedenborg, Blake" was now "running to seed . . . in Andrew Jackson Davis and the modern Spiritists." Charles Eliot Norton, the New England intellectual, a correspondent of Ruskin and of D. G. Rossetti, wrote in a review generally sympathetic to Blake that one could account for the most obscure and mystical passages in Blake only by reference to automatic writing as practiced by American spiritists.[15] Thomson saw Blake's inspiration as Divine; but automatic writing had more profane than sacred adherents. (The time was one in which spiritist phenomena, even of the table-knocking sort, interested and were found convincing by the cultivated. Wilkinson, Patmore [briefly], W. B. Scott, Tennyson [briefly], his brother Frederick, Mrs. Browning, and others were firmly persuaded; William Rossetti, Swinburne, D. G. Rossetti, Dickens, and Milnes attended seances in the 1860s. In 1882 the Society for Psychical Research was founded with Henry Sidgwick, Cambridge professor of moral philosophy, as its first president.)

From the point of view of the scientific spiritualist, Seymour Kirkup regretted Blake's lack of method. He wrote to William Rossetti in 1866,

> I don't think [Blake] a madman now. . . . [His] sanity seemed doubtful because he could only give his word for the truth of his visions. There were no other proofs; such as, with the most . . . scrupulous . . . investigation have been for eleven years by me directed to the subject. . . . [We] never die . . . [but after] a sleep of about twenty minutes . . . disencumbered like some of Blake's visions, [we] are free, and as happy as our temper will allow.[16]

15. Review of Pickering's editions of *SIE*, 1866, and *PS*, 1868; and of Hotten's facsimile of *MHH* (1868), *North American Review*, *108* (April 1869), 644–46. For Mrs. Gilchrist, see *Anne Gilchrist*, p. 159; for Conway, *Fortnightly Review*, p. 216.
16. *Rossetti Papers: 1862–70*, pp. 171–72.

The only Blakean of importance, before Yeats, who actually stated that Blake saw beyond the veil was William Bell Scott, who interpreted Blake through Varley's eyes. Scott helped the Blake revival by etching Blake's works, writing about him, and, most importantly, by preparing the first one man show of Blake's works after 1809, presented by the Burlington Fine Arts Club in April 1876. He also wrote an introduction for the exhibition's catalogue. To Scott Blake was a "practical mystic," who, though innocent of spiritism, had pre-intimated the "new Spiritualism" which was then flourishing. In Blake's "The Birth of Eve" he saw "the Creator evoking the Form of Eve out of Adam by an action of His hand, exactly similar to that of the Spiritualist of our day." [17] The catalogue introduction asserts that Blake's inspiration came from sources upon which no other artist had ever drawn.

Once it became clear that Blake was no longer a neglected genius, many began to be irritated by the cliquishness of his disciples and the extravagant claims they made for him. The Burlington Club exhibition became the occasion for reaction to express itself since it presented the non-Pre-Raphaelite public with its first exposure to a great deal of Blake's work. Indeed, for many who thought they admired Blake but whose enthusiasm had been based on their acceptance of the claims of Gilchrist, Rossetti, and Swinburne, the exhibition was a disappointment. W. B. Scott himself came to conclude that "too liberal praise" had made Blake "both as poet and painter, as much overestimated as he was [once] neglected." F. T. Palgrave reported to his friend W. E. Gladstone that there was "much puerility, much almost sensational spiritualism, much even (I suspect) of commonplace concealed by eccentricity of manner." Less sympathetically disposed observers of art and letters found occasion to attack Blake's status as mystical

17. "A Varley-and-Blake Sketch-Book," *Portfolio*, 2 (1871), 103; and *William Blake: Etchings from His Works* (London, 1878), p. 4.

prophet and teacher.[18] The Catholic poet Francis Thompson,
seeing his prejudices confirmed, thought

> It was nearly all utter rubbish. . . . . He does not seem
> to have been mad, but only to have assumed a sort of
> voluntary madness of freedom from convention in order
> to make himself original. . . . . He reminds me of that
> "pet lamb" we had . . . who imperceptibly grew into
> a strong pet ram, and was still called the "pet lamb,"
> until suddenly it dawned on us that it was not a lamb at
> all, but a very ill-behaved ram assuming the airs and
> privileges of his infancy.[19]

Two direct attacks appeared in reviews of the exhibition—
really reassessments of Blake—by Coventry Patmore and
Henry G. Hewlett.[20]

Hewlett, father of the novelist Maurice Hewlett, was an

18. Scott, *Autobiographical Notes, 1,* 23; G. F. Palgrave, pp. 146–
47. Scott's sonnet on again seeing his favorite designs to *The Grave*
explains, "I see/ An inspiration in art little skilled" (p. 24). See, too,
"An Exploded Idol," *Saturday Review, 41* (Apr. 15, 1876), 492–93;
and J. Beavington Atkinson, *Portfolio,* 71 and 68. Critics cited Blake's
plagiarisms from Michael Angelo, his over-literalism (in *NT*), his
faulty anatomy, and his obscurity—in fact, the conventional objections of an earlier day, but new to people who had not seen Blake's
work.

19. *Literary Criticisms,* ed. Rev. T. L. Connolly, S. J. (New York,
E. P. Dutton, 1948), p. 217. According to W. S. Blunt, young Thompson had no books but "Blake and his Bible" (*My Diaries . . . 1888–
1914* [2 vols. New York, Knopf, 1921], *2,* 182); if Blunt is to be
trusted, then apparently Thompson changed his opinion.

20. Patmore, "Blake" [1876], *Principle in Art, Etc.* (London,
1889), pp. 97–102; reprinted from *St. James' Gazette.* Hewlett, "Imperfect Genius," *Contemporary Review, 28* and *29* (Oct. 1876 and
Jan. 1877), 756–84 and 207–28 (see Chap. 5, n. 27). For information
on Hewlett's life see *The Letters of Maurice Hewlett,* ed. Laurence
Binyon, with an Introductory Memoir by Edward Hewlett (London,
Methuen, 1926), pp. 3–6. References to Patmore's life and views are
from J. C. Reid, *The Mind and Art of Coventry Patmore* (New York,
Macmillan, 1957), pp. 188–89; also pp. 66–68, 197, and 320.

Antiquarian lawyer for the Crown; he was an agnostic who felt betrayed when all his children turned into worshipping Christians. Politically he was a Liberal and a faithful Gladstonian. Patmore, the "mystical poet" and celebrator of married love, had been a Swedenborgian but became a Roman Catholic in 1857 or 1858. Politically, he was ultraconservative, even reactionary.

> [The] world is not and never will be made up of Swinburnes and [William] Rossettis, and . . . it is vain to denounce popular beliefs and institutions, when he [the poet of protest] has only to set up in their places others which are, and forever will be unintelligible by the great majority of mankind, and inapplicable to their demands. The people will always insist on having kings and priests.[21]

Although quite divergent in their basic beliefs, Hewlett and Patmore aimed at the same target—the claims that Blake's inspiration came from special sources, and the glorifying of madness, obscurity, and rebellion. Patmore, however, much the more partisan, reviles all forms of revolt, stigmatizes William Rossetti as "an enthusiast" for the Paris commune, and damns at once Blake, his "craziness," and the irresponsibility of his advocates.

> For the time, however, the manikin type of genius is all the fashion, especially with a class of critics who have it in their power to give notoriety, if they cannot give fame. Craziness alone passes at present for a strong presumption of genius, and where genius is really found in company therewith it is at once pronounced "supreme." This is partly because . . . the manikin mind is always red republican and ardent in its hatred of kings, priests,

21. "Mr. Swinburne's Selections," in *Principle in Art, Etc.,* p. 113. See also "The Poetry of Negation" in which Hugo and Carlyle are seen as fools when dealing with "real" problems.

"conventions," the "monopoly" of property and of women, and all other hindrances put in the way of virtue, liberty, and happiness by the wicked "civilizee."

[p. 101] [22]

Only "four or five lovely lyrics and here and there in the other pieces a startling gleam of unquestionable genius" constitute Blake's poetic claims; everything else is "mere drivel" (p. 97) or "delirious rubbish" (p. 99).

Hewlett's objections to the Blake clique are the protest of a nineteenth-century liberal who has rid himself of the worn-out mysteries of one religion only to find that more obscure and more exclusive inferior cults are rising up to replace it. The traditional regard for great poets as great teachers has been transformed into the religion of art, deification not only of the acknowledged great but of erratic genius as well, especially genius wrapped in "ever-thickening veils of enigmatic symbolism which may give it the aspect of revelation."

> There has been of late years, a growing tendency to the worship of indefiniteness in art, and the supply of candidates for divine honours is likely to grow with the demand. . . . Upon some minds another . . . influence [is] the exquisite fascination of belonging to the esoteric circle of disciples . . . who . . . possess the secret . . . denied to the multitude . . . [a] school [which] proclaims itself too palpably in the scornful words which they delight to fling at the Philistines and Boeotians, who will not, or cannot join them in adoration.
>   . . . The wilder his dreams and the more extravagant

22. For William Rossetti's allusion to "the much maligned Paris Commune" see Aldine, p. lxxxi. Patmore's virulence may also be a reaction to Rossetti's sympathetic explanation of Blake's view of "sensual indulgence": "Man the free divine spirit, was at liberty to do, and right in doing, whatsoever his spiritual essence dictated—he was a law to himself, and none other law existed" (see the entire passage, pp. lxxxiii–lxxxiv).

his utterances, the more likely are they to be accepted as gospel by those who find beauty in chaos, and have no scruple about upsetting social fabrics which they cannot rebuild.[23]

Reminding his readers that no one initially connected with the revival, with the possible exception of Gilchrist, ever claimed Blake's inspiration was supernatural, Hewlett then asks, if Blake's "credentials . . . are no higher than those of other artists and teachers in all ages, what justification is there for the emphasis so persistently laid upon them? Why should we be so often assured of his 'visionary' faculty and 'INSPIRED' utterance"? (pp. 773–74). He then applies particularly the criterion of poetic originality to Blake's writings in order to show Blake's limitations. He deals with him as a poet who wrote in an age of poetic revival, who took as his models the Elizabethans and whose works are part of the canon of late eighteenth-century poetry. Hewlett is the first (and only) nineteenth-century Blake critic systematically to list specific analogues for *Poetical Sketches* and, to a lesser extent, for *Songs of Innocence and of Experience,* from Spenser, Milton, and Shakespeare and from Ossian and Isaac Watts. Moreover, he says that Blake consciously adopted Elizabethan and Miltonic views of poetry in claiming divine inspiration.

Discrediting Blake as a great teacher, Hewlett concludes that his genius (as measured by standards of originality, fertility of ideas, fullness and maintenance of power, coherence of thought, and articulateness) was "imperfect," "eccentric," "fitful and nebulous." And one might be inclined to say that Hewlett's opinion is a fair example of what most of the prominent mid- and late Victorians thought about Blake, except that there appears to be no evidence that any of them ever did give him a thought. That the nature of the revival should cut him off from the mainstream of thought and letters was clear as early as 1864 when the anonymous *Westminster* re-

23. "Imperfect Genius," p. 759.

viewer objected to holding up as exemplary a personality
which was exclusive and inwardly directed rather than social
and humanitarian. Because they rely solely on inner conviction and repudiate the world outside as obstacle or deformity,
mystics like William Law, Behmen, and Blake are potentially
anarchical. The reviewer quotes, *"Wie ein jeder ist, so ist sein
Gott."* A mind such as Blake's sees each man as solitary and
beginning anew; it rejects the idea of a "race" of men or of
"progress of the race." [24]

There is no available evidence that Matthew Arnold,[25]
George Eliot, Charles Dickens, Leslie Stephen, Herbert Spen-
cer, or even William Morris ever read Blake's poems. Writing
in 1905 Paul Elmer More remarked:

> We find something closer to our understanding, some-
> thing for that reason wholesomer, in men like Words-
> worth and Goethe. . . . For after all it is not the office
> of the true poet to baffle the longing heart with the
> charms of self-deception, and we are men in a world of
> men.[26]

Whether seen as pure poet, pure mystic, or pure sensibility,
Blake apparently stood for the delusive appeal of idle dream-
worlds. He would scarcely appeal to ethical and humanitarian

24. *Westminster Review* (see Chap. 4, n. 22), p. 103.

25. In an essay on John Tauler Arnold wrote: " 'I love the mystics,
but what I find best in them is their single golden sentences, not the
whole conduct of their argument and the result of their work' "
(Lionel Trilling, *Matthew Arnold* [New York, Columbia University
Press, 1949], p. 377). Arnold's "The Study of Poetry" omits Blake
from the Company of great poets; this in 1880. Other omissions, as
Trilling notes, are Marlowe and Jonson; Donne, Marvell, Herbert, and
Vaughan.

26. Quotations from More in this paragraph are taken from "William Blake," *Shelburne Essays,* Ser. 4 (New York, 1906), pp. 237–38;
reprinted from the *New York Evening Post.* The essay was originally a
review of Sampson's edition.

The opposite of "sincerity" for More and his age would be "affectation" (which aestheticism frequently courted).

writers and thinkers. In addition, More saw Blake's *valuers* as humanly deficient and involved Blake in this estimate.

> The unmitigated admiration and the effective influence of Blake are to be found not among the greater romantic writers of the early nineteenth century, but among the lesser men—Rossetti, Swinburne and their school—who in one way or another have shrunk from the higher as well as the lower realities of life.

Defining the "realities of life" as ethical and social, and accepting Gilchrist's image of Blake, More sees Blake's readers willfully abdicating adult intelligence when they read the *Songs of Innocence.* He cannot picture Blake as intentionally insincere; the tradition of a simple child, never "double-minded," is too strong.

> The result of Blake's method is in one sense paradoxical. He was himself the sincerest of poets; his faculty of immediate contact is perfectly genuine, and yet the mood induced in most readers is one perilously akin to affectation. We feel the aerial transparency and the frail loveliness of his inspiration . . . —but only for awhile and at rare intervals. For the most part a little investigation will detect a slight note of insincerity in our enjoyment and, having discovered this, we fall back on the poets who accept fully the experience of the human heart.

CHAPTER EIGHT

The Ellis-Yeats Edition

Based on the work of the mid-century revival, Blake's position, that of a minor literary classic, rested on his lyrical poems; if anything, his prophetic books impeded any fuller reputation as a poet. During the 1880s these were appreciated mainly as beautiful *books* by the collectors, artists, and poet-painters in the Rossetti circle. As objects the engraved books influenced English Art Nouveau furniture and book design. But they were not printed, because those who thus admired them did not read them.[1]

Most critics never ventured beyond the lyrics and the *Marriage,* reading Swinburne only as confirmation that the prophecies were aberrations of an overwrought sensibility. Saintsbury spoke of Blake's "delight in sound . . . separated from sense." One reviewer thought that "No man [was] bound to

1. For the publication of Blake's prophetic books, including facsimile editions, see Appendix. Swinburne, who might have influenced publishers, was averse to printing Blake's text without his illustrations (*S. L.,* No. 259, *1,* 294). On the whole, therefore, Blake's audience and his promoters remained pretty well within the community of aesthetes (e.g., see n. 17 below). Bernard Quaritch, for instance, a most active collector, publisher of Blake facsimiles and also of EY which is sometimes referred to as the Quaritch Blake, was a man who never read a book, and never looked at a picture "except on vellum" (Allingham, *A Diary,* p. 349). Quaritch issued a series *Seen and Sung,* done by poet-painters, which took as model Blake's illuminated books; one of the volumes was *Seen in Three Days* (London, 1893), "Written, Drawn, & Tinted by Edwin J. Ellis."

See Robert Schmutzler, "Blake and Art Nouveau," *Architectural Review, 107* (Aug. 1955), 90–97. In 1883, Frederick J. Shields (see Chap. 7, n. 2) was working with Mackmurdo.

understand so vague a writer." W. B. Scott doubted that Blake had sufficient learning or the mental temper to read Paracelsus or Swedenborg as William Rossetti claimed; along with other sympathetic Blakeans, Scott would have been disappointed to discover that he had.[2]

In fact, Swinburne in the end had discouraged attempts to read the books for consistent meaning: "many voices might be heard crying in this wilderness before the paths were made straight" (p. 199). The popular Aldine edition reprinted the passage from Swinburne cautioning readers against attempting to "plant a human foot upon the soil of the newly-divided shires and counties" or to straighten out the sums and divisions "in the twelves, twenty-fours, and twenty-sevens" of *Jerusalem* (Swinburne, p. 282; Aldine, p. cxxviii). To a Blake analyst willing nevertheless to try, William Rossetti suggested that after a few years in solitary confinement devoted to reading the prophetic books one might possibly "piece together their myths, trace their connection, reason out their system" (p. cxxii). Enjoyment would increase with understanding, but Rossetti doubted whether Blake would turn out to be "free from a tinge of something other than sanity" (p. cxxii). Characteristically, mid-century criticism keeps circling back to the question of Blake's sanity.

Fifteen years after the Aldine Blake, Ellis and Yeats did begin to trace out the myths and their connections and called their account "The System." By positively exhibiting Blake's claim as a serious and coherent thinker—whether mystic, philosopher, theologian, or symbolist—rather than, at best,

2. Saintsbury, *Academy*, p. 600. Crawfurd, p. 490 n. Scott wrote that Blake's originality was guarded about by ignorance; "he was the most childlike manhood we are acquainted with." Reading Behmen and Cornelius Agrippa, Swedenborg and Paracelsus, is "entirely inconsistent with Blake's education, and reduces him besides, to the common level of derivatives, making him one of the educated million" (*Catalogue of the Burlington Fine Arts Club Exhibition of the Works of William Blake* [London, 1876], p. 10). See, too, *Letters of Smetham*, p. 377.

suggesting it as Swinburne and William Rossetti had done, Ellis and Yeats's work went a long way toward disarming the charge of madness and prepared the groundwork for an appreciation of Blake's prophetic books in the twentieth century.

The Works of William Blake, Poetic, Symbolic, and Critical published in 1893, albeit brilliant and revolutionary, must be one of the most idiosyncratic and poorly put-together among literary critiques. It does, however, still illuminate Blake despite dense, obscure, and dubious mystical doctrine. The book is in three volumes which include, in Volume *1,* a Preface, a "Memoir" of Blake, a preliminary exposition of the editors' approach entitled "The Literary Period," and a description of "The Symbolic System." Volume *2* contains the "Interpretations and Paraphrased Commentary" for all Blake's poetry (with texts for the major manuscript lyrics), except for *Poetical Sketches, Island in the Moon,* and some lesser manuscript lyrics; it includes also a section on "Blake the Artist" and a concordance of "Some References" to the Zoas. Volume *3* prints *Poetical Sketches,* the *Songs, Gates of Paradise,* the manuscript poems from the *Pickering MS* and the *Note-Book* not printed in Volume *2,* and "Notes" to the early poems; *Tiriel* and *Vala* appear in letterpress; the Lambeth prophecies, the *Marriage, Thel, Jerusalem,* and *Milton* are reproduced in lithograph. Some pages from *Vala* and the *Note-Book* are also facsimiled in Volume *3,* along with the designs to Blair's *Grave.*

Ellis and Yeats's collaboration began in 1888 or 1889 when Ellis showed the young Yeats a "scrap of notepaper on which he had written some years before an interpretation" of "The fields from Islington to Marybone" from *Jerusalem.*

The four quarters of London represented Blake's four great mythological personages, the Zoas, and also the four elements. These few sentences were the foundation of all study of the philosophy of William Blake that requires an exact knowledge for its pursuit and that traces the connection between his system and that of Swedenborg or of Boehme. I recognized certain attributions from what is sometimes called the Christian Cabbala, of which Ellis had never heard, and with this proof that his interpretation was more than fantasy he and I began our four years' work . . . [in about] the spring of 1889.[3]

Like critics before him, Edwin Ellis created a Blake in his own image. In his representation the Real Blake—later he wrote a biography entitled *The Real Blake*—turns out to mirror Ellis, a discernibly paranoid, spiritually henpecked magician with a split personality. Ellis was the son of a famous mathematician and Yeats remembered him saying, "I am a mathematician with the mathematics left out." He had a talent for verse which expressed itself in recasting and rewriting long passages of Blake's poems: Yeats reminisces about his gift of casting "something just said into a dozen lines of musical verse, without apparently ceasing to talk"; he would never "amend it." Joseph Hone describes Ellis as a man with two subjects—religion and sex; both were liberally indulged in explicating Blake.[4]

3. W. B. Yeats, *Autobiography* (New York, 1958), p. 108. The paragraphs that follow on Ellis, the progress of EY, the religion of art, and on Yeats's other interests in the eighties and nineties draw from the *Autobiography* (especially pp. 107–10); *Letters of W. B. Yeats,* ed. Allan Wade (New York, 1955), cited as "Yeats's *Letters*"; and W. B. Yeats, *Letters to Katherine Tynan,* ed. Roger McHugh (New York, McMullen Books, 1953).

4. Joseph Hone describes Ellis as a disciple of Rossetti, a student of Blake, Behmen, and Swedenborg, whom Yeats in 1922 credited with teaching him the " 'mastery of verse.' " *The Wanderings of Oisin* (1889) is dedicated to Ellis. Mrs. Ellis, also a student of the occult, would frequently drive Yeats out of her house for casting spells over her. Yeats complained to his friend the Fenian John O'Leary that her hysterics were holding up conferences on "The Symbolic System"

When the two met, Yeats—and subsequently Yeats's Blake, as Richard Ellmann notes—was an Irish symbolist poet working out his own occult system.[5] Both Ellis and Yeats experimented with practical magic and occult symbols; Ellis fell into a trance a number of times during the course of their collaboration. Yeats's interest in magic had begun around 1884 when he, George Russell (A. E.), and others founded a Hermetic Society in Dublin. In London he came under the influence of Madame Blavatsky, and from her Yeats picked up a good deal of unordered symbolism and mythology miscellaneously derived from various cultures. He also read her disciple, Alfred Percy Sinnett; "The Septenary Law" and "The Astral Shell" (from *Esoteric Buddhism*) turn up in his glossing of Blake's "Symbolic System."

In 1890 Yeats left Madame Blavatsky for a new Hermetic Society, the Order of the Golden Dawn, which had been founded three years earlier. In the Quaritch "Memoir" the editors suggest that there is "reason to believe" that Blake knew of the Kabala and Rosicrucian doctrines, that it is "possible that he received initiation into an order of Christian Kabalists then established in London, and known as 'The Hermetic Students of the G. D.' . . . He would have said

---

(Hone, *W. B. Yeats: 1865–1939* [London, 1942], pp. 75–76; Yeats's *Letters*, pp. 164–65).

In 1906 and 1907 Ellis published three books on Blake. *The Real Blake: A Portrait Biography* (London, 1907) included everything in the Quaritch biography (from the "Memoir" and "Literary Period") plus almost all of Blake's prose, parts of the exposition of his system, and Ellis' elaborations on Blake as husband, editor, and polemicist. His independent two-volume edition of *The Poetical Works of William Blake* (London, 1906) includes introductory exposition, annotations, and editorial notes, some of them exactly repeating parts of EY that he presumably wrote. After 1893 Ellis and Yeats wrote about Blake independently; they lost touch with one another entirely.

Ellis and Quaritch made an unsuccessful attempt to set up a "Blake Society," in the nineties (*Art Journal, N. S., 48* [1896], 30).

5. *The Identity of Yeats* (New York, Oxford University Press, 1954), p. 25 (see pp. 24–29).

nothing about such initiation even if he had received it" (EY, *1*, 24). Toward the end of his work on Blake Yeats wrote to his friend and mentor in the Irish nationalist movement, the Fenian John O'Leary, "If I had not made magic my constant study I could not have written a single word of my Blake book. . . . The mystical life is the centre of all that I do and all that I think and all that I write." [6]

Both Ellis and Yeats were personally drawn more to the Blake of D. G. Rossetti than to Swinburne's Apostle of Liberty. Ellis was himself a poet-painter; he, J. B. Yeats (a painter), and Jack Nettleship (a painter and critic) had formed their own "Brotherhood" in the 1860s and 1870s based on an admiration for Blake and Rossetti. In the 1880s Ellis was a typical aesthete, artificial, arch, and a little precious to judge from a set of drawings and prefaces in ten "Sugar'd Sonnets [of Shakespeare] . . . Resugar'd" which he did in 1884. The young W. B. Yeats absorbed the allegiances of his father's circle; when he was fifteen he was given Blake's poems. While J. B. Yeats and his friends turned from Rossetti to the new scientific French school of "Paint what you see," Yeats remained "pre-Raphaelite in all things" until he was past thirty, loyal to an ideal of Blake as poet-painter, with "Blake and his anti-materialist Art" [7] reinforcing his campaign against "Tyndall, Huxley, Bastien-Lepage and Carolus Du-

6. Yeats's *Letters,* p. 211. Three years earlier in 1889 he had written almost the same words to O'Leary, "You complain about the mysticism. It has enabled me to make out Blake's prophetic books at any rate" (p. 125).

The Order of the Golden Dawn was established by Dr. Woodman, Wynne Westcott, and S. Liddell Mathers in 1887 for the study and practice of ceremonial magic (Yeats's *Letters,* p. 183 n.).

7. Yeats's *Letters,* p. 150.

For the "brotherhood," see *The Letters of J. B. Yeats,* ed. Joseph Hone with a Preface by Oliver Elton (London, 1944). In the *Autobiography* W. B. Yeats notes that Ellis picked up his "passion for Blake . . . in pre-Raphaelite studios" (p. 108). For Nettleship's interest in Blake, see *D. G. Rossetti: His Family Letters, 1*, 281.

ran" (his "Bacon, Newton, & Locke" and Reynolds). Yeats
and his circle of poets and critics—Arthur Symons, Ernest
Dowson, Lionel Johnson—all followed Pater in accepting art
unconditionally as the only effective spiritual and religious
element in contemporary life.[8]

Yeats and Ellis' Blake emerged as the aesthetes' Blake
with a mystical symbolist superimposed. They also conferred upon Blake the distinction of being an Irishman.
During these years Yeats was becoming more and more
involved in the Celtic revival; he thought of himself as an
Irish poet, and he thought he had grounds to say that "we may
almost claim Blake for an Irish poet." Irishness and Irish myth
along with occultism and the religion of art entered into everything he wrote about Blake in the nineties.[9]

The exact division of labor in the edition is described to
us by Yeats in his *Autobiography* and, more specifically, in

8. The young Lionel Johnson writes while in school (Winchester)
that his adolescent treasures include Blake, Christina Rossetti, Arthur
O'Shaughnessy, Whitman, and Pater (Johnson, *Some Winchester
Letters* [New York, Macmillan, 1919], p. 182; letter dated 1885.)

9. Yeats's *Letters*, p. 136; letter dated "probably Sept., 1889."
Yeats's writings on Blake in the 1890s include his work on EY; he
edited and wrote the introduction to the Muses' Library collection of
The Poems of William Blake, containing *Thel, Tiriel,* the lyrics, and
passages from *MHH, VDA, Ahania, FZ,* and *Milt.* In 1897, Yeats
wrote two essays on Blake, "Blake and the Imagination" (a "Portrait"
for the *Academy*) and "William Blake and His Illustrations to *The
Divine Comedy"* (a three-part essay for the *Savoy*), which subsequently appeared in Yeats's *Ideas of Good and Evil* (London, A. H.
Bullen, 1903). References to these two essays are from W. B. Yeats,
Essays and Introductions (New York, 1961).

"William Blake and His Illustrations" shows Yeats's assimilation of
the work and writings of Samuel Palmer and Edward Calvert. A. H.
Palmer's *Life and Letters of Samuel Palmer* and S. Calvert's biography
of Edward Calvert with reproductions of the Blake-influenced woodcuts and of Calvert's later work, were published in 1892 and 1893,
respectively. For the influence of the works of Calvert and Palmer on
Yeats, see T. R. Henn, *The Lonely Tower* (London, Methuen, 1950).

a note he wrote on the flyleaf of his own copy of the Quaritch Blake, dated May 3, 1900:

> The writing of this book is mainly Ellis's. The thinking is as much mine as his. The biography is by him. He wrote and trebled in size a biography of mine. The greater part of the "symbolic system" is my writing; the rest of the book was written by Ellis working over short accounts of the books by me, except in the case of the "literary period," the account of the minor poems, and the account of Blake's art theories which are all his own except in so far as we discussed everything together.
>
> P. S.—The book is full of misprints. There is a good deal here and there in the biography, etc., with which I am not in agreement.[10]

The difficulty is to know where Yeats leaves off and Ellis begins adding.

Apparently the first thing the editors did was to discuss and read Blake together and to compile a "concordance of all Blake's mystical terms." This was done while they were copying Linnell's manuscript of *The Four Zoas* at Red Hill. Then Yeats wrote the running commentaries on the poems; he next undertook most of "The Symbolic System," simultaneously sketching out the "Memoir"; meanwhile Ellis wrote "Blake the Artist," "The Literary Period," and one section of the "Interpretations" ("Minor Poems") and saw to the texts and illustrations. Once past the early stages Yeats dreaded Ellis' interference; he wrote to O'Leary,

> The reason why I am afraid of leaving Blake for a time

10. Hazard Adams, *Blake and Yeats: The Contrary Vision* (Ithaca, Cornell University Press, 1955), pp. 47–48. For Adams' description of EY, see pp. 44–56. Adams is the only writer to treat EY in print at some length. An excellent one-paragraph description may be found in Frye's review of Blake research, "William Blake," *The English Romantic Poets and Essayists*, p. 12.

[to go to Dublin] is that Ellis is in a hurry and if I leave
it may do some of my chapters himself and do them
awry. Providence has stopped off his terrible activity for
the present with twelve lectures. . . . He may awake at
any moment however and attack my province with
horse, foot and artillery. The boundary between his and
mine being a not over well defined bourne. I had to
put up a notice against trespassers a couple of weeks ago.
Ellis is magnificent within his limits but threatens to over-
throw them, and beyond them he is useless through lack
of mystical knowledge.[11]

Ellis' additions were probably written after Yeats, leaving the
loose ends of Blake undone, went back to Sligo and Dublin
to devote himself to the Irish literary revival. Possibly some
of the very hasty seeming and poorly proofread chapters on
particular and miscellaneous points, such as clusters of symbols and the English names that were originally Ellis' contribution, are his additions to "The Symbolic System." The
observations on the married life of the four Zoas are undoubtedly his, since Ellis was interested more in personalities
than in poetry, particularly in anything that dealt with con-
flict between the sexes. Though certainly concerned with personality, Yeats did not share Ellis' taste or talent for melo-
dramatic reconstruction and may have restrained the wilder
imagination of his collaborator. Yeats, however, did share
Ellis' passion for signs, symbols, magic numbers, and abstractions; he probably is responsible for the proliferating correspondences with occult mythologies in "The Symbolic System" as well as for the significance of sounds, the patterns of
movement of the personages, and certainly (as a letter to
O'Leary tells us) for the charts. The moods, the emotional

11. Yeats's *Letters*, pp. 162–63; dated Jan. 21, [1891]. A letter to
Katherine Tynan, in 1889, shows Yeats deferring to Ellis' knowledge
(ibid., p. 112); at this time, he asked his most mystical friend (A. E.)
to send him "a letter with some Blake criticism" (ibid., p. 118, dated
Mar. 21). For visits to the Linnells at Red Hill see ibid., p. 145.

states, and the fourfold symmetry came from their mutual discussions.[12]

As an edition of Blake's work Ellis and Yeats's Blake is by far the most complete in the nineteenth century. It printed for the first time long extracts of the untitled manuscript that Ellis called *An Island in the Moon* after its opening sentence (EY, *2,* "The Literary Period") and *Vala* (EY, *3*) which the two editors considered Blake's "literary masterpiece" (EY, *1,* 46); some unpublished Annotations were printed and there are new pieces from the *Note-Book.*[13] Ellis also sup-

12. These attributions and others, below, are based upon information in Yeats's *Letters,* pp. 156–58 ("Ellis . . . exhibited a huge chart of mine, representing Blake's symbolic scheme in a kind of genealogical tree." Letter dated Oct. [1890]); pp. 133, 136, 145, 150, 153, 154, 155, 159, 161, 167, 184, 223, etc. See also Sampson (1905), Introductions, passim.

General collation of Yeats's Muses' Library Blake, Ellis' three volumes on Blake and an essay by Ellis, "William Blake," *Occult Review, 4* (July and Aug. 1906), 26–35 and 87–94 with passages and viewpoints in the Quaritch edition shows specifically that Ellis reprinted whole passages from EY, which I take to be his originally (e.g., *The Real Blake,* pp. 295 ff.) and indicates in a general way what each editor did. Also stylistic variations in EY sometimes make one confident about where Yeats (wavering, always rhythmical, always convincing to the ear) leaves off and Ellis (abrupt, testy, assertive, and often incoherent) begins.

13. *IM* (EY, *1,* 186–201) may be the "new Blake MS" just "turned up," that Yeats mentions in a letter dated late 1891 or early 1892 (Yeats's *Letters,* p. 199). Ellis describes the work in detail, but the editors could not print it in full because of a restriction imposed by its owner, the painter Fairfax Murray (EY, *1,* 186–87).

Earlier, in 1867, three lyrics from the manuscript (owned by Palmer at the time) appeared in a Cambridge University magazine, *The Light Blue, 1* (1867), 161 and *2* (1867), 240: "This city & this country" under the title "The Lawgiver's Song" (in *1,* 161) and two "Songs," "Phoebe drest like Beauty's queen . . ." and "Leave, oh leave me to my sorrow" [sic] (in *2*). The same issues of *The Light Blue* included a discussion of Blake in three parts ("Blake the Author," pp. 146–51 and "Blake the Artist," pp. 216–26 and 289–92) based mainly on Gilchrist's biography, but also containing an independent

plied a painstaking page by page account of the *Note-Book* plus the first full-scale attempt at dating its contents, based on position, handwriting, and placement on the page.

The editors provided facsimiles of the engraved poems, including the *Book of Los,* a recently published prophecy previously unknown,[14] but not what Blake needed most, accurate and readable printed texts. The printed texts they provide for the lyrics and manuscript poetry abound with misprints and errors, as a glance through the footnotes to the poems in Sampson's edition amply reveals. Most of their errors occur in the *Note-Book* poems and the drafts for *Songs of Experience.*[15] The text of *Vala* that Ellis prepared shows rearrange-

---

description of the one hundred Dante drawings, then in Linnell's possession, which the writer "P. M." had seen. It is also apparent that he knew Palmer or Linnell. Unfortunately, I have not been able to identify him.

Vala was mentioned in print for the first time by William Rossetti in the Aldine Preface.

14. The *Book of Los* was discovered, if happening to come across it in the B. M. constitutes discovery, by Frederick York Powell in 1874; however, Powell did nothing about making it known—possibly because this is one of the non-illustrated engraved books—until Ellis and Yeats were working on the Quaritch Blake. It was then published in a "magazine of exquisite ambitions," *The Century Guild Hobby-Horse,* 5 (1890), 82–89, with a short preface by Powell in which he noted that readers would find the book fully interpreted in the forthcoming Quaritch Blake. He also speculated that the reason for its remaining unknown was that it had been confused with Blake's *Song of Los.*

Powell (1850–1904) was one of W. B. Yeats's father's friends; a scholar, and an ardent admirer of Blake and Whitman. The *Hobby-Horse,* a magazine on the style of the *Savoy* or the *Yellow Book,* stated as its purpose "to deal . . . with the practical application of art to life" (Oliver Elton, *Frederick York Powell, A Life and A Selection . . . , 1,* 133–34).

15. Sampson (1905), p. 113. A glance at footnotes shows too that EY and the Muses' Library edition regularly follow the emendations of the Aldine edition and of Swinburne; if Swinburne and the Rossettis differ, they follow the Rossettis.

ment of many passages, adjustments in Blake's meter, and changed words. In 1906 when his own two volume edition of Blake's writings appeared he defended his editing, asserting that he found the manuscript "unpaged and unsorted." This is not entirely true, as the Yeats and Ellis facsimiles in Volume *3* evidence. He also said that the poem was "written at a headlong pace," that it has four hundred lines "so visibly and obviously different from what the author thought he had written, that an attempt to restore the missing words and cut off the redundant was one that imposed itself on the editor." The manuscript problems of *The Four Zoas* are staggering, but even so, as Keynes notes, the Ellis-Yeats version is "exceedingly inaccurate." [16] A Table indicating the changes Ellis made is incomplete (EY, *3*, 149 ff.). The intentional revisions and the choices of already revised texts of the *Songs of Experience* and the *Pickering* and *Note-Book* poetry, as well as the notes and explanations which appear in Volume *3* (pp. 88 ff.) and in Volume *2* (in "Minor Poems" and the separate accounts of other manuscript poems) are a tangled outgrowth of mid-century editing, the result of confusions (described above in Chapter 5) rather than of any editorial policy of Ellis and Yeats's own. Echoing Swinburne, they write that "with every year poetry tends to fall more and more into the clutches of the merely scholarly editors who prize the exact reproduction of an error above the enjoyment of ten beautiful songs" (EY, *1*, 183). There is confusion about the authority of the *Pickering MS* and the *Note-Book*. Ellis' approach, to *Vala* particularly, comes directly from Rossetti's defense of changes that can be made "without in the slightest degree

16. For Ellis see *Blake's Poetical Works,* ed. Ellis, *2*, 42 and "William Blake," *Occult Review*, p. 92. For a summary of problems connected with editing *FZ* see Blake, ed. Keynes, pp. 897–98; H. M. Margouliouth's edition of *Vala* (London, Oxford University Press, 1956); G. E. Bentley Jr., ed., *Vala; or, the Four Zoas:* A Facsimile of the Manuscript, a Transcript . . . and a Study of Its Growth and Significance (London, Oxford University Press, 1963); and E-B, pp. 737 ff.

affecting the original" and citations here and there in Swinburne of Blake's "slip[s] of mind or pen." [17]

Ellis' own edition of Blake dispensed with the Table (inadequate as it is) that showed his emendations of *Vala;* Ellis
smoothed the entire poem into a regular meter and extended
to *Milton* and *Jerusalem* his method of shifting passages and
changing words. He interpreted the poems and dated their
separate parts on the basis of presumed errors on the part of
Blake or on the basis of the symbolic definition of words.
(Ellis' edition was the only complete printed text of Blake's
prophecies before the publication of Geoffrey Keynes' Nonesuch Blake in 1925.)

As biographer Ellis found another positive source of interest in Blake's "errors." In *The Real Blake,* he writes,

> Blake's very smallest errors have so much narrative
> hidden in them,—narrative of the mind, for whose sake
> only that of the body is worth recollecting,—that this
> has its claim not to be passed over. Here, as in many
> other places, what seems merely literary criticism will
> often be found to help the personal story, as the personal
> story helps to direct literary criticism by explaining sym-
> bolic suggestions.

[p. 112]

In the Quaritch Blake, however, such freedom to emend was
not allowed Ellis. His policies were expressed in the general
arrangement of the book, with which Yeats probably agreed.
As textual editors Ellis and Yeats followed the Rossettis
without improving on them.

The Quaritch Blake opens with a "Memoir" which pre-
sented very much the same information about Blake's life as
Gilchrist's book did, together with some materials from
Tatham's Memoir, including the name of Blake's first love,
Polly or Clara Wood, who broke his heart. He then married

17. Rossetti, see above, Chap. 5, p. 110; Swinburne, p. 279 n.

Catherine Boucher because, as J. T. Smith first told the story, she pitied him in his misery. Yeats repeats the story, relating Catherine Blake to Enitharmon, the wife of Los (who *"is* Blake"), and to the "first female form," "Pity," in *Urizen* (EY, *1,* 12).

Beyond this Yeats does not explore the Blake marriage; he sees it as a series of poetic tableaux, first a "romance," then a "domestic drama," finally ending in Mrs. Blake's "tragic solitude of sorrow and dignity." There is, Yeats says, "nothing . . . wanting to the tale" (*1,* 13). However, at the end of the next chapter there is a cryptic, somewhat conflicting, comment that "Blake was not in love with his wife, though he loved her. Mrs. Blake was in love with her husband" (*1,* 33).

The near contradiction is explained in Ellis' *The Real Blake,* where we find that Ellis has brooded on the name Polly Wood, the childlessness of the Blakes, and D. G. Rossetti's interpretation of "William Bond" (describing some "terrible and difficult crisis" that took place in "poor Catherine Blake's married life"—the story Gilchrist told and Swinburne retold of Blake's wanting to take a second wife) and has come up with a domestic drama in which Mrs. Blake is shocked into a violent faint and fall. This leads to the loss of an unborn child, whose existence no one ever dreamed of until Ellis invented it, and to subsequent barrenness. There is no substantiation for what Ellis intuits from "William Bond," only his conviction that "this was so because it must have been." [18]

18. *The Real Blake,* pp. 88 ff., and 186. Ellis expanded Yeats's Memoir" in EY from "about 60" original pages (Yeats's *Letters,* p. 184). For D. G. Rossetti's interpretation of "William Bond," arrived at after reading Swinburne's *Blake,* see *Life, 2,* 87.

Twentieth-century writers have been more clinical about the marital problems of the Blakes than Ellis was; no one, however, speaks of them anymore as an ideal married couple (see J. Middleton Murry, *William Blake* [London, J. Cape, 1933]; Margaret Lowery, *Windows of the Morning;* Margaret Rudd, *Organiz'd Innocence* [New York, Routledge & Kegan Paul, 1956]). Erdman has a sidelight on the

The one genuinely novel piece of information in the "Memoir" is Yeats's claim that Blake was an "Irish poet." "Blake's grandfather I have found out by chance was a Cornelius O'Neal who took the name of Blake to dodge his creditors," Yeats writes to a friend in about 1889.[19] The particular appeal of the story to Yeats was that it conferred upon Blake a personal legacy with the dignities and sanctions that come from a living tradition. The Celtic imagination had been defined for Yeats and his contemporaries in Matthew Arnold's "On the Study of Celtic Literature" and Ernest Renan's *The Poetry of the Celtic Races*. The Celt is preeminently a man who by nature "reacts against the despotism of fact." His literature is pervaded with "natural beauty and natural magic." In the qualities of Blake's divided personality, fiery as "that potent Elizabethan, Shawn O'Neil" (*1, 9*), or courteous in the "O'Neil tradition of good manners" (*1, 27*), either exalted in vision or else sunk in despair, Yeats saw manifested the characteristics of the typical Irish temperament. Ellis applies the cruder side of racial determinist psychology when he terms Blake a "red-headed Irishman." [20]

With his own fluent Celtic capacity for making myths,

---

second wife story (p. 142). For a unique note on Mrs. Blake's supposed long-suffering nature, see Wilfred Partington, "Some Marginalia," *TLS* (Jan. 28, 1939); in *Life*, ed. Todd, p. 396.

Ellis is responsible for a number of other unfounded assumptions about Blake, which only David Erdman has examined. For Blake's having grown up in a Swedenborgian household with a library of Swedenborgian books (many of which had not been published at the time when Ellis claims Blake read them) see Ellis, *The Real Blake*, pp. 106–08; "William Blake," *Occult Review*, p. 29; and Erdman, "Blake's Early Swedenborgianism: A Twentieth Century Legend," *Comparative Literature*, 5 (1953), 247–57.

19. Yeats's *Letters*, p. 136; dated Sept. 1889.

20. "William Blake," *Occult Review*, p. 89 (see also *The Real Blake*, pp. 186 and 196). Arnold, *On the Study of Celtic Literature and On Translating Homer* (1866) (New York, Macmillan, 1924), p. 77. Yeats quotes from both Arnold and Renan, in "The Celtic Element in Literature" (1902) (*Essays and Introductions*, p. 173).

Yeats shaped to heroic legend the story of his subject's parentage. Blake's personal history as it appears in the "Memoir" does not refer to a totally unplaced Irishman, Cornelius O'Neal. It is told there that the grandfather of William Blake was an Irish aristocrat named John O'Neil who took the name of his wife, "an unknown woman," and became "Blake" to escape imprisonment for debt. Yeats selected and interpreted events in terms of their relevance to the spiritual biography of one of the world's great mystics. Finally, he created an analogue or perhaps an Imitation of a Great Myth,[21] beginning with Blake's birth to an unknown mother into a station lower than his (grand)father's, through the years of appren-

---

21. A passage Yeats wrote in 1898 on the nature and the impetus of symbolic art is relevant to his treatment of Blake's life-story as symbol:

> All Art that is not mere story-telling, or mere portraiture, is symbolic. . . . A person or a landscape that is a part of a story or a portrait, evokes but so much emotion as the story or the portrait can permit without loosening the bonds that make it a story or a portrait; but if you liberate a person or a landscape from the bonds of motives and their actions, causes and their effects, and from all bonds but the bonds of your love, it will change under your eyes, and become a symbol of an infinite emotion, a perfected emotion, a part of the Divine Essence: for we love nothing but the perfect, and our dreams make all things perfect, that we may love them.

[*A Book of Images* by W. T. Horton, intro. W. B. Yeats (London, 1898), p. 10]

That the story of Blake's Irish ancestry is one Yeats chose to believe has been confirmed by Adams. Yeats's authority for Blake's Irish ancestry, according to his marginal note in his own copy of EY (2, 2), was Dr. Carter Blake who claimed to be a descendant of the O'Neil Blakes. A letter to Yeats from Carter Blake's daughter, now in Mrs. Yeats's possession, says only that two brothers of John O'Neil were beheaded; it offered Yeats no confirmation at all of her father's story (Adams, pp. 46–47). Adams suggests that this letter was written before the publication of EY. For a wildly inaccurate life of Blake which names Ireland as his birthplace, see *Encyclopaedia Britannica*, 8th ed. (1854), *4*, 153 (in B-N, item 672).

ticeship which "contain very little of active teaching" (*1*, 2)
—the years when *Poetical Sketches* and *Songs of Innocence*
were written—to the christological year when Blake awoke
into full mystical life. This rebirth was concurrent with Blake's
three-day sleep after the death of his brother Robert; then
Blake rose to write *The Marriage of Heaven and Hell*, "when
his thirty-three years of mystical apprenticeship were over"
(*1*, 33, 7). The early poems then, the work of Blake's years
of apprenticeship before he was called to higher mystical
works, are "mere literature" (*1*, 186) and preparation for the
prophetic books which Ellis and Yeats, according to their understanding of Blake, redesignated the "symbolic books."

"The Literary Period" (*1*, 175 ff.), written by Ellis, is defined in the phrase "first, and merely literary period" (*1*,
200). It deals with *Poetical Sketches* to some extent, but the
most important sections are devoted to the *Note-Book* and to
An Island in the Moon (now credited as Blake's first intellectual satire)—a collection of character portraits, conversations,
and songs, about middle-class literati and other intellectuals.
The editors make the supposition, which was generally accepted, that "we are being taken behind the scenes at many of
the literary evenings in Mr. Matthew's [sic, Mathew's] drawing room" (*1*, 187);[22] it is suggested that "Inflammable Gas"
is meant to represent the Reverend Mathew. There are one
or two allusions in the discussion to "Shandeyism" or "playful prose," but never to satire or satiric purposes, as govern-
ing the writer's intelligence. The editors see two possible kinds

22. The only twentieth-century scholar seriously to question *IM*'s
being a satire upon the Mathew circle is Erdman (*William Blake:
Prophet Against Empire*, pp. 86–87, n. 12; see, too, pp. 86 ff.).

In his independent commentaries Ellis regards *IM* and the *Note-
Book* doggerel as outbursts of personal resentment, not as symbolic
vision at all; Yeats, writing on *IM* in the Muses' Library Blake, echoes
EY—satire and "pre-mystic" touches (pp. xxviii–xxix). Speaking of
the tone of *IM* in *The Real Blake*, Ellis says Blake "was too young and
good-natured to keep up the mood of bitter derision for long at a
time" and turned into the way of *SI* (p. 82).

of significance in the piece, biographical revelation or else movement toward symbolic perceptions and symbolic vocabulary. Perhaps the current image of Blake, remote from common concerns, operated to exempt him from so worldly a mode as satire.

An Island in the Moon is characterized as "pre-mystic," its words not granted the "importance which would belong to a later production, if part of the great myth" (*1*, 187). This is qualified, however, when the song "When old corruption first begun" is termed "Blake's first true symbolic book" (*1*, 193). The difference between literary exercise and mystical vision is made clear in Ellis' remark that Blake was reluctant to "put himself unreservedly" in the hands of his visions and of his improvising faculty; symbolic vision is still restrained by literary judgment:

> These people of the moon, though often speaking words caught up from people of the world, when the author was "among his own friends" yet presented themselves to his literary faculty as types, not individuals. They assembled before his mind's eye in a waking dream of slowly increasing clearness and completeness. Blake watched them, as he watched later his mystic visions, for the sake of the interest that belonged to them as types, and for their visionary attractiveness, which is like that of a theatrical performance, to anyone who possess the visionary faculty. But he never put himself unreservedly in their hands, and when one of the dream personages began to over-do his visionary antics, then the improvising side of Blake's mind was checked by its judicial side, and compelled to confess that it had been trying to make a fool of him.

[*1*, 191–92]

The *Note-Book,* however, "forcibly demonstrates how superiour Blake the mystic was to Blake the penman" (*1*,

204–05). Ellis' object (and method) in dating the *Note-Book* contents was to see when individual words and names began to be used in their spiritual or symbolic sense, as words too became "spiritual forms." To Ellis and Yeats, "[The] mystic value [of the *Note-Book*] is chiefly . . . the lesson to be learned as to the effect of mysticism in raising Blake above the literary weaknesses which continually infected him from the poetry of the day" (*1*, 229). Earlier commentators, Ellis writes, "not having the least idea of what Blake really meant by his whole system of writing . . . were simply groping for beauties or oddities in a mass of confusion of which they knew neither the mystic nor the biographic value" (*1*, 229). By "biographic value" Ellis and Yeats mean Blake's increasing rejection of nature as shown by his increasingly symbolic use of ordinary words. Their intention is neither to explicate individual poems nor to point out "beauties," but to show that everything Blake wrote fits into or approaches a complex mystical system. Ellis says of the word "Swallow," in "The Swallow sings in Courts of Kings," that "It is one of the very few merely literary, non-mystical corrections left by Blake" (*1*, 221).[23]

Ellis' section on the *Note-Book* shows how the language of the developing mystic transforms ordinary words in Blake's most casual private jottings. Earlier, in the "Memoir," he and Yeats demonstrated at length that the expressions "Villain" and "bereave my Life" in "On H[ayley]'s Friendship" ("And when he could not act upon my wife/ Hired a Villain to bereave my Life") which William Rossetti had quoted in evidence of Blake's paranoia are to be understood as applying to the life of the spirit and to the enemies of the life of the spirit—not to adultery, murders, and various atrocities of the flesh. In his *Note-Book* comments Ellis refers back to this passage repeatedly (*1*, 213, 223, 231, and so on), using it as a basis for glossing other words such as "action" in "I

23. In fact, there is no indication at all of any "correction," by Blake (see E-B, pp. 505 and 789).

assert for My self that . . . the Outward Creation . . . is
hindrance and not Action" ("VLJ," E-B, p. 555), here referring to "mental action" (1, 231). Ellis applies his symbolic
vocabulary systematically and rigidly, ignoring the possibility
that the purport of certain terms may be ironic, and not always considering the symbolic word as affected by differing
contexts. Blake's use of the word "cloud" "in a feminine sense"
is traced to his scorn of Joanna Southcote who claimed she,
like the Virgin Mary, was a cloud and would bear a new
Messiah (1, 210); justice is not done to the variety of attitudes that Blake could be counted on to bring to "cloud" in
such a context, nor is there enough allowance in Ellis' rigidity
for concrete meanings of clouds and cloudiness that vary from
poem to poem. "Ornament" (with "ornamental") in "Sir
Jo[s]hua praised Rubens with a Smile/ By calling his the
ornamental Style" (E-B, p. 503) is a "religious" term meaning "intended for eternity" or else, if having reference to
natural things, "nature used for symbol" (1, 214). The force
of the lines consists in "ornamental" ultimately meaning precisely the opposite; Reynolds damns himself. Ellis probably
has in mind Blake's annotation to Reynolds' statement in the
Discourses that "The regular progress of cultivated life is from
necessaries to accommodations, from accommodations to ornaments." Blake writes: "Satan took away Ornament First.
Next he took away Accomodations & Then he became Lord
& Master of Necessaries" (E-B, p. 626). Neither Rubens nor
Reynolds is an "ornamental" painter in the reversed, approv-
ing sense of Blake's comment. Reynolds' smiling sneer is
halfway toward Blake's viewpoint in which both painters are
inessential because they are both sunk in Nature not as symbol. Rubens and Reynolds belong among "all the Copies [sic]
or Pretended Copiers of Nature" who "Prove that Nature becomes . . . to its Victim nothing but Blots & Blurs" ("PA,"
E-B, p. 563).

Insofar as Ellis and Yeats showed that ordinary words (even
in annotations or in Blake's perplexing conversations with

Crabb Robinson) were used in a symbolic sense, they made
Blake himself appear more intelligible and more sane. They
also indicated, and justified to some extent, the complexity
and difficulty of his system. Yeats and Ellis saw Blake's "Symbolic System" (*1*, 235–420) as an ascending Jacob's Ladder
of emotional "states" or moods forming "spaces" about them
which reached to God. This is the first articulation of
Blakean (dialectic) progression found in nineteenth-century
criticism. (Yeats adapted this motion into his image of the
gyres.) The missing links in what Yeats and Ellis presumed
to be a continuous and also hierarchical system were to be
found in the missing books—the ones Tatham burned (*1*,
333) or that Blake "published in heaven." [24] Every state and
space is fourfold. Each state is symbolized by a person; their
source is Universal Mind as it passed through Blake's personal
consciousness while the poet was in a state approaching trance.
The chief persons are the four Zoas, introduced as such for
the first time, and identified as Tharmas, Urizen, Luvah, and
Urthona; their symbols, genealogies, and histories are also
indicated. This is probably the most important contribution
Ellis and Yeats made to interpretation of the prophetic books.

Between the extremes of The Divine World (Jerusalem),
whose condition is Divine Unity or Freedom, and Nonentity,
whose condition is Mundane Unity or Law (Satan), are the
four levels or "abodes" of existence which correspond to the
darkening Ages of the Earth (Golden, Beulah; Silver, Alla;
Brazen, Al-ulro; Iron, Or-ulro). To each level belongs a
different and increasingly fallen group of characters whose
very names, according to Yeats, represent a withdrawal from

24. Crabb Robinson recalled Blake's telling him, "I write . . .
when commanded by the spirits and the moment I have written I see
the words fly abt the room in all directions. It is then published"
(*Blake, Coleridge, Wordsworth, Lamb, Etc.*, p. 12). See too the
letter to Flaxman beginning "Dear Sculptor of Eternity," dated Sept.
21, 1800 (Blake, ed. Keynes, p. 802).

the purely intuitive and mystical to the allusive and finally to the representational or merely natural: the Zoas (whose names are purely symbolic); the characters like Tiriel, Theotormon, and others (offspring of the Zoas) whose names embody recognizable and allusive syllables but are mainly symbolic or mystical; the Brazen citizens of Al-ulro, Reuben, Simeon, and the rest whose names are the names of the Old Testament; and finally the Iron age, Hand, Hyle, Peachy, and so on—the real names of living Englishmen (*1,* 258, chart facing 280, 328–30).

Twentieth-century students have agreed that the four levels of existence or states as Blake terms them, are Ulro, Generation, Beulah, and Eden or Eternity.[25] Ellis and Yeats use the phrase "four states of humanity" for their four levels (*1,* 262); apparently they derived both phrase and conception from a passage on plate 34 of *Milton* which describes the "Four States of Humanity *in its Repose*" (l. 8, italics mine), a qualification and condition they do not take into account. The passage in its entirety explains the only diagram to be found in all of Blake's engraved writings (plate 33); this may account for appeal [26] and its importance for Yeats's exposition. Blake writes,

> And the Four States of Humanity in its Repose,
> Were shewed them. First of Beulah a most pleasant Sleep
> On Couches soft, with mild music, tended by Flowers of
> Beulah

25. See S. Foster Damon, *William Blake: His Philosophy and Symbols* [1924] (New York, 1947), Chap. 24 ("Cosmography").

26. Describing the sketch-book of Blake's designs to the *Divine Comedy,* Yeats speculates about the possibility of incipient diagrams: "There are certain curious unfinished diagrams scattered here and there among the now separated pages of the sketch-book, and of these there is one which, had it had all its concentric rings filled with names, would have been a systematic exposition of his animosities and of their various intensity" ("William Blake and His Illustrations to *The Divine Comedy*" [1897], p. 132).

Sweet Female forms, winged or floating in the air
  spontaneous
The Second State is Alla & the third State Al-Ulro;
But the Fourth State is dreadful; it is named Or-Ulro:
The First State is in the Head, the Second is in the Heart:
The Third in the Loins & Seminal Vessels & the Fourth
In the Stomach & Intestines terrible, deadly, unutterable
And he whose Gates are opend in those Regions of his
  Body
Can from those Gates view all these wondrous Imagina-
  tions

. . .

Four Universes round the Universe of Los remain
  Chaotic
Four intersecting Globes, & the Egg form'd World of Los
In midst; stretching from Zenith to Nadir, in midst of
  Chaos[.]
One of these Ruind Universes is to the North named
  Urthona
One to the South this was the glorious World of Urizen
One to the East, of Luvah: One to the West; of Tharmas.

                    [E-B, p. 133, pl. 34, ll. 8–18 and 32–37]

Not only is the interpretation of the states based on this
passage, but also Ellis and Yeats's conception of Blake's
engraved books as a unified and systematic opus. Each book
is conceived as having its place in a master scheme of Head,
Heart, or Loins (which correspond to the Zoas in their separated or fallen state); within each book the chapters or sections are assigned aspects such as the Heart of the Head, the
Loins of the Head, and so on; the fourth of any series is seen
as a bringing together or realization of the preceding three.
The "fours" are infinite: each engraved book and each person-
age is given a fourfold significance. There was an attempt on
Ellis' part to fit Irish counties and provinces (with the four

provinces seen as gates) into the groupings of four quarters of London, four points of the compass, four Zoas, and so on: "Verulam - Munster - Reuben's Gate; London - Connaught - Joseph's Gate; York - Ulster -   Edinburgh - Leinster." [27] Richard Ellmann records that fours never lost their fascination for Yeats; in 1897 he was still trying to form a system of fours based on the "four talismans" in Celtic lore.[28]

The sources for the many charts and tables that map the circulation of the Zoas or the movement of Albion or mankind through the twenty-seven Churches (divided into Heart, Head, and Loin groups), for the symbols of the Zoas, for the significance of names, numbers, and colors ranged from Swedenborg to the gossip of practical magicians Yeats happened to know. The only mystical authors mentioned by name are Swedenborg and Behmen. Some of the parallels and interpretations resulted from experiments which the editors performed to see what images and symbols Blake's names evoked from the minds of subjects who had never heard of Luvah or Bowlahoola (EY, *1,* 327); some came from information Yeats picked up from mystics of his acquaintance. In the margin next to a passage on "The Symbolism of Color" which refers to "A certain order of occultists who have made the symbolism of sun worship their special study" (*1,* 311–12), Yeats later noted that: "Boodie Innis, a member of this order told me of this symbolism" WBY.[29] Opposite a statement that "Tharmas, as is also the case with the water-god in a certain Hindu system of occult mythology, never travels

27. Private letter from Hazard Adams, Jan. 1962. Mr. Adams thinks that the letter from Ellis means that he had a hand in the "Irish business."

28. Ellmann, p. 29.

29. Letter from Adams. In the same chapter Yeats alludes to a "system of totems as taught by Hindu occultists" (EY, *1,* 313).

Yeats's sources of information also included his friend, poet and classicist Lionel Johnson, and Frederick York Powell, whom he consulted about possible Greek and Celtic derivations of Blake's names. For Johnson, see EY, *1,* 335–37; for Powell, *1,* 329.

from the West" Yeats later wrote, "Authority H. P. B. a
doubtful authority—I would never quote her now." [30] In the
1900 memo he wrote that some of

> my own constructive symbolism is put with too much
> confidence . . . parts should be used rather as an inter-
> pretitive [sic] hypothesis than as a certainty. The circula-
> tion of the Zoas, which seems to me unlike anything in
> traditional symbolism, is the chief cause of uncertainty.
> . . . There is also uncertainty about the personages who
> are mentioned . . . too seldom to make one know them
> perfectly.[31]

Other important sections in "The System" deal with
"Albion and the Zoas" and the Contraries, that is, "dual aspects" of "all divisions" which are allied to the "typical contraries—the sexes." "All symbols but the final symbol—the
'Human Form,' or 'Man'—are found grouped in sexes"
(EY, *1*, 320). Whereas Swinburne noted the rhetorical uses
of paradox and inversion (in the *Marriage*) or opposed Theism and Pantheism, Yeats saw Blake's use of paradox and
the contraries as itself symbolical. Explaining why Ulro, the
"selfish Centre," is outside Beulah ("What is above is within
. . . the circumference is within, outside the selfish Centre"
[sic], *Jer.*, pl. 71, ll. 6–7),[32] Yeats writes:

30. EY, *1*, 265; Adams, p. 48. Yeats affixed a note (EY, *1*, 314)
to a table of colors with their "physical" and "mental" meanings: "I
am now convinced that Blake's colour scheme is founded on Boehme's
color scheme. March 1902, WBY" (Letter from Adams).
31. Adams, p. 48.
32. The text of *Jer* reads:

> What is Above is Within, for every-thing in Eternity is translu-
> cent:
> The Circumference is Within: Without, is formed the Selfish
> Center

[E-B, p. 223]

EY's quotation of the line suggests more the language of the mystic.

The apparent contradiction disappears when looked at
in the light of Blake's religious belief in the essential
brotherliness of Imagination . . . and the essential egotism and isolation of Reason. The one being Christ, the
other Satan; the one having for its function and result,
Forgiveness; the other, Accusation. Each is endowed
with a centre and circumference. The centre of brotherhood, or its essence, is its quality of expansiveness. But
this is an inner expansiveness. Each man opens his own
mind inwards into the field of Vision and there, in this
infinite realm, meets his brother-man. Blake believed
that all could do this sooner or later. The substitute for
those who could not, was to open the affections inwards
to the seat of sympathy and there to find not the isolated
heart, but the brotherhood of all hearts. The selfish
centre which is "outside" is outside in an unexpansive
sense, for non-entity is not expanse, though it be limitless
as error. The selfish centre is made of the exterior reason
and the five senses. It is the mortal personality, that
which death inevitably dissolves, but which it is life's
business to destroy, for this is "Salvation." Hence salvation is the opposite of morality, and the centre is outside
the circumference. The paradox turns out to be a symbol,
not a contradiction.

[EY, *1*, 404–05]

Yeats paid tribute to what Blake's system taught *him* when
he wrote that it had liberated his thinking "from formulas
and theories of several kinds." [33]

The individual "Interpretations and Paraphrased Commentary" (EY, 2) of the prophecies and "The Minor Poems"
apply the technical vocabulary of symbols and the principle
of dating on the basis of mystical usages to fit each poem into
a place in the overall system. The poems are arranged accordingly; hence *Thel* is made to follow the *Marriage, Tiriel*

33. Yeats's *Letters*, pp. 152–53; dated May ?1890.

is printed almost at the end of the canon because of its more
developed symbolism, and the *Ghost of Abel* is moved ahead
because it is less mystical.

The Rossettis and Thomson tended to oversimplify the
Songs of Innocence into children's poems; Ellis and Yeats
make them esoteric puzzles. This holds for the *Songs of Experience* also, with the poems in both sets being read primarily
as pieces which fit into the "System." "London" is glossed as a
literary version of a passage in *Jerusalem* (EY, 2, 15). (Difficulties in following their interpretations are increased by inaccurate cross-references.) In "The Little Black Boy" "The
mother . . . [who] is the 'vegetative [sic] happy,'—Mnetha
herself—points to the East while she teaches symbolism"
(EY, 2, 9). The phrase "Vegetater happy" occurs in the
Song of Enion at the end of "Night the Eighth" of *Vala* (E-B,
p. 370, l. 23), which both Ellis and Yeats (in the Muses' Library editon) extracted. It was for them a key passage aside
from its lyrical beauty, doubtless because it expresses a condition in which all external nature becomes symbol; as man
collects "the scattered portions of his immortal body/ Into
the Elemental forms of every thing that grows" and "stores
his thoughts/ As in a store house in his memory" (ll. 7–8
and 12–13) against Apocalypse, there is a disappearance of
the "mortal" through "improved knowledge" (l. 32). Ellis
uses the passage to illustrate how words function in their
"Blakean sense." In the line "The furrowd field replies to the
grave" (l. 28), "Furrowed fields [sic]" means "married
women" and "grave" is "reserve of unused physical force."
Vala is the storehouse of symbolism, the source poem, Blake's
literary and symbolic masterpiece—Ellis thought it the greatest poem ever written.[34]

The Ellis and Yeats edition is strongest in two areas:
Yeats's essay on "The Necessity for Symbol" and the exposition of "nature" in Blake's system. Ellis and Yeats are the first

34. "William Blake," *Occult Review,* pp. 95 and 92.

critics to suggest how absolute Blake's polemic was: "Nature [Blake] tells us, is merely a name for one form of mental existence" (EY, 2, xii). The relationship of nature and imagination is eloquently stated in the preface to the edition.[35] Following the sentence quoted above the passage continues:

> Art is another and higher form. But that art may rise to its true place, it must be set free from memory that binds it to Nature.
>
> Nature,—or creation,—is a result of the shrinkage of consciousness,—originally clairvoyant,—under the rule of the five senses, and of argument and law. Such consciousness is the result of the divided portions of Universal Mind obtaining perception of one another.
>
> .   .   .
>
> In Imagination only we find a Human Faculty that touches nature at one side, and spirit on the other. Imagination may be described as that which is sent bringing spirit to nature, and seemingly losing its spirit, that nature being revealed as symbol may lose the power to delude.
>
> [EY, *1*, xii]

In the "Symbolic System imagination is related in detail to Christ and nature to his Incarnation.

Poetry, as a "higher form . . . of mental existence" which puts on nature to assert universal symbols, is itself symbolic. Poetic language is a kind of magical incantation; accordingly Blake's names, as Yeats discusses them—each isolated sound having some occult meaning—are spells that call up universal images and forms. Los is "Between water and fire" because

35. Although the passage in question from the preface to EY certainly sounds like Yeats's writing, there is reason to believe it may be by Ellis. Earlier in this preface, there is an allusion to Swinburne's ignorance of the four Zoas; in 1906 W. B. Yeats writes to his father that "The passage about [Swinburne] in the Blake book was by Ellis" (Yeats's *Letters*, pp. 474–75).

"th" and "l" suggest *"water,* with all its symbolic uses" and
"s" is "light fire." "O" is darkness, being a "dark vowel."
This makes "Thel" a "girl of the watery valley" and Alla-
manda "Rivers of nerves—male power in light" (EY, *1,*
339–40). The lesson to be learned from this is that "Art and
poetry, by constantly using symbolism, continually remind us
that nature itself is a symbol" (*1,* xiii).

Yeats's essay on symbolism is a full statement of what he
learned (and confirmed for himself) from his work on Blake
about imagination, nature, symbol, and the function of poetry.[36] "The Necessity for Symbol" authorizes poetry by identifying it with all religious and mystical teaching, in a recon-
ciliation that was then central to Yeats. "Blake's system of
thought . . . is profoundly Christian—though wrapped up
in a queer dress—and certainly amazingly poetical. . . .
[This] Blake interpretation . . . has for me [opened up] new
kinds of poetic feeling and thought." [37]

According to Yeats's essay the first principle of both
mysticism and symbolist poetry is to recognize the "absolute
difference" in kind between natural and spiritual things (*1,*
236); in their common use of symbol or correspondences the
symbolist poet and the mystic are one.

> The chief difference between the metaphors of poetry
> and the symbols of mysticism is that the latter are woven
> together into a complete system. The "vexed sea" [of
> Lear's mind] would not be merely a detached compari-
> son, but, with the fish it contains, would be related to
> the land and air, the winds and shadowing clouds, and
> all their totality compared to the mind in its totality.

> [EY, *1,* 238]

36. Yeats describes "The Necessity for Symbol" as a "very important essay" in a letter written soon after he finished it, having made
some alterations suggested by Ellis (Yeats's *Letters,* p. 170; dated
June 1891).

37. Ibid., pp. 152–53; dated May ?1890. Like Swinburne, Yeats was
defining his own poetic principles through his writing on Blake.

The sources of both poetry and mystic doctrines, however, are in the occult world. In the "Memoir" Yeats defined Blake's conception of poetic imagination in purely occult terms: seeing with the "mental eye" is not, Yeats asserts, what most men say it is, a

> grandiloquent way of describing ordinary fancy. The final secret of the long processions of the figures in true "vision" remains with the visionary beings themselves— those universal powers the hem of whose garments man may touch and cling to for a moment in deepest trance. Blake, Swedenborg and Boehme are but men who have overheard and recorded a few words spoken by the spiritual forms among themselves for their own delight.
>
> [EY, *1*, 48]

Yeats's view of vision as overhearing, recording, touching the hems of unseen garments conveys the notion of being attuned to some eternal and present dimension of the Universal Mind; Yeats saw this as true of many poets (himself included) and all mystics and occultists. As an interpretation of Blake— engaged in ceaseles "mental fight" and "intellectual warfare" —it seems incongruously passive; it recalls both the earlier criticism that compared Blake's work with the productions of automatic writing and the fact that automatic writing would eventually furnish Yeats with an avowed source of poetic images. The highest state—to which the element of "Divine fire" is assigned—is regarded by Yeats as "Divine Unity" (called "Jerusalem" in "The System") and the energy of Blake's state of Eden tends to stiffen into Byzantine iconography. The active and combative elements found in Blake seem, in nineteenth-century criticism, to have been read as an unattractive side of his personality. They were almost never related to vision or prophecy, never by Yeats who fitted these qualities into his Image of Blake but not into the "System":

> The errors in the handiwork of exalted spirits are as the more fantastical errors in their lives . . . as Blake's

anger against causes and purposes he but half understood; as that veritable madness an Eastern scripture
thinks permissible among the saints; for he who half
lives in eternity endures a rending of the intellectual
body.[38]

The nineteenth-century tradition of Blake criticism made it
natural for Yeats to see Blake's imagination as receptive and
passive and to think that Beulah is the highest human state
to Blake. (For Yeats himself, to go beyond Beulah is to pass
into trance or the rapt motion of the dance. Inspiration which
comes from such a source descends and begets.[39]) Possibly
the "Four States of Humanity in its Repose" were accepted
by Yeats as definitive and final because "Repose" suggested
an ultimate perspective to him.

The "System" is for Yeats enriched and legitimized by being
an aesthetic analogue to a typical and perennial mystical hierarchy:

This poetic genius or central mood in all things is that
which creates all by affinity—worlds no less than religions and philosophies. First, a bodiless mood, and then
a surging thought, and last a thing. This triad is universal
in mysticism, and corresponds to Father, Son, and Holy
Spirit. In Swedenborg it is divided under the names

38. "William Blake and His Illustrations to *The Divine Comedy*,"
p. 128.

39. Frye remarks that what "seals off the upper limit of Yeats'
Vision," from Blake's viewpoint, is its "uncreative mental condition."
Yeats stands, he says, "at his own Phase One," in abject passivity, an
"aristocratic ideal above him, impossibly remote and lost in the
turning stars" ("Yeats and the Language of Symbolism," *University
of Toronto Quarterly, 17* [Oct. 1947]; reprinted in Frye, *Fables of
Identity* [New York, 1963], p. 234)

Frye goes on to remark that Yeats as poet did not submit to this
passive doctrine of the theorist: "Yeats never entrusted anything
except the *Vision* to his spirits" (Idem).

celestial, spiritual and natural degrees; in the Kabala as
Neschamah, Ruach and Nephesch, or universal, particular and concrete life. In Theosophical mysticism we hear
of the triple logos—the unmanifest eternal, the manifest
eternal, and the manifest temporal; and in Blake we
will discover it under many names and trace the histories
of the many symbolic rulers who govern its various sub-
divisions.

[*EY, 1,* 241]

In "The Celtic Element in Literature" (1902) Yeats redefined
Celtic "natural magic" as one branch of the "ancient religion
of the world, the ancient worship of Nature"; hence Celtic
myth and story are seen not only as accidents of a racial impulse but as an available living source of ancient, poetic, and
sacred images. Absorbing himself increasingly in the ancient
myths and the unconscious poetry of the Irish peasantry,
Yeats noted that Blake's myth seemed to him deficient and
unpoetic at times because it was not tied to a living tradition.
In 1897 he wrote in "Blake and the Imagination,"

He was a man crying out for a mythology, and trying to
make one because he could not find one to his hand. Had
he been a Catholic of Dante's time he would have been
well content with Mary and the angels; or had he been
a scholar of our time he would have taken his symbols
where Wagner took his, from Norse mythology; or have
followed, with the help of Professor Rhys, that pathway
into Welsh mythology which he found in *Jerusalem;* or
have gone to Ireland and chosen for his symbols the
sacred mountains, along whose sides the peasant still
sees enchanted fires, and the divinities which have not
faded from the belief, if they have faded from the prayers, of simple hearts; and have spoken without mixing
incongruous things because he spoke of things that had

been long steeped in emotion; and have been less obscure
because a traditional mythology stood on the margin of
his sacred darkness.[40]

Insofar as Blake in "[A Vision of the Last Judgment]" had
given him a gospel of the Imagination, Yeats was prepared to

40. Pp. 176 and 114. Yeats makes the same point concerning
Shelley ("The Philosophy of Shelley's Poetry" [1900], *Essays and
Introductions*, p. 95). Yeats may have had in the back of his mind a
passage in Swinburne's book:

> A single man's work, however exclusively he may look to in-
> spiration for motive and material, must always want the breadth
> and variety of meaning, the supple beauty of symbol, the in-
> fectious intensity of satisfied belief, which grow out of creeds
> and fables native to the spirit of a nation, yet peculiar to no
> man or sect, common yet sacred, not invented or constructed,
> but found growing and kept fresh with faith.
>
> [Swinburne, p. 194]

In "The Celtic Element," Yeats writes that Arnold's provincialism
(he does not term it that) was due to his narrow knowledge of "folk-
song and folk-belief" (p. 176). The forty years that intervened between Arnold's *On the Study of Celtic Literature* and Yeats's essay
saw a rise in the status of non-Christian myth, partly through the
perhaps involuntary agency of Higher Criticism and also through the
many independent efforts of scholars and literary men in translating,
printing and describing Welsh, Norse, Celtic, and Germanic legend
and folk story. Such studies helped to establish a context for the
appreciation of Blake's prophecies.

In 1839, J. J. Garth Wilkinson condemned Blake for rejecting true
Christian revelation for false, naturalistic mythologies (see Chap. 3,
pp. 50 ff.). Swinburne writing in 1864 had to deal with the "likeli-
hood of offensive misconstruction" when he discussed Blake's myth of
Urizen, the "vision of a creator divided against his own creation" (p.
151). By the 1880s, Wilkinson's researches into Norse myth (the
main study of his life after about 1850) had convinced him that all
mythologies partook of Divine Revelation. Ellis and Yeats treat all
figures in Blake—Christ, Urizen, Mary, Hindu gods, and so forth—
as equal and equally symbolic; "Christ himself must have been one of
the followers of Aengus. Has not some body identified him with
Hermes?", Yeats writes to a friend (Yeats's *Letters*, p. 324; dated
Aug. 27, ?1899).

worship. He preferred the collective to the individual imagination, however, and he looked to collective sources for valid
and beautiful images. His *Savoy* articles of 1897 on Blake's
drawings for the *Divine Comedy* and his introduction to *A
Book of Images* by W. T. Horton (1898) quote at length
from Blake's "[Vision]," but in both pieces Yeats criticizes
Blake as artist for being a "too literal realist of imagination,
as others are of nature," and therefore unsusceptible to "grace
of style" [41] and ultimately to the decorative elegance that for
Yeats could have talismanic significance:

> What matter if in his visionary realism, in his enthusiasm
> for what, after all, is perhaps the greatest art, he refused
> to admit that he who wraps the vision in lights and
> shadows, in iridescent or glowing colour, until form be
> half lost in pattern, may, as did Titian in his *Bacchus
> and Ariadne,* create a talisman as powerfully charged
> with intellectual virtue as though it were a jewel-studded
> door of the city seen on Patmos? [42]

Although Yeats began to feel that the essential symbolist
poetry to be found in pattern and tradition had been sacrificed
by Blake, still Blake remained to him "the chanticleer of the
new dawn." [43] With all he wrote on Blake in the nineties the
Quaritch edition was in Yeats's eyes a contribution to what
he had called "a greater renaissance" in which he felt himself
a part, "the revolt of the soul against the intellect—now be-

41. "William Blake and His Illustrations to *The Divine Comedy,*"
pp. 119–21; *A Book of Images,* p. 7.
42. "William Blake and His Illustrations to *The Divine Comedy,*"
p. 121. In this essay Yeats comments on the traditional criticism that
Blake's technique was "cloudy and indecisive," noting that "The
technique of Blake was imperfect, incomplete as is the technique of
wellnigh all artists who have striven to bring fires from remote summits; but where his imagination was complete, his technique has a
like perfection" (p. 127). This is essentially what Blake said about
his powers of invention and his powers of execution.
43. *A Book of Images,* p. 12.

ginning in the world," [44] another standard raised against
science and in behalf of the teaching of "the Rule of the Free
Imagination" (EY, *1*, 2). The antimaterialism of Yeats's time
was much more hostile to contemporary life in its utter rejection of nature and of mundane experience and even more
esoteric than Pre-Raphaelite aestheticism. The religion of art
that would banish the religion of the churches is expressed in
Yeats's belief that "the poets were uttering, under the mask
of phantasy, the old revelations." "Our commentary," wrote
Yeats of his and Ellis' intentions in their edition, "will, I believe, give to the world a great religious visionary who has
been hidden." [45] Revolutionary ethics and democracy, Blake
the libertarian evangelist of Swinburne's book are simply irrelevant. Walt Whitman makes no appearance in the Quaritch
edition. The editors write:

> The false idea that a talent or even a genius for verse
> tends to give a man a right to make laws for the social
> conduct of other men is nowhere supported in Blake's
> works. The world in which he would have the poet, *act-*
> *ing as a poet,* seek leadership is the poetic world. That
> of ordinary conduct should be put on a lower level.
>
> [EY, *1*, xi–xii]

What influence the Yeats and Ellis edition had was not due
to ordinary usefulness. Its expensiveness and its intrinsic
drawbacks, the errors and misprints, precluded that. As an
accurate, readable text of Blake's poetry, the Quaritch Blake
did not supplant the Aldine Blake; neither did Yeats's cheap
Muses' Library edition. It did, however, stimulate enough interest in the prophetic books to cause Sampson, Maclagan
and Russell, and later Keynes to produce a respectable text.[46]

44. Yeats's *Letters,* p. 211.
45. Review of *Homeward: Songs by the Way,* by A. E., *Bookman,*
6 (Aug. 1894), 147–48; Yeats's *Letters,* p. 156.
46. Early twentieth-century editions are Sampson's in 1905 and
1913. The latter, Oxford, edition contains *FR* printed in full for the

Contradictions, mistakes, obscure or else unverifiable allusions prevented the Yeats-Ellis edition from shedding specific light on single poems or books. The "Interpretations" have never been analyzed by any scholar.[47] The most influential part of the book, "The Symbolic System," was a stimulus, rather than an authority, for later Blakeans such as E. R. D. Maclagan who urged the formation of a Blake society to recover

first time (it was first quoted by George Saintsbury, in *The History of English Prosody* [3 vols. New York, 1906–10], *3*, 23–25) and selections from the prophetic books. Also *Jerusalem*, eds. E. R. D. Maclagan and A. G. B. Russell (London, A. H. Bullen, 1904) and *Milton*, eds. E. R. D. Maclagan and A. G. B. Russell (London, A. H. Bullen, 1907). And finally *The Writings of William Blake*, ed. Geoffrey Keynes (3 vols. London, The Nonesuch Press, 1925); also *The Prophetic Writings of William Blake*, eds. D. J. Sloss and J. P. R. Wallis (Oxford, Clarendon Press, 1926).

47. Virginia Moore makes this point, suggesting that Yeats's readings deserve serious study (*The Unicorn* [New York, Macmillan, 1954]).

Harold Bloom, in a public lecture on Yeats, has remarked that EY's many mistakes, not so much in interpretation as in recounting the narrative, lead him to think that Yeats may not have read through the long poems.

Northrop Frye's analysis of the book's difficulty (especially in the "Interpretations") is that Ellis and Yeats "approached Blake from the wrong side of Blavatsky."

> they had already acquired a smattering of occultism and they expected to find in Blake an occult system or secret doctrine instead of a poetic language. . . . Again, Blake though a very systematic thinker, sharply warns his readers against what he calls "mathematic form," and this includes all the Euclidean paraphernalia of diagrams, figures, tables of symbols and the like, which inevitably appear when symbolism is treated like a dead language. The result is an over-schematized commentary full of false symmetries, which itself more difficult to understand than Blake, is still further confused by centrifugal expositions of Boehme and Swedenborg. As Yeats truly remarks in the course of this work: "The student of occultism . . . should particularly notice Blake's association of black with darkness."

["Yeats and the Language of Symbolism," *Fables of Identity*, pp. 231–32; see EY, *1*, 313 for black and "darkness"]

the one great English mystic, whose thought is so sin-
gularly congenial to the temper of the present age: the
one great mystic of all time who has chosen for his
vehicle no mortal system of dogma or metaphysic, but an
immortal art.[48]

The work of Ellis and Yeats did, then, sanction and provoke
serious scholarship based on Blake's prophetic books; it gave
plausible initial answers to all the unresolved nineteenth-century hesitations and questions: Was Blake really a poet or
simply a Personality? Was he a madman? Was one to take his
visions seriously, and how did one take them? And was there
a plausible explanation, short of insanity, for the difference
between *Songs of Innocence* and *Jerusalem?* Swinburne supplied an exposition of Blake's "leading ideas," but Ellis and
Yeats described a "System." Swinburne spoke of inversions of
recognized institutions; Ellis and Yeats described an organic
spiral, an image of a dialectical progression, in which contraries were understood as provisional, symbolic of creative
oppositions. Swinburne had said that all Blake's personages
reenacted the same themes wearing different names and
(grotesque) garbs. Ellis and Yeats demonstrated that each
was different and part of a plan, both vertical (the natural,
intellectual, emotional hierarchy) and lateral (head, heart,
loins in each state overlapping). Once the existence of the
four Zoas, the principle of fourfold meaning, the dialectical
progression, and the theory of symbol had been absorbed,
the "System" was open to addition, qualification, documen-
tation, and comparative studies.

48. E. R. D. Maclagan, "Four Recent Books on William Blake,"
Occult Review, 5 (Feb. 1907), 74. Maclagan describes Blake's system
as being more "uncompromisingly difficult of access" than that "of all
those who have formulated . . . a system of speculative mysticism"
(p. 69).
A Blake society was formed in 1913.

AFTERWORD

It is observable that the traditional "anthology" Blake is becoming, if it is not already, so much "linen clothes folded up." *The Four Zoas, Milton,* and *Jerusalem* are claiming their pre-eminence in Blake's achievement. Nineteenth-century editors and critics lifted Blake and his lyrical poems from oblivion. Twentieth-century editors and critics have gradually recovered the prophetic books as well. In 1924 S. Foster Damon, Blake's first truly modern commentator, wrote:

> I confess frankly that when I began collecting comments on Blake, I thought him mad and *Jerusalem* trash. But as the work went on, and plane after plane of sanity was opened, my conversion began. Now I firmly believe that the last of Blake's works are greatest. . . . Blake . . . tried to solve problems which concern us all, and his answers to them are such as to place him among the greatest thinkers of several centuries.[49]

The alienated roles in which Blake had been cast by his commentators—madman, mystic, and magician—began to give way to the symbolist, to the psychologist, indeed to the poet, and to Blake "in This World" as Harold Bruce titled his biography in 1925. The hard dying image of Blake as the singer of inspired baby talk also began to fade. With changing tastes, other Romantic poets, Shelley, Wordsworth, and Keats, began to be studied more in their longer works, for values other than the simplicity of their pure lyrical

49. Damon, *William Blake,* p. ix.

voices. Damon compared contemporary attitudes to Blake
with former attitudes toward Beethoven.

> The world at large . . . admitted that Beethoven had
> written many charming things in his younger days; but
> that his last twenty years were matters for the maddest
> enthusiasts only. . . . And so with Blake. The *Songs of
> Innocence* are read everywhere; yet we lack a correct
> text of *The Four Zoas!* [50]

Tracing the reputation of most poets means seeing how
they dress to suit different times and places; in the nineteenth
century, more than in other times perhaps, it also means seeing how they are recreated in the images of their individual
critics. All this is true of Blake's reputation. Blake's story,
however, is also peculiarly a history of reclamation. From
nothing—no printed texts, no reading public, no confidence
in a man presumed insane—Blake's nineteenth-century editors cleared a narrow path for readers to approach him. It
has since been widened and twentieth-century criticism has
made Blake generally accessible in a way that the impression-
ism and the brilliant mystifications of Swinburne, Ellis, and
Yeats never did. Nevertheless their work led ultimately to
Damon's undertaking, to the humanistic and literary analysis
of Blake's poetry which has made it theoretically possible for
him to be understood through those faculties which Blake asserted that all men might possess if they would.

50. Ibid.

APPENDIXES

Blake into Print—Appearances of
Blake's Writings

The editors listed are those whose texts are directly based on Blake's manuscripts, engraved works, or, in the case of *Poetical Sketches,* on the first edition. *The French Revolution,* Blake's only other printed poem, was not reprinted until the twentieth century. The listings for *Thel, Poetical Sketches,* and *Gates of Paradise* are not continued past the appearance of complete, generally accurate texts. For *Songs of Innocence and of Experience,* only separate printings before 1863 are given; the translated texts in Crabb Robinson's "William Blake, Künstler, Dichter und Religiöser Schwärmer" are not included. I also list facsimile editions for works printed only in extracts. For American printings of poems from *Poetical Sketches* and *Songs of Innocence and of Experience,* based on Blake's texts, see B-N, item nos. 221, 226, 259 and 280.

Editors' names are abbreviated as follows:

Malk	B. H. Malkin, *A Father's Memoirs of His Child*
Cunn, 1	Allan Cunningham, "Life of Blake," *Lives of the Most Eminent Painters* . . . , 2 (1830)
Cunn, 2	Allan Cunningham, "Life of Blake," enl. ed., *Lives of the Most Eminent Painters* . . . , 2 (1830). Only cited for poems not in the earlier edition. These printings are not noted in Sampson (1905).

JTS	J. T. Smith, "Blake," *Nollekens and His Times, 2* (1828)
Wilk	J. J. Garth Wilkinson, ed., *Songs of Innocence and Experience,* by William Blake (1839)
Gil	Alexander Gilchrist, *Life of Blake, 1*
DGR	D. G. Rossetti, ed. Selections, *Life, 2*
Shep	R. H. Shepherd, ed., *Poetical Sketches* (1868); *Songs of Innocence and Experience* (1866); *Poems of Blake* (1874)
Swin	Algernon Charles Swinburne, *William Blake* (1868)
WMR	William Michael Rossetti, ed., *Poetical Works of Blake* (Aldine, 1874)

Page numbers are given for Malk, Cunn, JTS, Gil, Swin, and other references where texts appear in the course of biography or criticism. Emendations of special interest are given in footnotes. Except for those in *Songs of Experience, Gates of Paradise,* and the manuscript poetry, the changes cited here do not appear in Sampson (1905). For the first appearances of Blake's prose, see Chap. 5, n. 6.

Poems and Prose Pieces from
Poetical Sketches

The Original Edition, 1783, through Shepherd's Edition, Pickering, 1868

Contents appear in the original order (E-B, pp. 400–36; Blake, ed. Keynes, pp. 1–40). Bracketed numbers for *Edward the Third* are scene numbers.

Song: "Fresh from the dewy hill,"	Gil, p. 40, ll. 1–16 Shep
Song: "When early morn walks forth"	Gil, p. 40, ll. 1–16 Shep
To the Muses	Cunn, *1*, 145 DGR Shep
Gwin, King of Norway	Cunn, *2*, 187–88, ll. 41–42, 45–60, 65–68, 75–80 Shep
An Imitation of Spenser	Shep
Blind-Man's Buff	DGR Shep
King Edward the Third	Cunn, *1*, 146–47, [3], ll. 220–31; [5] ll. 21–35, 36–38 DGR, [1], ll. 25–52; [3], ll. 96–183, 220–93; [5], in full; [6], in full except for ll. 3–4, 31–33, 45–48, and 53–56 Shep
Prologue to Edward the Fourth	Shep
Prologue to King John	Shep
A War Song	Shep
The Couch of Death	Shep
Contemplation	Shep
Samson	Shep

Songs of Innocence and of Experience

Up to 1863

For J. J. Garth Wilkinson's complete edition of *Songs of Innocence and Experience*, 1839, see Chap. 3, pp. 47 ff.

POEMS PRINTED SEPARATELY BEFORE 1863

Songs of Innocence

Introduction	Cunn, *1*, 151
The Lamb	Cunn, *2*, 185 [a]
The Chimney Sweeper	James Montgomery, ed. *Chimney-Sweeper's Friend . . .* (1824) Cunn, *1*, 151–52
The Divine Image	Malk, pp. xxxiii–xxxiv "The Inventions of William Blake," *London University Magazine*, 2 (Mar. 1830), 321[a]
Holy Thursday	Malk, pp. xxix–xxx Cunn, *2*, 184 [a]
Laughing Song	Malk, p. xxvi Cunn, *2*, 184–85 [a]

Songs of Experience

Introduction	"The Inventions of William Blake," pp. 321–22 [a]
The Tyger	Malk, pp. xxxix–xl Cunn, *1*, 145–46 [Allingham], *Nightingale Valley* (1860), pp. 95–96 [a]

The Garden of Love	"The Inventions of William Blake," p. 322 [a]
A Poison Tree	"The Inventions of William Blake," p. 322 [a]

a. Not noticed in Sampson (1905).

D. G. Rossetti's Emendations to *Songs of Experience, Life*, 2 *

TITLE	LINE	DGR	BLAKE TEXT	PAGE IN E-B	KEYNES EDITION
Holy Thursday	15	Babes should never hunger . . .	Babe can	20	pp. 211–12; no. 51, p. 181
Ah! Sun-Flower	3	. . . sweet golden prime	clime	25	p. 215
The Garden of Love		(ADD 2 stanzas at beginning)	"I laid me down" N	459	no. 4, p. 162
The Little Vagabond	4	The poor parsons with wind like a blown bladder swell.	Such usage in heaven will never do well. (For The . . . swell, see draft in N)	718	no. 45, p. 179, l. 5
A Poison Tree		(Titled Christian Forbearance)	see draft in N	721	no. 10, p. 165
		(ADD A Cradle Song)	N	459	no. 9, pp. 164–65

* See the first and third paragraphs of the table immediately following for abbreviations and underscoring.

237

Poems in Manuscript:

In Gilchrist's *Life of Blake,* Shepherd's Editions, Swinburne's *William Blake,* and the Aldine Blake; and D. G. Rossetti's Texts of "Broken Love" and "The Woman Taken in Adultery!"

The manuscript poems, "Poems Hitherto Unpublished," are listed below in the order in which they were printed in the Selections, 1863, and with D. G. Rossetti's titles. Additions and changes appearing in the 1880 edition are indicated by the use of square brackets with "ADD" to indicate the addition of a passage, "OM" an omission, and "SUB" a substitution. All changed words are underscored; the correct reading is given in column two following title, line and manuscript citations.

Manuscript poems printed in the Life (that is, in Volume *1*) are given with chapter and page references in both first and second editions. The poems remaining in manuscript that Shepherd, Swinburne, and William Rossetti printed in 1866, 1868, and 1874 respectively are listed according to each editor's titles. (Shepherd, it should be noted, did not supply or change titles.) These lists are not taken past the mid-century editions. (For *The Four Zoas* and *An Island in the Moon,* see Chap. 8, pp. 199–202 and n. 13.)

Blake's manuscript title appears after each poem in a parallel column if it differs from the editor's, or in the case of untitled poems, the first line appears in quotation marks; the manuscript reference is also given in this column. ("N" is used to designate the *MS Note-Book,* in this section.) The next two columns list page references in E-B and in Keynes. E-B page numbers and, when necessary, line numbers are given for the *Note-Book* poetry; also given are Keynes's number (or numbers) for the poem, as well as the page and lines in his edition.

Where poems have been formed from more than one fragment or poem by Blake (and this happens frequently in selections from Blake's manuscript poetry) the nineteenth-century editor's ordering of these passages has been followed in giving the E-B and Keynes references (see Riches, p. 242 below). In the one instance where more than one version of the same poem is used, both versions are cited: in DGR's printing of "The Golden Net" (p. 241, below) where the title and manuscript citation (column two) is *"Pick MS* and 'Beneath the white thorn lovely may' N," the Pickering version of "The Golden Net" is the basic text, with DGR's incorporations from a draft in the *Note-Book* beginning "Beneath the white thorn lovely may." The E-B page reference is accordingly "pp. 474–75 and p. 77," the Keynes reference is "p. 424 and no. 9, pp. 421–22," with the "and" in both cases indicating the compounding of fragments. In a few cases there will be one reference in E-B and more than one in Keynes (see "The Wild Flower's Song," p. 241); this is due to their different apparatus for handling manuscript poetry.

Footnotes identify printings or changes not noted in Sampson (1905), and occasionally comment on changed titles in later printings.

MANUSCRIPT POEMS IN THE SELECTIONS, EDITED BY D. G. ROSSETTI

SELECTIONS	TITLE OR FIRST LINE IN BLAKE (IF DIFFERENT) AND MS	PAGE AND LINES IN E-B	NUMBER (FOR N), PAGE AND LINES IN BLAKE, ED. KEYNES
Poems Hitherto Unpublished [SUB *Ideas of Good and Evil*]			
The Birds		pp. 469–70	no. 10, pp. 422–23
Broken Love (See p. 253)	"My Spectre around me night and day" N (See p. 253 below.)	pp. 467–68 (See p. 253 below.)	no. 1, pp. 415–17 (See p. 253 below.)
The Two Songs	"I heard an Angel singing" N	pp. 461–62	no. 8, p. 164
The Defiled Sanctuary	"I saw a chapel all of gold" N	p. 458	no. 6, p. 163
Cupid	"Why was Cupid a Boy" N	p. 470, ll. 1–16	no. 72, p. 552, ll. 1–16

The Woman Taken in Adultery (See p. 249 below.)	The Everlasting Gospel N (See p. 249 below.)	p. 516 [a]: ll. 1–2, 5–14; pp. 512–14 [e]: ll. 7–16, 19–20, 27–32, 39–50, 53–64	p. 748, a: ll. 1–2, 5–14; pp. 753–55, e: ll. 7–16, 19–20, 27–32, 39–50, 53–64
Love's Secret	"Never pain to tell thy love" N	pp. 458, 768	no. 2, p. 161
The Wild Flower's Song	N	pp. 463–64	no. 30 and no. 20, p. 175 and p. 170
The Crystal Cabinet	Pick MS	pp. 479–80	pp. 429–30
Smile and Frown	The Smile Pick MS	p. 474	pp. 423–24
The Golden Net	Pick MS and "Beneath the white thorn lovely May" N	pp. 474–75 and p. 777	p. 424 and no. 9, pp. 421–22
The Land of Dreams	Pick MS	p. 478	p. 427
Mary	Pick MS	pp. 478–79	pp. 428–29
Auguries of Innocence (See Chap. 5 above.)	Pick MS	pp. 481–84	pp. 431–34
The Mental Traveler	Pick MS	pp. 475–77	pp. 424–27

241

MANUSCRIPT POEMS IN THE SELECTIONS, EDITED BY D. G. ROSSETTI (*Continued*)

SELECTIONS	TITLE OR FIRST LINE IN BLAKE (IF DIFFERENT) AND MS	PAGE AND LINES IN E-B	NUMBER (FOR N), PAGE AND LINES IN BLAKE, ED. KEYNES
[In a Myrtle Shade] (Moved to precede William Bond)	(See p. 243 below.)		
William Bond	*Pick MS*	pp. 487–89	pp. 434–35
Scoffers	"Mock on Mock on Voltaire Rousseau" N	pp. 468–69	no. 4, p. 418
The Agony of Faith	The Grey Monk *Pick MS* and "I saw a Monk of Charlemaine" N	pp. 480–81 and pp. 199–200 with notes on pp. 732–33	pp. 430–31 and no. 5, pp. 418–20, ll. 19–48, 57–61
Daybreak	Morning N	p. 469	no. 6, p. 421
Thames and Ohio	"Why should I care for the men of thames" N	p. 464	no. 12, p. 166
Young Love	"Are not the joys of morning sweeter" N	p. 463	no. 24, p. 172
Riches	"Since all the Riches of this World" N and Riches N	p. 508 and p. 461	no. 86, p. 557 and no. 49, p. 181

Opportunity	"If you trap the moment before its ripe" N and Eternity N	p. 461 and p. 461	no. 42, p. 179 and no. 43, p. 179
Seed Sowing	"Thou hast a lap full of seed" N	p. 461	no. 16, p. 168
Barren Blossom	"I feard the fury of my wind" N	p. 458	no. 11, p. 166
Night and Day	"Silent Silent Night" N	p. 462	no. 14, p. 168
In a Myrtle Shade	To my Mirtle N (Title from in a mirtle shade N)	p. 460 (p. 460)	no. 34, p. 176 (no. 18, p. 169)
[ADD Love and Deceit]	"Love to faults is always blind" N (How to know Love from Deceit is a deleted title.)	p. 463	no. 29, p. 175

Couplets and Fragments

I "I walked abroad on a snowy day"	Soft Snow N	p. 464	no. 32, p. 176

243

MANUSCRIPT POEMS IN THE SELECTIONS, EDITED BY D. G. ROSSETTI (*Continued*)

SELECTIONS	TITLE OR FIRST LINE IN BLAKE (IF DIFFERENT) AND MS	PAGE AND LINES IN E-B	NUMBER (FOR N), PAGE AND LINES IN BLAKE, ED. KEYNES
II "Abstinence sows sand all over"	N	p. 465	no. 40, p. 178
III "The look of love alarms"	N and "Soft deceit & idle-ness" N	p. 465 and p. 466	no. 53, p. 182 and no. 54, p. 182 (See, too, no. 59, p. 184, stanzas 2 and 3.)
IV "To Chloe's breast young Cupid slily stole"	N	p. 508	no. 87, p. 557
V "Great things are done when men and mountains meet"	N	p. 502	no. 64, p. 550
VI "The errors of a wise man make your rule"	N	p. 502	no. 61, p. 550, ll. 6-7
VII "Some people admire the work of a fool"	N	p. 508	no. 83, p. 556

245

MANUSCRIPT POEMS IN THE SELECTIONS, EDITED BY D. G. ROSSETTI (*Continued*)

SELECTIONS	TITLE OR FIRST LINE IN BLAKE (IF DIFFERENT) AND MS	PAGE AND LINES IN E-B	NUMBER (FOR N), PAGE AND LINES IN BLAKE, ED. KEYNES
[ADD XVI "Prayers plough not, praises reap not"]	*MHH*, pl. 9	pl. 9, p. 37, ll. 59–60	pl. 9, p. 152, ll. 20–21
[ADD ᶜ XVII "The sword sang on the barren heath"]	N sung	p. 464	no. 39, p. 178
[ADD ᵈ XVIII "O Lapwing, thou fliest across the heath"]	N around	p. 460	no. 15, p. 168
[ADD XIX "The Angel that presided at my birth" See p. 260 below.]	N oer	p. 493	no. 26, p. 541
Epigrams and Satirical Pieces on Art and Artists			
1 "I asked of my dear friend orator Prig"	N askd my	pp. 506–07	no. 74, pp. 553–54, ll. 1–14

2 "O dear mother Outline, of wisdom most sage"	N knowledge	p. 507	no. 74, pp. 553–54, ll. 16–21
3 On the Great Encouragement Given by English Nobility and Gentry to Correggio, Rubens, _____ Reynolds, Gainsborough, Catalani, _____ and Dilberry Doodle	N Rubens Rembrandt Reynolds . . . Catalani Du Crowe & _____ and "All Pictures thats Panted with Sense & with Thought" N	pp. 506 and 502	no. 53, p. 548 and no. 56, pp. 548–49
4 "Seeing a Rembrandt or Correggio"	"When I see a Rubens Rembrandt Correggio" N	p. 506	no. 63, p. 550
5 To English Connoisseurs	N	p. 505	no. 46, p. 546
6 "Sir Joshua Praises Michael Angelo"	N	p. 503	no. 15, p. 539
7 To Flaxman	To F _____ ("You call me Mad . . .") N	p. 499	no. 34, p. 544

247

MANUSCRIPT POEMS IN THE SELECTIONS, EDITED BY D. G. ROSSETTI (*Continued*)

SELECTIONS	TITLE OR FIRST LINE IN BLAKE (IF DIFFERENT) AND MS	PAGE AND LINES IN E-B	NUMBER (FOR N), PAGE AND LINES IN BLAKE, ED. KEYNES
8 To the same	To F―― ("I mock thee not . . .") N	p. 499	no. 10, p. 539
9 "Thank God, I never was sent to school"	"You say their Pictures well Painted be" (2 lines) N	p. 502, ll. 3–4	no. 61, p. 550, ll. 3, 5

b. Not noted in Sampson (1905). For "Smack" Sampson has "smart."
c. First printed by WMR. See pp. 268, 269.
d. Not noted in Sampson (1905).

D. G. Rossetti's texts of *The Everlasting Gospel* and "My Spectre around me" (titled "The Woman Taken in Adultery" and "Broken Love") are printed below at the left. In a parallel column, I have indicated the line numbers for sections of *The Everlasting Gospel* (see list, p. 241 above), and Blake's stanza number and lines for "My Spectre around me." Changes in Blake's words or phrases (as distinguished from omissions and/or rearrangements of whole lines or passages) are underscored. The correct versions appear in column two for "The Woman Taken in Adultery"; they are appended to "Broken Love," according to line numbers for Rossetti's text. I omit changes in punctuation, spelling, and capitalization.

The Woman Taken in Adultery

(Extracted from a Fragmentary Poem, entitled, 'The Everlasting Gospel')[e]

The vision of Christ that thou dost see
Is my vision's greatest enemy.
Thine is the fare of all mankind,—
Mine speaks in parables to the blind;
Thine loves the same world that mine hates;
Thy Heaven-doors are my Hell-gates.

The Everlasting Gospel

Section a: E-B, p. 516; Keynes, p. 748

1
2
5   friend
6
7
8

249

e. For Swinburne and WMR's printings, see pp. 265, 267.

The Woman Taken in Adultery (continued)

Socrates taught what Meletus
Loathed as a nation's bitterest curse,
And Caiaphas was in his own mind
A benefactor to mankind.
Both read the Bible day and night;
But thou read'st black where I read white.

Jesus sat in Moses' chair;
They brought the trembling woman there
Moses commands she be stoned to death;
What was the sound of Jesus' breath?
He laid his hand on Moses' law:
The ancient heavens in silent awe,
Writ with curses from pole to pole,
All away began to roll.
The earth trembling and naked lay,
In secret bed of mortal clay,

250

The Everlasting Gospel (continued)

9
10
11
12
13
14

Section e: E-B, p. 512–14; Keynes, pp. 753–55

7   was sitting
8
9
10
11
12
13
14
15
16

And she heard the breath of God	19	
As she heard it by Eden's flood:—	20	heard by
'To be good only, is to be	27	
'A God, or else a Pharisee.	28	
'Thou Angel of the Presence Divine,	29	
'That didst create this body of mine,	30	
'Wherefore hast thou writ these laws	31	
'And created Hell's dark jaws?	32	
'Though thou didst all to chaos roll	39	
'With the serpent for its soul,	40	
'Still the breath Divine doth move,	41	does
'And the breath Divine is Love.	42	
'Woman, fear not; let me see	43	Mary
'The seven devils that trouble thee;	44	torment
'Hide not from my sight thy sin,	45	
'That full forgiveness thou may'st win.	46	That forgiveness
'Hath no man condemned thee?'	47	Has
'No man, Lord.'	48	
'Then what is he		
'Who shall accuse thee? Come ye forth,	49	

The Woman Taken in Adultery (continued)

'Ye fallen fiends of heavenly birth!
'Ye shall bow before her feet,
'Ye shall lick the dust for meat;
'And though <u>ye</u> cannot love, but hate,
'Ye shall be beggars at love's gate.
'What was thy love? Let me see't!
'Was it love, or dark deceit?'

'Love too long from me hath fled;
''Twas dark deceit, to earn my bread;
''Twas covet, or 'twas custom, or
'Some trifle not worth caring for.
'But these would <u>call</u> a shame and sin
'Love's temple that God dwelleth in.'

252

The Everlasting Gospel (continued)

50 Fallen Fiend
53 You
54 You
55 you
56 Shall
57
58
59 has
60
61
62
63 That they may call
64

Broken Love   "My Spectre around me"

Line Number in Selections	Poem	Blake's Stanza No.	Lines (Stanza and Page if Needed) in E-B, pp. 467–68[f]	Lines in Keynes, pp. 415–17[f]
	My Spectre around me night and day	1	1	1
	Like a wild beast guards my way;		2	2
	My emanation far within		3	3
4	Weeps incessantly for my sin.		4	4
	A fathomless and boundless deep,	2	5	23
	There we wander, there we weep;		6	24
	On the hungry craving wind		7	25
8	My Spectre follows thee behind.		8	26
	He scents thy footsteps in the snow,	3	9	27
	Wheresoever thou dost go;		10	28

f. Lines from stanzas Blake neither deleted nor numbered, which E-B groups as a "[Postscript]" (p. 468) and Keynes as "Additional Stanzas (p. 417), are indicated here by the use of parentheses.

253

What transgressions I commit
Are for thy transgressions fit,—
They thy harlots, thou their slave;
And my bed becomes their grave.

36

5 Seven of my sweet loves thy knife
Hath bereaved of their life:
Their marble tombs I built, with tears
And with cold and shadowy fears.

40

6 Seven more loves weep night and day
Round the tombs where my loves lay,
And seven more loves attend at night
Around my couch with torches bright.

44

7 And seven more loves in my bed
Crown with vine my mournful head;
Pitying and forgiving all
Thy transgressions, great and small.

48

8 When wilt thou return, and view
My loves, and them in life renew?
When wilt thou return and live?
When wilt thou pity as I forgive?

52

(5)   17   (5)   35
(6)   18   (6)   36
(7)   19   (7)   37
(8)   20   (8)   38

21   39
22   40
23   41
24   42

25   43
26   44
27   45
28   46

29   47
30   48
31   49
32   50

"My Spectre around me" (continued)

14	53	71
	54	72
	55	73
	56	74

Broken Love (continued)

56	Throughout all Eternity
	I forgive you, you forgive me.
	As our dear Redeemer said:
	"This the wine, and this the bread."
	(Omits stanzas 9, 10, 11, 12, and 13.)ᵍ

Line 15	And never will from sin be free
Line 16	Till she forgives & comes to me
Line 18	didst
Line 20	Bind around
Line 24	Fill
Line 25	Thou sit
Line 27	thou sit
Line 28	thy
Line 29	shall
Line 32	Till she forgives & comes to me
Line 38	Has
Line 40	shuddering
Line 43	each
Line 46	wine
Line 50	to
Line 53	& Throughout

g. Printed by Swinburne, pp. 278–79. He gives stanzas 8–14 in the order 8, 9, 10, 12, 11, 13, 14—noting that Blake "by some evident slip of mind or pen" has "put [st. 12] before the preceding one." WMR follows DGR. EY prints Blake's 14 stanzas,

MANUSCRIPT POETRY IN GILCHRIST'S *Life, 1*

PAGES IN *Life, 1*, 1863:1880	TITLE, FIRST LINE IN *Life, 1*	TITLE OR FIRST LINE IN BLAKE AND MS	PAGE AND LINES IN E-B	NUMBER (FOR N) PAGE, AND LINES IN BLAKE, ED. KEYNES
	Chapter 20			
181:222	On Hayley the Pickthank	On H____ the Pick Thank N	p. 498	no. 57, p. 549
181:OM	"Friends were quite hard . . ." (See p. 245, "XIV Epitaph.")	Another N	p. 494, ll. 3–4	no. 43, p. 546, ll. 3–4
181:223	"Thy friendship oft . . ."	To H____ N	p. 498	no. 39, p. 545
181:224	"My title as a genius"	"My . . . [a] genius" N	p. 497	no. 44, p. 546
181:224	To Hayley ("You think Fuseli . . .")	To H N	p. 497	no. 9, p. 538 (Titled To H[unt])

MANUSCRIPT POETRY IN GILCHRIST'S *Life, 1* (continued)

PAGES IN *Life, 1* 1863:1880	TITLE, FIRST LINE IN *Life, 1*	TITLE OR FIRST LINE IN BLAKE AND MS	PAGES AND LINES IN E-B	NUMBER (FOR N) PAGE, AND LINES IN BLAKE, ED. KEYNES
		Chapter 22		
208:254	"Cromek loves artists . . ."	"Cr___ loves . . ." N	p. 500	no. 17, p. 540
208:254	"A petty, sneaking . . ."	N	p. 501	no. 18, p. 540
208:255	"I always take my judg- ment"	Cromek Speaks	p. 501	no. 58, p. 549
		Chapter 29		
257:305	Advice of the Popes . . .	Annotations to Reynolds' *Discourses*	p. 625	p. 445
258–59: 307	"When nations grow old . . ."	Annotations to Reynolds' *Discourses*	p. 631	p. 452
259:307	"Some look to see the . . ."	Annotations to Reynolds' *Discourses*	p. 627	p. 447

258

259:307	"When Sir Joshua Reynolds died"	Annotations to Reynolds' *Discourses*	p. 630	p. 451
264:312	On the Venetian Painter	Annotations to Reynolds' *Discourses*	p. 640	p. 463
265:313	"Raphael sublime . . ."	N and "The Cripple every step Drudges & labours" N	pp. 505–06, ll. 1–4 and p. 504, ll. 1–4	no. 50, p. 547, ll. 1–4 and no. 52, p. 548, ll. 1–3, 5
265:313	On Colourists	"Call that the Public Voice" (In "[A Public Address]" N)	p. 567	p. 597
266:314	"No real style of colouring"	N	p. 502	no. 1, p. 536

Chapter 34

307:350	"The fox, the owl, the spider and the bat"	On S——— ("The Fox . . . Beetle & . . .") and "The fox, the owl, the spider, and the mole" DC	p. 500, ll. 3–4 and p. 531	no. 37, p. 545, ll. 3–4 and p. 575

MANUSCRIPT POETRY IN GILCHRIST's *Life, I* (continued)

PAGES IN *Life, 1,* 1863:1880	TITLE, FIRST LINE IN *Life, 1*	TITLE OR FIRST LINE IN BLAKE AND MS	PAGES AND LINES IN E-B	NUMBER (FOR N) PAGE, AND LINES IN BLAKE, ED. KEYNES
309–10: 352–53	"I rose up at the dawn of day" (See p. 264 below.)	N	6 stanzas, pp. 472–73: ll. 1–4, 5–8, 9–12, 21–22 and 13–14, 13–14 and 17–18, 25–28	no. 91, 6 stanzas, pp. 558–59: ll. 1–4, 5–8, 9–12, 21–22 and 13–14, 13–14, 17–18, 25–28
311:353	"The Angel who presided at my birth" (See p. 246 above.)	N "... that ... oer ..."	p. 493	no. 26, p. 541

260

POEMS FROM BLAKE'S LETTERS TO BUTTS, FIRST PRINTED IN GILCHRIST'S *Life*, 1863, 2 (APPENDIX 1)

PAGES IN *Life*, 1863, 2	PAGES IN *Life*, 1880, 1	FIRST LINE IN *Life*	PAGES IN E-B	PAGES IN BLAKE, ED. KEYNES
180–81	152–53	"To my friend Butts I write"	683–84	804–06
181	153	"Wife of the friend of those I most revere"	685	806
189–91	181–83	"With happiness stretched across the hills"	692–93	816–18
198	193	"O why was I born with a different face?"	700	828–29

261

MANUSCRIPT POEMS FIRST PRINTED BY SHEPHERD, *Songs of Innocence and Experience*, 1866

(Note: Shepherd's edition contains generally accurate texts for all the poems in the *Pickering MS.*)

TITLE IN SHEPHERD	BLAKE'S TITLE (IF DIF- FERENT) AND MS	PAGE IN E-B	PAGE IN KEYNES
Song: By a Shepherd [h]	Song 1st by a Shepherd	457	63
Song: By an Old Shepherd [h]		457	64
Long John Brown and Little Mary Bell	*Pick MS*	487	434

h. The Shepherds' Songs were found in a copy of *PS* owned by Mrs. Flaxman. Gilchrist probably never saw them.

MANUSCRIPT POEMS IN SWINBURNE'S *William Blake*, 1868

PAGE IN SWINBURNE	TITLES, EXTRACTS IN SWINBURNE	TITLE (IF DIFFERENT) OR FIRST LINE IN BLAKE AND MS	PAGE AND LINES IN E-B	NUMBER (FOR N) PAGE AND LINES IN BLAKE, ED. KEYNES
31–32	14 lines from "When Klopstock England defied"	N	pp. 491–92, ll. 11–18, 21–26	no. 61, pp. 186–87, ll. 11–18, 21–26
38	"Of Hayley's birth . . ."	"Of H s birth . . ." N	p. 497	no. 14, p. 539
53 n.	Mr. Stothard to Mr. Cromek	N	p. 500	no. 23, p. 541
53 n.	Mr. Cromek to Mr. Stothard	N	p. 500	no. 24, p. 541
53 n.	To F. and S.	On F_____ & S_____ N	p. 500	no. 31, pp. 543–44
55–56	"The caverns of the grave I've seen"	N	p. 472	no. 90, p. 558
61	"The bleat, the bark, bellow and roar"	2 lines of Auguries of Innocence *Pick* MS	p. 482	p. 437, ll. 71–72
123 n.	3 lines of Tiriel	plate 5	p. 279, ll. 1–3	p. 106, ll. 1–3

MANUSCRIPT POEMS IN SWINBURNE'S *William Blake*, 1868 (continued)

PAGE IN SWIN-BURNE	TITLES, EXTRACTS IN SWINBURNE	TITLE (IF DIFFER-ENT) OR FIRST LINE IN BLAKE AND MS	PAGE AND LINES IN E-B	NUMBER (FOR N) PAGE AND LINES IN BLAKE, ED. KEYNES
124	Motto to the Songs of Innocence and—Experience	. . . & of . . . N	p. 490	no. 56, p. 183
127 n.	4 lines of "There souls of men are bought and sold"	The human Image N	p. 719	no. 28, p. 174, ll. 29–32
128	Prayer[1] (See p. 260 above.)	"I rose up at the dawn of day" N	pp. 472–73, stanzas 1, 2, 3, 6, 4, 5, 7	no. 91, 558–59, stanzas 1, 2, 3, 6, 4, 5, 7
137–38 n.	2 stanzas from in a mirtle shade	N	p. 460, ll. 1–4, 9–12 (stanzas 1, 3)	no. 18, p. 169, ll. 7–14 (stanzas 1, 3)
137–39	Infant Sorrow	N	p. 28 (Infant Sorrow of Songs of Experience), pp. 719–21 (for rest)	no. 13, pp. 166–67
141	The Will and the Way	"I askéd a thief to steal me a peach" N	p. 459	no. 7, p. 163
142	The Marriage Ring	The Fairy N (The Marriage Ring is a deleted title)	p. 466	no. 38, p. 178

264

143–44	"A fairy leapt upon my knee"	"A fairy skipd . . ." MS	p. 473	p. 188
144	4 lines of "Why was Cupid a Boy" (See p. 240.)	Cupid (See p. 240.)	p. 470, ll. 17–20	no. 72, p. 552, ll. 17–20
157–74	253 lines (scattered) of The Everlasting Gospel (See The Woman Taken in Adultery, pp. 241, 249–52 above.)	(For *EG* see pp. 241, 249–52 above.)	pp. 510–16, 791–96 (given in order they appear in E-B) pp. 510–12 [d]: ll. 1–4, 11–16, 35–38, 43–106; pp. 512–14 [e]: ll. 1–80, 83–96; pp. 514–15 [b]: ll. 17–40, 47–57; p. 516 [a]: ll. 5–6; p. 794 [i]: ll. 1–16, 24–38, 47–48; p. 795 [h]: ll. 1–4; p. 796 [f]: ll. 1–2	pp. 748–59 (given in order they appear in Keynes) *a*: ll. 5–6; *b*: ll. 17–40, 47–59; *d*: ll. 1–4, 11–16, 35–38, 43–108; *e*: ll. 1–80, 83–96; *f*: ll. 1–2; *h*: ll. 1–4; *i*: ll. 1–16, 25–38, 47–48

MANUSCRIPT POEMS IN SWINBURNE'S *William Blake*, 1868 (continued)

PAGE IN SWIN- BURNE	TITLES, EXTRACTS IN SWINBURNE	TITLE (IF DIFFER- ENT) OR FIRST LINE IN BLAKE AND MS	PAGE AND LINES IN E-B	NUMBER (FOR N) PAGE AND LINES IN BLAKE, ED. KEYNES
182	"What is it men in women do require?"	Several Questions Answerd N	p. 466, ll. 11–14	no. 46, p. 180
264 n.	"Why are thou silent and invisible?"	To Nobodaddy N	pp. 462–63	no. 21, p. 171
278–79	9 stanzas from "My Spectre around me" (See Broken Love, pp. 253–56 above.)	Stanzas 8, 9, 10, 12, 11, 13, 14 and 2 deleted stanzas (See Broken Love, pp. 253–56 above.)	pp. 467–68 and p. 774, deleted stanzas [3] and [4]	no. 1, pp. 415–17 (Deleted stanzas are ll. 9–12 and ll. 19–22.)

i. WMR follows the text in the Life (see p. 260 above) and titles the poem "Mammon." (W. B. Yeats titles it "The Two Thrones" in the Muses' Library Blake)

266

MANUSCRIPT POEMS FIRST PRINTED BY WILLIAM ROSSETTI IN THE ALDINE BLAKE

WMR	TITLE (IF DIFFERENT) OR FIRST LINE IN BLAKE AND MS	PAGE AND LINES IN E-B	NUMBER (FOR N) PAGE AND LINES IN BLAKE, ED. KEYNES
313 lines from The Everlasting Gospel (See The Woman Taken in Adultery, pp. 241, 249–52, 267.)	N	pp. 510 ff. and notes. Printed in full except [c], pp. 510–12. Minor omissions	p. 748 ff. Printed in full except c, pp. 750–51
Lafayette	"Let the Brothels of Paris be opened" and (in E-B) "Who will exchange his own fire side" (9 stanzas in all) N	9 stanzas, pp. 490–91 and p. 491 (plus notes, pp. 779–80): p. 490, ll. 1–4; p. 490, ll. 13–16; p. 490, ll. 9–10 and 6–7; p. 779, "Fayette beheld the queen," 4 lines; p. 491, ll. 17–18 and p. 779, note to l. 18 of "Let the Brothels," 2 lines; p.	9 stanzas, no. 60, pp. 185–86: stanza 1, ll. 1–4; stanza 4, ll. 5–8; stanza 3, ll. 16–17 and [stanza 2, ll. 11–12]; [ll. 27–30]; [ll. 31–34]; ll. 20–21 and [22–23]; ll. 35–38; [stanza 1, ll. 56–59]; [stanza 2, ll. 52–55]. (Brackets indicate stan-

WMR	TITLE (IF DIFFERENT) OR FIRST LINE IN BLAKE AND MS	PAGE AND LINES IN E-B	NUMBER (FOR N) PAGE AND LINES IN BLAKE, ED. KEYNES
		491, "Who will ex-change . . .", ll. 5–8 ("Fayette beheld the King & Queen"); p. 779, "Fayette Fayette thourt bought & sold," 4 lines; p. 780, "Will the mother exchange," 4 lines	zas and lines deleted by Blake.)
Idolatry	"If it is True What the Prophets write" N	pp. 492–93	no. 30, p. 543
Couplets and Fragments			
V "Grown old in love"	N	p. 508	no. 71, p. 552

VI "The Sword sang on barren heath"	N sung	p. 464	no. 39, p. 178
XV Reason	"You dont believe I wont attempt to make ye" N	p. 492	no. 2, p. 536
XVI Friends and Foes	"Was I angry with Hayley who usd me so ill" (2 lines) N and "Anger & Wrath my bosom rends" N	p. 496, ll. 7–8 and p. 494	no. 4, p. 538, ll. 8–9 and no. 5, p. 538
XVII "Here lies John Trot"	Another N	p. 494	no. 43, p. 546
XVIII "I was buried near this dyke"	Another N	p. 494	no. 42, p. 546
XIX Blake's Friends	William Cowper Esqre N	p. 498	no. 68, p. 551
XX "False Friend, fie" j	"If Men will act like a maid smiling over a Churn," 2 lines N	pp. 493–94, ll. 5–6	no. 81, p. 556, ll. 5–6

j. Not noted in Sampson (1905).

MANUSCRIPT POEMS FIRST PRINTED BY WILLIAM ROSSETTI IN THE ALDINE BLAKE (continued)

WMR	TITLE (IF DIFFERENT) OR FIRST LINE IN BLAKE AND MS	PAGE AND LINES IN E-B	NUMBER (FOR N) PAGE AND LINES IN BLAKE, ED. KEYNES
Epigrams			
V To Venetian artists	N	p. 507	no. 75, p. 554
XII Raphael and Rubens	A Pretty Epigram . . . Flemish Ooze N and "Rafeal Sublime Majestic Graceful Wise" N	p. 505 and pp. 505–06	no. 48, p. 547 and no. 50, p. 547
XV Fuseli	"The only Man that eer I knew" N	p. 498	no. 69, p. 551
On Hayley's Friendship (In Prefatory Memoir, pp. xciii–xciv.)ᵏ	On H——ys Friendship N	p. 497	no. 35, p. 544
Tiriel		pp. 273–82	pp. 99–110

k. See p. 288.

Engraved Writings

(Other than *Songs of Innocence and of Experience*) Complete or in Extracts, Up to the Ellis-Yeats Edition; with the dates of Facsimile Editions

In the table below, column one indicates plate and line numbers for each engraved book. The four columns to the right list printings: the number of the chapter in which an extract appears is given for the first edition of Gilchrist's Life; page references are given for Swinburne's *William Blake* and the 1880 edition of the Life. (For engraved writings printed in the *Life of Blake, 2,* only the volume number is indicated.) The last column lists other printings, including the dates of facsimile editions.

Extracts are listed in the order of their occurrence in Blake's works according to E-B. Footnote references are to work, plate, and line.

BLAKE (PLATE)	(LINES)	LIFE 1863 (CHAPTER)	SWINBURNE (PAGES)	LIFE 1880 (PAGES)	OTHER
		There is No Natural Religion			
In facsimile					2 in 1886
		The Book of Thel			
{ 3	{ 7–31				"The Inventions of William Blake," p. 322
{ 6	{ 11–22				Wilk
6	1–8				
In full		Vol. 2		Vol. 2	
In facsimile					1876, 1884
		The Marriage of Heaven and Hell and *A Song of Liberty*			
2	The Argument	10		78–79	
3–4	9 to end of pl. 4	10		79–80	
3–7	to end of A Memorable Fancy in pl. 7		213		
7–10	Proverbs of Hell only[1]	10[1]		80–81[1]	

8	21–25 (2–5 in Keynes)		208	
8 in facsimile			opposite 208	
11			214	
12–13			214–15	
12–13	10 to end of pl. 13	10		82–83
14			215	
14	12–15	10		82–83
15–17	1–26 of A Memorable Fancy	10		82–83
15–17	17 to end of A Memorable Fancy		216	
17–20	A Memorable Fancy except for last line		218–20	
17–20, 21–22 m		10 m		82–83 m
21–22			221	
22–24			222	

l, m. See p. 288.

BLAKE (PLATE)	(LINES)	LIFE 1863 (CHAPTER)	SWINBURNE (PAGES)	LIFE 1880 (PAGES)	OTHER
25–27	(*A Song of Liberty*)		223–24		1868, 1885
In facsimile					*Century Guild Hobby Horse*, 2 (1887), 137 ff.
In full					

Visions of the Daughters of Albion

BLAKE (PLATE)	(LINES)	LIFE 1863 (CHAPTER)	SWINBURNE (PAGES)	LIFE 1880 (PAGES)	OTHER
iii	The Argument	12		102–03	
1	1–15	12		103–04	
2	6 ("wearing . . .")–8		229		
2	11–28	12		104–05	
2–4	23–pl. 4, line 12		229–30 [n]		
3–4	7–pl. 4, line 7	12		105	
5	3–9		231		
5	33–40		231		

7	10–15	233			
7	17–18	233			
7	21–22	233			
8	6–13	234			
In facsimile			12	106	1875, 1884

America, a Prophecy

1	1–17 (". . . fold")		12	107	
2	1–2	235			
2	6–9	235 [o]			
3–4	1–pl. 4, line 2		12	107	
5 in facsimile			12	opposite 110	
6	1–10		12	108	
9	4–6, 9–10 (". . . lightnings")	235–36			
9	14–15 (". . . Heavens!")	235–36			
9	17 ("red . . .")–19	235–36 [p]			

n, o, p. See p. 288.

BLAKE (PLATE)	(LINES)	LIFE 1863 (CHAPTER)	SWINBURNE (PAGES)	LIFE 1880 (PAGES)	OTHER
10	6 ("call'd . . .")–10		236		
11 in facsimile		12		opposite 108	
11	6–15		236–37		
15	11	12		108	
15	23–25		237		
15 and 16	26 and pl. 16, lines 2–5 (". . . sublime")		237		
In facsimile					1875, 1887

Europe, a Prophecy

1–2		14		126–27	
9 in facsimile		14		opposite 124	
9	1, 4–5 (". . . years")	14		125	
10	10–23		242		

12 in facsimile		14			opposite 126
13	6–8		244		
14	32–36		244		
15	10–11		245		1887

In facsimile

The Song of Los

3	11–14	14		129
3	25 ("the . . .")–26 (". . . places")	14		129
3	28–30	14		130
4	1–4	14		130
4	13–17		255	
4	16–21	14		130
6	1–14	14		130
7	14–23		256	
7	19–23	14		131

277

BLAKE (PLATE)	(LINES)	LIFE 1863 (CHAPTER)	SWINBURNE (PAGES)	LIFE 1880 (PAGES)	OTHER
7	31 to end of pl.		257 [q]		1890
In facsimile					

The First Book of Urizen

BLAKE (PLATE)	(LINES)	LIFE 1863 (CHAPTER)	SWINBURNE (PAGES)	LIFE 1880 (PAGES)	OTHER
3	36–39		246 [r]		
5	25–27		246 [r]		
18–19	6–pl. 19, line 9	14		127–28	
20	26–29		247 [r]		
23	21–22		247 [r]		
23	23 ("he . . .")–25		247 [r]		
25	11–12		248 [r]		
25	29–36		248 [r]		
25	39–42		248 [r]		
28	1–7		248 [r]		
28	19–23		248 [r]		
In facsimile					1888

The Book of Ahania

2	21–26	14	131
2	27 ("laughing . . .")–29	14	132
2	38–43	14	132
4–5	45 to end of pl. 5		252–53 [s]
4–5	52 ("Ah . . .")–55, 65–pl. 5, line 2	14	132
In facsimile			1892

The Book of Los

In full — *Century Guild Hobby Horse, 5 (1890), 84–89 (see Chap. 8, n. 14)*

Milton

1	Preface, in full	21	258–59

q, r, s. See p. 288.

BLAKE (PLATE)	(LINES)	LIFE 1863 (CHAPTER)	SWINBURNE (PAGES)	LIFE 1880 (PAGES)	OTHER
	Lyric ("And did . . .") in full	21	258–59	241	
	1 line ("Would . . . 29v")	21	258–59	241	
2	1–3 (". . . lustre")	21		242	
2	1–15		260		
2	25	21		241	
6–7	35–pl. 7, line 4		261		
9	4–6		262	223	
9	21–29		262		
9	46–47		263		
11	17–26		264		
12	29 ("I . . .")–30, 32–34 (". . . Serpent!")		265		
13	30–34		265		

t, u. See p. 288.

BLAKE (PLATE)	(LINES)	LIFE 1863 (CHAPTER)	SWINBURNE (PAGES)	LIFE 1880 (PAGES)	OTHER
24	68–73		270	242	
25	26–29 (". . . Nations"), 32 ("The . . .")–37		271		
27	3–10		271	243	
27	19–20		271	243	
27	23–31		271	243	
27	37–41		271	243–44	
28	46–47, 50–57		273		
31	28–48	21 ᵛ			
31	28–63		273–74 ᵛ	244–45 ᵛ	
36	21–28	21 ʷ		245	
In facsimile					1886

Jerusalem

3	Beginning to "... as kindly received," and last sentence of paragraph 2 ("... Read-er ... talent.")	21		225–26
3	Poem ("Reader ...") in full, one sentence following ("We ... Sleep ...")		285–86	
3	Passage from "Of the Measure" ("When this ... to each other.")	21		227
5	16–30	21		228
10	7–16	21 [x]		235 [x]
12	30–37	21		237 [y]
13	34–36	21		237
13–14	59–pl. 14, line 1	21 [z]		235 [z]

v, w, x, y, z. See pp. 288–89.

	BLAKE	LIFE 1863	SWINBURNE	LIFE 1880	OTHER
(PLATE)	(LINES)	(CHAPTER)	(PAGES)	(PAGES)	
16	61-67	21		236	
17	33-35	21		236	
17	59-63			229 [aa]	
20	5-18			236	
27	Poem ("The fields from . . .") in full	21		232-34	
37 in fac-simile			opposite 282		
34 [38] [bb]	41-48			227 [cc]	
38 [43] [bb]	47 ("Hark! . . .")–52			229 [dd]	
52	Poem, 1, 25-28	21		238	
52	Poem				WMR
55	60-64	21		235	
56	3-10	21		237	

284

56	33	21 [ee]	237 [ee]
56	44	21	236
57	10		235
61	11 ("if I were . . .") –13 (". . . his anger")	21 [ff]	237 [ff]
61	16 ("I . . .")–22	21	237
64	24	21 [gg]	236 [gg]
69	19–25	21 [hh]	237 [hh]
71	10 ("these . . .")		229
71	38–39		229 [ii]
77	4 lines "To the Christians" ("I give you . . . wall")	Vol. 2, 2	Vol. 2, opposite 1
77	One sentence ("Imagination . . . no more"). E-B, p. 229, lines 9–12 of prose. Blake, ed. Keynes, p. 717, top, lines 1–4	21	236

aa, bb, cc, dd, ee, ff, gg, hh, ii. See pp. 289–90.

BLAKE (PLATE)	BLAKE (LINES)	LIFE 1863 (CHAPTER)	SWINBURNE (PAGES)	LIFE 1880 (PAGES)	OTHER
77	Poem, lines 24–28 (". . . sick") and 31–35; "England! awake!" in full		291–92		
77	Poem, in full (35 lines)				WMR
78 in facsimile		21		opposite 226	
81 in facsimile			276–77		
91	2	21		236	
99	2–5		292		
In facsimile					1877

For the Sexes: The Gates of Paradise

"Prologue" in full	12	100–02
"Keys of the Gates" in full	12 [jj]	100–02
"Epilogue" in full	12	100–02
In facsimile			1888

On Homers Poetry and On Virgil

In full	Vol. 2	Vol. 2
In facsimile		1886

The Ghost of Abel

In full	Vol. 2	295–97

jj. See p. 290.

287

k. Not noted in Sampson (1905).

l. *MHH*, plates 7–10: From *Proverbs of Hell* Mrs. Gilchrist omitted lines 5, 15, 16, and 19 on plate 7; lines 21–25 on plate 8 (lines 1–5 in Keynes' edition); lines 41, 43, and 55 on plate 9 (lines 2, 4, and 16 in Keynes); and lines 61, 65, and 67 on plate 10 (lines 1, 5, and 7 in Keynes). Most of these deal with repressive religion and the evils of unacted desire. Subsequently many were either extracted, facsimiled, or printed in the course of exposition in Swinburne.

m. *MHH*, plates 17–20 and 21–22: Mrs. Gilchrist has omitted lines 6–10 (E-B, p. 41; p. 156, lines 38–42, in Keynes) and lines 17–20 (E-B, p. 41; p. 157, lines 4–7, in Keynes) from plates 17–20; also lines 1–3 and 6–18 of plates 21–22. (Same in Keynes.)

n. *VDA*, plate 2, line 25: Swinburne substitutes "green" for "ripe corn." For plate 2, line 32, "my infinite brain," Swinburne has "my infinite beam."

o. *Amer*, plate 2, line 7: For "I know thee . . ." Swinburne has "I love thee . . ."

p. *Amer*, plate 9, line 19: For "enormous circles" Swinburne has eternal circles."

q. *SLos*, plate 7, lines 31–32: For ". . . dead dust rattling bones to bones/Join: shaking convuls'd the . . ." Swinburne has ". . . dead dust rattling bones to bones/Came shaking convulsed, the . . ."

r. All Swinburne's extracts are verbatim, but written as continuous text—without quotation marks.

s. Printed verbatim in continuous sentences as in *U*.

t. *Milt*, plate 15, lines 40–41: For "Against the rock, which was inwrapped with the weeds of death/Hovering over the cold bosom, in its cold vortex Milton bent down" Life has "Against the rock which . . bosom. In . ."

u. *Milt*, plate 22, line 61: For "He sent his two Servants Whitefield & Westley . . ." Swinburne (followed by Life, 1880) has "God . . . Wesley . . ."

v. *Milt*, plate 31: Lines 46–49 read:

46   Thou perceivest the Flowers put forth their precious Odours!
47   And none can tell how from so small a center comes such sweets
48   Forgetting that within that Center Eternity expands
49   Its ever during doors that Og & Anak fiercely guard[.]

Notes

Life, 1863, ends the passage at line 48 "... expands." (p. 198). Swinburne remarks that "This line [i.e. 49] appears to have been too much for the writer in the Life, who breaks the quotation short ... annihilating ... at once grammar, sense, and sound." Mrs. Gilchrist drew on Swinburne's explication and quoted the passage in full in the 1880 edition.

w. *Milt*, plate 36: The illustration with Blake's inscription "Blake's Cottage at Felpham" is reproduced.

x. *Jer*, plate 10, line 10: For "them" Life has "these."

y. *Jer*, plate 12, line 34: For "iron braces" Life, 1880, has "traces." (Life, 1863, has "braces" however.)

z. *Jer*, plate 13: For line 65, "... wailing to be Created." Life has "waiting to ..." For line 65, "But to those who enter into them they seem the only substances" Life has "... only realities."

aa. *Jer*, plate 17, line 62: For "tell Hand & Skofield they are ..." Life has "Tell him, Hand and Skofield, they are ...". The additional passages from *Jer* represent the editorial decisions of DGR who wrote about six new paragraphs on *Jer* for the 1880 Life. See my article, "Blake in 1863 and 1880: The Gilchrist *Life*," *BNYPL* (April 1967), pp. 216–38.

bb. The two numbers (printed as in E-B) refer to two arrangements found for plates 29–46 of *Jer*. The order followed by E-B, found in three copies, is designated by the unbracketed numbers. Keynes' edition follows the order shown in brackets and found in two copies of the poem.

cc. *Jer*, plate 34 [38]: For line 44, "I see thee awful Parent Land in light, behold I see!" DGR has "Behold I see!/I see the awful ..."

dd. *Jer*, plate 38 [43], line 51: For "my Saxons" DGR has "the Saxons."

ee. *Jer*, plate 56, line 33: For "And rock the Cradle while! Ah me! Of that Eternal Man" Life has " Rock the cradle,   ah me! of that eternal man!"

ff. *Jer*, plate 61, lines 11–13: For "... if I were pure, never could I taste the sweets/Of the Forgive[ne]ss of Sins! if I were holy! I never could behold the tears/Of love! of him who loves me in the midst of his anger in furnace of fire." Life has "If I ... sins/If I were holy ... tears [/] of love/Of him ... of His anger."

289

gg. *Jer,* plate 64, line 24: For "Without Forgiveness of Sin, Love is Itself Eternal Death" Life has " . . . Love itself is . . ."

hh. *Jer,* plate 69, line 21: For "Closed in by a sandy desart" Life has "by _____ sandy deserts."

ii. *Jer,* plate 71, lines 38–39: For "Skofeld had Ely Rutland Cambridge Huntingdon Norfolk/Suffolk Hartford & Essex: & his Emanation is Gwinevera" Life has "Skofeld had Ely, Rutland, Cambridge, Huntingdon,/Norfolk,I/]Suffolk, Hertford, _____ Essex, and his emanation is Guinivere." The editor (DGR) adds "(!!!)."

jj. *GP,* "Keys," plate 5: For Blake's "Two Horn'd Reasoning Cloven Fiction" Life has "Two Horrid Reasoning Cloven Fictions." In plate 12, for Blake's "And in depths of my Dungeons" Life has "icy Dungeons." Swinburne's running commentary on *GP* (pp. 18–28), apparently based on the text in the Life, alludes to prison-houses "of ice and stone." For plate 5, Swinburne glides over the problem of identifying two cloven fictions—one the shield and the other the spear ("Blind in Fire with Shield and Spear,/Two Horrid Reasoning Cloven Fictions,/In Doubt which is Self Contradiction,/ A dark Hermaphrodite I stood" (Life, *I*, 101). He glosses it: " . . . and the fire wherein man is blind; ashamed and afraid of his own nature and its nakedness, surrounded with similitudes of severance and strife . . ." (p. 21). Sampson (1905) has "Two Horrid Reasoning, Cloven Fiction" (p. 374).

SELECTED BIBLIOGRAPHY

Allingham, William, "Some Chat About William Blake," *Hogg's Weekly Instructor, N. S.,* 2 (1849), 17–20.

[――, ed.], *Nightingale Alley,* ed. "Giraldus," London, 1860.

Bentley, G. E. Jr., and Martin K. Nurmi, *A Blake Bibliography: Annotated Lists of Works, Studies, and Blakeana,* Minneapolis, Minn., University of Minnesota Press, 1964.

Blake, William, *The Complete Writings,* ed. Geoffrey Keynes, London, Oxford University Press, 1966.

――, *Letters of William Blake,* ed. Geoffrey Keynes, New York, Macmillan, 1956.

――, *Letters of William Blake, Together with a Life by Frederick Tatham,* ed. A. G. B. Russell, New York, C. Scribner's Sons, 1906.

――, *The Marriage of Heaven and Hell,* facsim., London, Hotten, 1868.

――, *The Note-Book of William Blake,* facsim., ed. Geoffrey Keynes, London, Nonesuch, 1935.

――, *The Poems of William Blake: Comprising Songs of Innocence and Experience Together with Poetical Sketches and Some Copyright Poems* not in any other collection, ed. Richard Herne Shepherd, London, 1874.

――, *Poems of William Blake,* ed. William Butler Yeats, London, Muses' Library, 1893.

――, *Poetical Sketches . . .* Now first reprinted from the Original edition of 1783, ed. Richard Herne Shepherd, London, 1868.

――, *The Poetical Works of William Blake, Lyrical and Miscellaneous,* ed. with a Prefatory Memoir by William Michael Rossetti, London, Aldine, 1874.

――, *The Poetical Works of William Blake,* ed. John Sampson, London, Oxford University Press, 1905.

――, *The Poetical Works of William Blake,* ed. Edwin J. Ellis, 2 vols. London, Chatto & Windus, 1906.

――, *The Poetical Works of William Blake,* ed. John Sampson, London, Oxford University Press, 1913.

————, *The Poetry and Prose of William Blake,* ed. David V. Erdman with Commentary by Harold Bloom, New York, Doubleday, 1965.

————, *Songs of Innocence and Experience,* ed. with Preface by J. J. Garth Wilkinson (1839), London, New-Church Press, 1925.

————, *Songs of Innocence and Experience,* with other poems . . . , ed. Richard Herne Shepherd, London, 1866.

————, *There is no Natural Religion,* facsim., London, Pickering, 1886.

————, *The Works of William Blake, Poetic, Symbolic and Critical,* eds. Edwin J. Ellis and William Butler Yeats, 3 vols. London, 1893.

————, *Works by William Blake,* in facsim., including *SI, SE, Thel, VDA, Amer, Eur, U,* and *SLos,* ltd. ed. for F. S. Ellis, London, 1876.

————, *Works,* in facsim., executed by W. Muir and associates, Edmonton, and issued as follows: *SI,* 1884; *SE,* 1885; *Thel,* 1884; *There is no Natural Religion,* 1886; *MHH,* 1885; *VDA,* 1884; *Amer,* 1887; *U,* 1888; *Eur,* 1887; *SLos,* 1890; *Milt,* 1886; *GP,* 1888; *On Homer's Poetry and On Virgil,* 1886.

Buckley, Jerome, *The Victorian Temper,* Cambridge, Mass., Harvard University Press, 1951.

Caine, Hall, *Recollections of Dante Gabriel Rossetti,* Boston, 1898.

Calvert, Samuel, *A Memoir of Edward Calvert, Artist,* London, 1893.

Carlyle, Thomas, *The Life of John Sterling* [1851], *Works of Carlyle, 11,* Centenary ed., London, n.d.

————, *On Heroes, Hero-Worship and the Heroic in History. Works of Carlyle, 5,* Centenary ed., London, n.d.

Coleridge, Samuel Taylor, *Collected Letters,* ed. Earl Leslie Griggs, 4 vols. London, Oxford University Press, 1956–59.

Conway, Moncure D., Review of Swinburne's *William Blake. Fortnightly Review,* N. S., *3* (Feb. 1868), 216–20.

Crompton, Louis, "Blake's Nineteenth Century Critics," diss. University of Chicago, 1953.

Cunningham, Allan, "Life of Blake," *Lives of the Most Eminent British Painters, Sculptors, and Architects, 2,* 6 vols. London, 1830.

————, "Life of Blake," *Lives of the Most Eminent British Painters, Sculptors, and Architects, 2,* rev. and enl. ed. 6 vols. London, 1833.

Damon, S. Foster, *William Blake: His Philosophy and Symbols* (1924), New York, P. Smith, 1947.

Ellis, Edwin J., *The Real Blake: A Portrait Biography*, London, Chatto and Windus, 1907

————, "William Blake," *Occult Review*, 4 (July and Aug. 1906), 26–35, 87–94.

Ellmann, Richard, *The Identity of Yeats*, New York, Oxford University Press, 1954.

Erdman, David V., *William Blake: Prophet Against Empire*, Princeton University Press, 1954.

Esdaile, K. A., "An Early Appreciation of William Blake," *The Library*, 5 (July 1914), 229 ff.

Farington, Joseph, R. A., *The Farington Diary*, ed. J. Grieg, 6 vols. London, n.d.

Frye, Northrop, *Fearful Symmetry*, Princeton University Press, 1947.

————, "William Blake," *The English Romantic Poets and Essayists: A Review of Research*, New York, Modern Library Association, 1957.

————, "Yeats and the Language of Symbolism," *Fables of Identity*, New York, Harbinger Books, 1963.

Gilchrist, Alexander, *The Life of William Blake, "Pictor Ignotus," with Selections from His Poems and Other Writings*, 2 vols. London, 1863.

————, *The Life of William Blake: With Selections from His Poems and Other Writings*, enl. ed., 2 vols., London, 1880.

————, *The Life of William Blake*, ed. W. G. Robertson, London, John Hall, 1906.

————, *The Life of William Blake*, ed. Ruthven Todd, rev. ed. with additional notes, New York, Everyman, 1945.

Gilchrist, Herbert H., *Anne Gilchrist, Her Life and Writings*, with a Prefatory Notice by William Michael Rossetti, London, 1887.

Grigson, Geoffrey, *Samuel Palmer: The Visionary Years*, London, K. Paul, 1947.

Hewlett, Henry G., "Imperfect Genius," *Contemporary Review*, 28 and 29 (Oct. 1876 and Jan. 1877), 756–84 and 207–28.

Hone, Joseph, *W. B. Yeats: 1865–1939*, London, Macmillan, 1942.

Horne, H. P., "William Blake's *Marriage of Heaven and Hell*," *The Century Guild Hobby Horse*, 2 (1887).

H[unt], R[obert], "Blake's Edition of Blair's *Grave*," *Examiner*, No. 32 (Aug. 7, 1808), pp. 509–10.

[————], "Mr. Blake's Exhibition," *Examiner*, No. 90 (Sept. 17, 1809).

[Hutton, R. H.], "William Blake," *The Spectator*, No. 1847 (Nov. 21, 1863), pp. 2771–73.

"The Inventions of William Blake," review in *London University Magazine*, 2 (Mar. 1830), 318–23.

Keynes, Geoffrey, *A Bibliography of the Writings of William Blake,* New York, Grolier Club, 1921.

———, *Blake Studies,* London, R. Hart-Davis, 1949.

———, and Edwin Wolf, *William Blake's Illuminated Books: A Census,* New York, Grolier Club, 1953.

Lamb, Charles, *The Letters of Charles and Mary Lamb,* ed. E. V. Lucas, 3 vols. New Haven, Yale University Press, 1935.

"Last of the Supernaturalists, The," review in *Fraser's Magazine, 1* (Mar. 1830), 217–35.

"Life of Blake, The," review in *Westminster Review, N. S., 25* (Jan. 1864), 101–18.

"Life of William Blake, The," review in *Athenaeum*, Nos. 1880 and 1881 (Nov. 7 and Nov. 14, 1863), 599–601 and 642–44.

Malkin, Benjamin Heath, Esq., *A Father's Memoirs of His Child,* London, 1806.

[Montgomery, James, comp.], *The Chimney-Sweeper's Friend and Climbing Boys' Album,* London, 1824.

More, Paul Elmer, "William Blake" (1905), *Shelburne Essays,* Ser. 4, New York, G. P. Putnam's Sons, 1906.

Palmer, A. H., *The Life and Letters of Samuel Palmer,* London, 1892.

Patmore, Coventry, "Blake," *Principle in Art, Etc.,* London, 1889.

Powell, Frederick York, "William Blake. *The Book of Los," The Century Guild Hobby Horse, 5* (1890).

Robinson, Henry Crabb, *Blake, Coleridge, Wordsworth, Lamb, Etc.,* ed. Edith J. Morley, New York, Longmans, Green, 1922.

———, *On Books and Their Writers,* ed. Edith J. Morley, 3 vols. London, J. M. Dent & Sons, 1938.

———, "William Blake: Künstler, Dichter und Religiöser Schwärmer," *Vaterländisches Museum, 2* (Jan. 1, 1811), 107–31.

Rossetti, Dante Gabriel, *Works,* ed. William Michael Rossetti, rev. and enl. ed., London, Ellis, 1911.

———, *Dante Gabriel Rossetti: His Family Letters With A Memoir,* by William Michael Rossetti, 2 vols. London, 1895.

———, *Letters to William Allingham, 1854–1870,* ed. George Birbeck Hill, New York, [1897].

Rossetti, William Michael, *Letters to Anne Gilchrist Concerning Whitman, Blake, and Shelley,* eds. Clarence Gohdes and Paull Franklin Baum, Durham, N. C., Duke University Press, 1934.

———, *Some Reminiscences,* 2 vols. New York, C. Scribner's Sons, 1906.

————, comp., *Rossetti Papers: 1862–1870,* London, Sands, 1903.

————, ed., *Ruskin; Rossetti; Preraphaelitism: Papers 1854–1862,* London, 1899.

Ruskin, John, *Works,* ed. E. T. Cook and Alexander Wedderburn, 39 vols. London, G. Allen; New York, Longmans, Green, 1903–12.

Saintsbury, George, *A History of English Prosody,* 3 vols. New York, Macmillan, 1906–10.

————, *A History of Nineteenth Century Literature (1780–1895),* New York, Macmillan, 1931.

————, review of the Aldine Edition of *The Poetical Works of William Blake, Academy,* N. S., No. 35 (Dec. 5, 1874), pp. 559–601.

Scott, William Bell, *Autobiographical Notes, . . . 1830–1882,* ed. W. Minto, 2 vols. London, 1892.

————, *Catalogue of the Burlington Fine Arts Club Exhibition of the Works of William Blake,* London, 1876.

————, "A Varley-and-Blake Sketch-Book," *The Portfolio,* 2 (1871), 103–05.

————, *William Blake: Etchings from His Works,* London, 1878.

Smetham, James, "Gilchrist's *Life of William Blake*," *London Quarterly Review, 31* (Jan. 1869), 265–311.

————, *Literary Works,* ed. William Davies, London, 1893.

————, *The Letters of James Smetham,* with a Memoir by William Davies, eds. Sarah Smetham and William Davies, London, 1892.

Smith, John Thomas, *Nollekens and His Times: Comprehending A Life of That Celebrated Sculptor; and Memoirs of Several Contemporary Artists, from the Time of Roubiliac, Hogarth and Reynolds, to that of Fuseli, Flaxman and Blake,* 2 vols. London, 1829.

Southey, Robert, *The Correspondence of Robert Southey with Caroline Bowles,* ed. Edward Dowden, London, 1881.

————, *The Doctor,* 7 vols. London, 1847.

Stirling, A. M. W., *The Richmond Papers,* London, W. Heinemann, 1926.

Story, Alfred T., *The Life of John Linnell,* 2 vols. London, 1892.

Swinburne, Algernon Charles, *The Complete Works of Algernon Charles Swinburne,* eds. Sir Edmund Gosse and Thomas J. Wise, Bonchurch ed., 20 vols. London, W. Heinemann, 1925–27.

————, *The Swinburne Letters,* ed. Cecil Lang, 6 vols. New Haven, Yale University Press, 1959–62.

————, *William Blake: A Critical Essay,* London, 1868.

————, *William Blake: A Critical Essay,* with a new preface, London, Chatto & Windus, 1906.

Symons, Arthur, *William Blake*, New York, E. P. Dutton, 1907.

Thomson, James ("B. V."), *Biographical and Critical Studies*, London, 1896.

[————] "B. V.," "The Poems of William Blake," *National Reformer*, *N. S.*, 7 (Jan. 14, 21, 28, and Feb. 4, 1866), 22–23, 42–43, 54–55, 70–71.

————, "A Strange Book," *The Liberal* (Sept., Oct., Nov., and Dec., 1879).

Wade, Allan, *A Bibliography of the Writings of W. B. Yeats*, London, R. Hart-Davis, 1951.

[Wainewright, Thomas Griffiths], "Janus Weathercock," "Mr. Weathercock's Private Correspondence," *London Magazine*, 1 (Sept. 1820).

Warren, Alba H., Jr., *English Poetic Theory, 1825–1865*, Princeton Studies in English, No. 29, Princeton University Press, 1950.

Wilkinson, Clement John, *J. J. Garth Wilkinson: A Memoir of His Life*, London, K. Paul, 1911.

Wilson, Mona, *The Life of William Blake*, rev. ed. with additional notes, New York, Oxford University Press, 1949.

Wolf, Edwin, "Blake-Linnell Accounts," *Papers of the Bibliographical Society of America*, 37 (1943), 1–22.

Yeats, J. B., *The Letters of J. B. Yeats*, ed. Joseph Hone, with a Preface by Oliver Elton, London, Faber & Faber, 1944.

Yeats, William Butler, *Autobiography*, New York, Anchor Books, 1958.

————, Introduction to *A Book of Images*, by W. T. Horton, London, Unicorn Press, 1898.

————, *Essays and Introductions*, New York, Macmillan, 1961.

————, *The Letters of W. B. Yeats*, ed. Allan Wade, New York, Macmillan, 1955.

GENERAL INDEX

Names of artists and engravers mentioned once appear under "Art." Secondary sources are selectively indexed, as is the Appendix. Cross references to the Blake Index refer to the listing of his works beginning on p. 309. For abbreviations of Blake's works, see pp. vii–viii.

INDEX TO BLAKE'S POETRY, PROSE, AND ART WORKS

Poems and prose are listed under the collection or manuscript in which they appear. The listing of names of characters and places is incomplete (see "names" under "Blake" in the General Index). The Appendix is selectively indexed. Asterisks indicate titles from Gilchrist's *Life of Blake, 2,* edited by D. G. Rossetti.

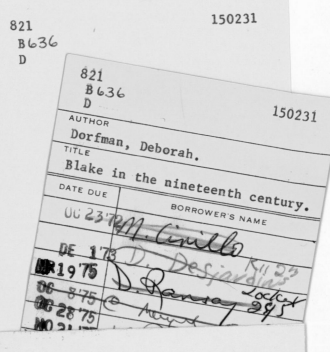